The New Isolationism

A STUDY IN
POLITICS AND FOREIGN POLICY
SINCE 1950

NORMAN A. GRAEBNER

THE RONALD PRESS COMPANY · NEW YORK

Library of Congress Catalog Card Number: 56–11573

To
Walter Johnson

Preface

This book is a study of the unfortunate effects on American diplomacy of certain internal political forces in the United States since 1950. There is nothing unusual or objectionable in the use of foreign policy issues in the struggle for domestic political power, provided that the discussion hinges on responsible alternatives based on world realities and national limitations. But for politicians the temptation is always present to ride to political victory on promises that can never be fulfilled—only to find on achieving office that their utopian commitments to domestic political elements have left them without bargaining power in the give-and-take of international diplomacy. Such hazards to effective diplomacy have appeared from time to time in every democratic country. Nowhere can they be more clearly seen than in the breakdown of American bipartisan foreign policy in the past half-decade.

The roots of an unrealistic attitude toward foreign policy lie deep in American history. In the nineteenth century American success in all fields came so quickly and cheaply that the majority of the people never understood the role of power in that success. America's freedom to develop along her own lines depended essentially on the British Navy and the European balance-of-power structure. Under this vitally important but unobtrusive protection Americans gradually lost their sense of reality in foreign affairs.

The result was the characteristic frame of reference of

isolationist opinion in the first half of the present century with its assumption that the United States had the power and virtue to achieve its way in the world. Americans came to believe that their first duty to themselves and to the world was to preserve the internal institutions and economy that had developed under the impact of a unique moral purpose. Thinking of power in moral terms, they overestimated their own influence and underestimated that of others. They came to expect that unilateral action aimed at utopian moral goals would be uniformly successful in America's international relations. Such attitudes can be clearly seen in the pronouncements of Wilson's Fourteen Points and the Kellogg-Briand Pact, and even in Roosevelt's Atlantic Charter and the Truman Doctrine.

The vast majority of Americans were shaken loose from these easy presuppositions by World War II and the events that followed. But the old views died hard. As the cold war dragged on, with the Communist success in China and the apparently permanent Sovietization of Eastern Europe, increasing numbers among politicians and the general public began to lose patience. On the old assumption of limitless power, they could find only one explanation for the seeming failures of foreign policy—incompetence and even betrayal by successive administrations. The resulting outbreak of charges and investigations was firmly based on the old concepts of invincibility, moralism, and utopianism. Its protagonists accepted the *fact* of American leadership in the struggle against militant communism, but they could not on their own terms accept its implications. They advocated unlimited goals for American foreign policy—the return of Chiang Kai-shek to the mainland and, after 1952, the liberation of Eastern Europe. But they would not recognize the changing world power relations that made these goals exceedingly difficult to achieve.

Concentrating on a purely internal solution, these "new isolationists" were the true heirs of an old tradition.

The present book is a study of the impact of these attitudes and demands on the foreign policies of the Truman and Eisenhower Administrations. It shows how, even before 1952, pressure from the new isolationists had led to serious modifications in the Truman-Acheson diplomacy that made negotiated solutions increasingly difficult. It traces Eisenhower's gradual accommodation during the 1952 campaign to the political demands of the extremist wing of his party. Finally, it points out how commitments made for political purposes during the campaign have impeded the subsequent Administration's freedom of action in pursuing a realistic foreign policy.

Since 1955 the relaxation of the American people suggests that the new isolationism is receding as a powerful force in American politics and foreign policy. The symbols of recent years—Tehran, Yalta, and Potsdam—are losing their political effectiveness. But the era of their influence is not yet at an end, for the new isolationism has created a powerful tradition of unilateralism toward both Russia and China that still demands nothing less than total surrender as a condition of genuine negotiation. The United States Congress has not yet been willing to challenge the utopian goals of American diplomacy and thereby create the foundations for future accommodation.

There is little that is unique in this recent venture of politics into foreign policy. In analyzing the years since 1950 the author has used the frame of reference that he created in a previous study of the Oregon question of 1844-1846. President James K. Polk, having accepted the utopian goal of 54° 40′ during the 1844 campaign, discovered in the White House that he was trapped between the ultimate necessity of finding the diplomatic means of living peacefully with England and the immediate necessity of living at peace with his party. In the crisis his political commitments effectively ruled out all diplomacy with Britain on the boundary question. Eventually in 1846 the British assumed the diplomatic initiative that brought peace.

The Editors of *Current History* and *World Affairs Quarterly* have kindly extended permission to use materials which have appeared in their journals. Hans J. Morgenthau, Walter Johnson, Carol L. Thompson, and Richard W. Van Alstyne, as well as my colleagues at Iowa State College, Donald Boles, C. H. Matterson, and Wayne S. Cole, have read the entire manuscript and have given me the benefit of their knowledge and insight. To these, who have aided so unselfishly, I am grateful. Whatever the errors in fact and judgment, they would be far greater without their generous suggestions. To my wife, Laura, I am indebted for her critical judgment and for the freedom from responsibilities so essential for uninterrupted writing and research. For the mistakes and shortcomings that must inevitably remain in such a work I alone am responsible.

                                        Norman A. Graebner

Ames, Iowa
July, 1956

Contents

The New Isolationism

1

Foundations: 1950

§ 1

Playing politics with foreign policy is an American game as old as the Republic. At most critical junctures since the adoption of the Constitution—whenever the external affairs of the nation have become matters of vital concern—policy formulation has been subjected to partisan assault. Neither party nor age has been totally exempt from its lure of political gain. In the notable attacks on the policies of George Washington, James Madison, James K. Polk, Abraham Lincoln, and Woodrow Wilson there was much that had no apparent object other than domestic partisan advantage. For that reason it is difficult in reading United States diplomatic history to find much justification for some of the past onslaughts on American diplomacy. Whatever the success this nation's foreign policies have achieved, it has never been the product of partisanship.

Since 1950 the American people have been subjected again to a tumultuous discussion of foreign policy. This debate, like those of previous generations, stemmed from the conviction that United States foreign policy, like domestic policy, must be the subject of continued political scrutiny. Senator Robert A. Taft of Ohio, for example, when asked if it were wise to make of foreign affairs a

3

major political issue, replied: "I certainly do. . . . In our form of government there must be no sacred cows. If there had been more publicity and open debate in years now gone, we might have a sounder foreign policy than we do have. The public was never even told the most important decisions made at Yalta and Tehran and Potsdam. There was no open debate about selling Chiang Kai-shek down the river."

Taft was correct in his insistence that he had the right to criticize what he termed the blunders of Democratic policy. His pronouncement merely followed the American democratic tradition which assumes that under debate the best ideas, by the force of their validity, will rise to the surface and be adopted as policy. Democratic discussion rests on the free and continuous introduction of new concepts, and it is entirely feasible that the foreign policy views of the opposition at any moment might be superior to those of the party machine in control of the nation's diplomacy. For that reason any sound discussion of foreign affairs which calls attention to failures in understanding or performance, and even builds political fences while it adds some needed correctives, is not only salutary but is actually demanded by the national interest. The real test of wisdom that confronts any party which attempts to expand its influence through the successful use of foreign policy symbols is whether its assumptions will form the basis of responsible alternatives that recognize national limitations.

This is essential. Foreign policy formulation is not primarily the determination of objectives; it consists of the evaluation of means. Only a nation that is all powerful can equate policy with aspirations. Since no nation is omnipotent, external relations must ever be governed by limits. This necessitates, therefore, that debate not force the acceptance of assumptions which will burden future policy by promising too much. To denounce a failure of American purpose abroad might be good politics. But if that purpose was beyond the capability of American power to achieve, then the insistence that success was possible might expose United States policy to untold intellectual and diplomatic handicaps.

Strangely enough, this assurance of perfect success has usually accompanied the use of partisanship in American foreign policy discussion. The reason is clear. Successful partisan exploitation of diplomatic issues is evidence that either the questions at issue have been oversimplified or they have been made to contain some outrageous proposition which will play upon certain nationalistic emotions held by the American people. In either case, it means that the more politically rewarding the partisan venture, the more difficult it will be for national leadership to balance policy goals with the actuality of limited power.

§ 2

The extraordinary power of domestic politics in the United States to subvert foreign policy rests on a dual foundation: the capriciousness of the American people in the realm of diplomatic concepts and the distribution of political power in the American constitutional system. In this nation three groups share control of policy: the Executive and his advisers, the Congress, and foreign policy interest groups who ostensibly represent the public. In practice no course of action can go beyond the point at which these three forces meet. There is no guarantee in the American political system that foreign policy will ever rise above the least common denominator of Executive, Congressional, or public opinion. In a democracy it is the character of public opinion that in the long run will determine the quality of the nation's foreign relations.

Mass opinion has always been the one undeniable power in any genuine democracy, but in recent decades it has enjoyed an expanding influence. Under conditions of modern technology the public not only fills the traditional role of selecting officials; it imposes direct limitations on government. To this striking phenomenon Walter Lippman, in *The Public Philosophy*, has attributed the decline of democratic power and influence since World War I. It is this "mass negative," as he defines it, that has made it difficult for most democracies to play decisive roles in world affairs for the reason that popular opinion is always out of phase. "The unhappy truth is," Lippmann has written, "that the prevailing public opinion has been destructively wrong at the critical junctures. The people have imposed a veto upon the judgment of informed and responsible officials."[1]

Whether the public be informed, uninformed, or misinformed, it will play an important role in the formulation of foreign policies. And in the United States public opinion polls reveal the disturbing reality that the American people generally are neither informed nor concerned with the nation's external affairs. Even at that it is apparent that mass opinion becomes the real political disease of democracy only when it exists in combination with other determining factors. Public sentiment has no separate entity except as it is given direction, strength, and vitality by powerful foreign policy elites or by political leaders. The public becomes destructive of clear and informed public policy when its ignorance is not removed, but exploited. If the American people have been wrong at the critical junctures, it is because they invariably have been offered pleasing and inexpensive panaceas which have driven them into irrational judgments. When the public mood has not been aroused or misled by partisan debate, it has permitted a national administration broad latitude in policy formulation. Between 1947 and 1950 the American people with singular unanimity assumed peacetime responsibilities and burdens unprecedented in American history.

Over the long haul public opinion may be reliable, but at critical moments short-term opinion, or what is accepted as opinion in Washington, is so vulnerable to subjectivity and emotionalism that it becomes a poor and inadequate guide for national action.[2] It is the extreme instability of short-run American foreign policy thinking that invites partisanship and constantly threatens the proper performance of American diplomacy. It presents limitless opportunities to small, well-organized groups to capture the moods and opinions of an unorganized public. It permits them to confuse issues of primary and secondary importance—those that are essential for American security and those that are decidedly negotiable—and thus create national objectives which appear reasonable intellectually but become hopeless diplomatically. It gives them the power to distort the nation's vision and force its diplomacy into inflexible patterns.

One reason why the American people are so susceptible to foreign policy stereotypes is that, in a day of crisis and complexity in world affairs, they tend to be distrustful of complicated answers. American impatience may go far to explain the amazing industrial triumphs of the nation. But in foreign affairs this characteristic leads to limitless expectations. Dean Rusk, until his recent retirement one of our abler diplomats, has described this American trait:

There are few fields of human endeavor where wishful thinking and self-delusion are as common, or as dangerous, as in foreign policy. We demand simple answers to the most complex questions confronting human intelligence. We expect consistency in policy, though the facts themselves are full of contradictions. We should like an easy way to carry a heavy burden, an agreeable way to perform disagreeable tasks, a cheap way to bring about an expensive result.[3]

Even more fundamental to this problem is the fact that various ethnic groups in the United States have been conditioned to respond to questions of foreign policy primarily through emotion. For that reason they can be made to react violently to clichés and symbols that tap the wellsprings of isolationism, nationalism, hyphenism (special appeals to national groups), and even of religion. This was especially true at mid-century. American involvement in World War II had prepared the staunch isolationists of the thirties, especially among German-Americans, for what Samuel Lubell has termed the "politics of revenge" against former Democratic administrations. In addition, various ethnic groups after the war were driven by the desire to appear as loyal Americans, and this became the key to their politics. During the war those who had found it difficult to become assimilated sought vigorously with the coming of peace to demonstrate their patriotism by their vocal opposition to communism.[4] For them hostility to Russia was more than the normal reaction to a troublesome and aggressive antagonist; it was the very essence of Americanism.

Perhaps these tendencies toward emotionalism would be permitted to lie dormant were it not for the distribution of powers in the Constitution. Professor E. S. Corwin once observed that its vagueness on diplomatic matters has become "an invitation to struggle for the privilege of directing American foreign policy." In no area of public discussion can that struggle be resolved more speedily and with greater finality than by exploiting the predilections and prejudices of the public in diplomatic affairs. Such partisanship merely engrafts the instability of the public mind to the instability of the American political and constitutional system.

Under the Constitution the Executive must take the responsibility for policy formulation, but Congress can play a formative role in strengthening or destroying that policy. Its very power comprises the major challenge of partisanship to the quality of the nation's policy, for Congress can alter any program through its control of the purse, through investigation, and through debate. Congress has wielded its authority over appropriations with telling effect since the end of the war. It has reduced grants for aid to Western Europe, for military assistance, and for the Voice of America. It has attached riders to appropriations to provide expenditures for objects not contemplated by the administration. At times such action, as in the case of China, can affect considerably a policy based on Executive judgment.

As a major instrument of power Congressional investigation can alter policy for good or evil in a fashion that is without parallel in any other democracy. The object of this procedure is to force accountability in the Executive branch, both as to conformity with law and as to efficiency in performance. The service a successful investigation can render the country is considerable. But, George B. Galloway once observed, "Any adequate analysis of the inquiries of Congressional committees must take account of their political motivation; for it is evident that the influence of a party has sharpened the edge of the inquisitorial sword."[5] Through extensive questioning of past diplomatic policy a Congressional committee can modify Executive judgment or destroy the effectiveness of State Department officers. Such investigations can convince an administration that it is losing public support and prompt it to desert policies based on the national interest. Reviewing the influence of past Congressional hearings, Congressman James P. Richards concluded: "It is undeniable that they have a noticeable effect on how our officials conduct relations with other countries and on the attitudes of other countries toward the United States."[6]

Perhaps Congress's greatest influence over foreign policy is exerted through the power of debate, for through this device it educates or miseducates the American public. President Washington advised in his Farewell Address: "In proportion as the structure of government gives force to public opinion, it is essential that public opinion should be enlightened." During the past century and a half that principle has become increasingly valid. Public opinion, like other human phenonema, is not static, but can be elevated or stunted according to its nurture. Partisan debate not only misleads the public, but often reduces its will to act on difficult, costly policy. Any partisan effort to make foreign policy palatable through oversimplification renders the nation no service. It has been said that when the uninformed are taught to doubt, they do not know what to believe.

To the extent that the American people have traditionally been reluctant to make hard decisions, American leadership has failed. "The malady . . . ," writes Lester B. Pearson, Canadian Secretary of State for External Affairs, "is not . . . inherent in democracy as a political and constitutional system. It is, rather, the result of an internal derangement within individual men. This malady, which is contagious, can hit *any* society if enough men in positions of political influence abdicate their own responsibilities in favour of their special or selfish or superficial interests."[7] The disease of democracy is demagoguery and the refusal of leaders to follow their honest judgment in the quest for immediate and easy political success.

The adequate performance of any democracy must rest on the individual character. There is no institutional framework that can produce policy that is morally responsible except through leadership that is morally responsible. Whether this leadership might better reside in the Executive than in Congress is not at issue, for under the Constitution both branches will share the burden of determining American policy. Nor is any alternative required, for Congress has contributed markedly to past success in American foreign policy.[8] But cooperation between Executive and Congress should not have as its object the avoidance of conflict. The purpose of debate is to find the best policy, and to restrain discussion would eliminate some vital ingredient. What matters is simply the quality of the discussion.

Perhaps the chief obligation of political leadership in the United States is the elevation of public opinion to a level commensurate with the national interest. Rather than attempt to underbid one another through appeals to the nationalistic emotions of the public, national leaders, both in Congress and the Executive, might better acquaint the American people with the inherent limits of foreign policy so that issues may turn on questions of alternate courses to achieve limited goals rather than on vain propositions of perfection. Congress must share this responsibility because its influence exceeds that of the State Department and often that of the President himself. Because foreign affairs for the vast majority of American citizens are remote and esoteric, the repetitive effect of one partisan viewpoint will frequently penetrate more deeply into the public consciousness than the less readily plausible views which might emanate from the Executive, Congress, or the experts.

Partisan debate can as easily mislead and confuse friends and allies over the world as the American public. Thomas E. Dewey has written in *Journey to the Far Pacific* that "the most irresponsible statement of a Congressman or Senator, speaking for nobody but himself, is headlined around the world and is often mistaken to represent American policy." Their power to influence alone should compel national spokesmen to limit their statements on foreign affairs to astute analysis or proved fact. *Bipartisanship* suggests the conditions under which the search for adequate policy remains reasoned and wise and prepares the public for the acceptance of action that satisfies the minimum requirements of the national interest.

§ 3

Bipartisanship in foreign policy was reached in a limited field during the postwar years. It continued, ever precariously, until 1950, largely because of the minority leadership of Senator Arthur Vandenberg of Michigan. Through a period of four years the active bipartisanship of Congress and the Executive on European policies had created a remarkable sense of national solidarity. Those years witnessed the creation of a balancing power to offset that of the Soviet world. American policy was aimed at building a coalition of free nations as the surest reliance for living through the present troubled times without war. As late as 1950 there seemed to be a united front in the United States on matters of foreign policy. When the crisis came, wrote John Foster Dulles in *War or Peace* (1950), "The major parties were united, the nation was united, and the calculations of our enemies were confounded." And Vandenberg echoed, "It was a meeting of minds. . . . Our Government did not splinter. It did not default. It was strong in the presence of its adversaries."[9]

Despite these successes of American policy, since 1949 the Republican party had been on the verge of revolt. The policies of Harry Truman had held Russian expansion in check, but they had cost billions and the end of the burden was not in sight. Powerful elements in the party, more-over, had always believed bipartisanship wrong as a matter of principle. "Bipartisan foreign policy has resulted in a blackout—a blackout of intelligent debate in Congress and the press," charged Alfred M. Landon in December, 1948. "Both the Republican party and the Democratic party have bypassed Congress and party responsibility. Instead a few people in both parties set foreign policy and everybody has to accept." John M. Vorys of Ohio added in March, 1949, "Unity solely for the sake of unity may be disastrous. History is strewn with the wreckage of countries that were united, but in the wrong course."[10]

Such critics believed it the obligation of the minority party to attack and expose. As practical politicians they saw that policies bearing the biparty trademark emerged as policies of the administration. These were the simple lessons of the bitter Republican loss to Truman in 1948. Many Republicans leaders were convinced by this cam-paign that the G.O.P. was dependent on the isolationist foreign policy vote which Wendell Willkie had captured in 1940 to offset the party's weakness on economic issues.

Still, the immediate challenge to bipartisanship in 1950 lay elsewhere. The year 1949 had been a critical one for United States relations with the Far East and with China in particular. By December, Chiang Kai-shek had taken refuge on the island of Formosa which the Allies had promised him at Cairo in 1943, the victim of the rising tide of Communist power on the China mainland. For many Americans his new isolation was a bitter reality. Through-out the recent war the United States had regarded him as a staunch ally. In fact, United States diplomacy with Japan had reached an impasse because President Franklin D. Roosevelt refused to sacrifice his China to Japanese ambitions. It was upon Chiang that Washington had pinned its hopes for the creation of a stable Orient in the postwar years.

Chiang's collapse brought partisan friction to a higher stage than at any time since 1945, for Republicans were not immediately involved in the creation of China policy. By October, 1949, Vandenberg was disturbed over the future of bipartisanship. He noted that the Republican party showed signs "of 'splintering' into various degrees of isolationism which could be ominous for a free America in a free world." The Washington *Star* apprised its readers of an impending partisan outburst. "For some time," observed the editor,

there has been a restless stirring in the Republican ranks, a rising revolt against the "me-tooism" which some hold responsible for the succession of G.O.P. disasters at the polls. And there is more than suspicion that some influential Republicans have been playing with the idea of carrying this revolt to the extent of junking the bipartisan foreign policy in the hope that some partisan advantage could be salvaged from the resulting discord.

Vandenberg deplored this trend and moved to stop it. He attacked those who blamed Truman for past Russian gains. "On many counts I don't like him better than they do," he admitted. "But he is the *only* President and the *only* Commander-in-Chief we have got or are going to have for three more critical years." Nor could Vandenberg see any clear alternative to American policy in China. ". . . China aid," he wrote in August, 1949, "is like sticking your finger in the lake and looking for the hole. . . ." It was easy to criticize, looking backward, but he added, "I am not disposed to do much of it."[11]

Vandenberg reminded his colleagues of the true meaning of bipartisanship. He admitted readily that a successful bipartisan policy tended to strengthen the party in power. But, he added, bipartisanship "is not an iron curtain behind which specious unity would stifle the traditional American debate" in the area of foreign affairs. To the Senator bipartisanship was "a united effort, under our indispensable two-party system, to unite our official voice at the water's edge so that America speaks with maximum authority against those who would divide and conquer us and the free world."

Bipartisanship, as he defined it, insisted only that argumentation look to national security rather than to partisan advantage. It meant simply that all criticism of administration policy be derived from the merit of the proposal rather than from the belief that since the party in power pursues a specific policy the minority must take exception for no other reason than that the majority pursues it. There is a subtle, but essential, difference between a "national union" in which all groups automatically support administration policy, and bipartisanship which allows and encourages opposition if it is based on a factual or analytical evaluation of the case. What is necessary is that both parties in Congress face issues with a sense of responsibility. In essence, then, bipartisanship is the continuing search for truth through cooperative effort.

Dulles joined Vanderberg in warning his fellow Republicans that since United States coalition policy was "impressed with a trust for the benefit of mankind," the American people should not play with it as something that belonged to them alone. It was essential that the nation remain unified "on the main features of our foreign policy, so that there can be confidence that our policies will be sustained and continuous." Another Republican spokesman, Paul Hoffman, in his *Peace Can Be Won*, declared that Americans could not "afford to indulge in the luxury of blaming a particular party or group of individuals for our present troubles. We should be too busy to search for scapegoats." Margaret Chase Smith of Maine in June, 1950, spoke out in a similar vein in Congress. "Certain elements of the Republican party," she said, "have materially added to this confusion in the hopes of riding the Republican party to victory through the selfish exploitation of fear, bigotry, ignorance, and intolerance. There are enough mistakes of the Democrats for Republicans to criticize constructively without resorting to political smears."[12]

For the Democrats, Senator John Sparkman of Alabama took up the cause of bipartisanship. In a pamphlet which he presented to the Senate he emphasized his conviction "that the security of the United States requires that the leaders of both political parties, whether in Congress, the executive branch, or among the people, must do their utmost to see that we approach our world obligations in a nonpartisan spirit." He reminded the critics of American China policy that until Chiang began to fail badly they had not criticized the policy or proposed concrete alternatives. He cited the records of the Foreign Relations Committee which indicated that there had not been a word of criticism of American policy in China or a single suggestion of change.

Many Democrats, while reluctant to differ with the administration openly, did not rush to the defense of the State Department, for Democratic leaders as well as Republican had been almost completely ignored in the construction of Far Eastern policy. In their arrogance toward Congress, State Department policy-makers had ignored the power of Congress over foreign policy and had failed to build support which might defend them from partisan assault.

During 1950 bipartisanship ground to an abrupt halt. In February a Joint Committee of the Republicans in the House and Senate agreed on a new statement of party principles. The basis of attack was implicit in one sentence which reminded the American people that they had won the war five years earlier but had still to win the peace. The President anticipated the move and complained to Vandenberg: "I am sorry that they can't find a domestic issue on which to carry on the campaign. It seems to me that that could be done if an intelligent approach were made to the subject."

It now appears evident that the relations between Senator Vandenberg and President Truman will long remain a model in bipartisan cooperation. The President placed major reliance upon Vandenberg's support, for none understood more clearly than he the complete dependence of successful diplomacy on the support of Congress. Quite logically he showed grave concern over the Senator's final illness. "I sincerely hope that the Lord will be good to the country and hurry along your physical recovery, so that you can come back and take your proper place as the Minority Leader of the Program," he addressed the Senator in March, 1950. Four days later he wrote again, "You don't realize what a vacuum there has been in the Senate and in the operation of our foreign policy since you left. That has always been one of the difficulties in the continuation of policy in our government."[13]

With Vandenberg's death the President attempted to fill the breach with appointments of John Foster Dulles and John Sherman Cooper, both former Republican Senators, to high echelon positions. But nothing the President might do could prevent the ensuing debate on the past record of American foreign relations.

Democratic policy had been based on the concept of limited power. It accepted the great tragedy of our time that the United States at the height of her power is caught in historic forces which make her less the director of her destiny than ever before. It was aimed primarily at the "containment" of Russia through the bolstering of free nations with economic and military aid. In the Far East it recognized both the existence of a political and social revolution and the inevitability of change. To these two factors the Truman administration attributed the fall of Chiang Kai-Shek. Since east Asia was in a momentous internal upheaval, the Democratic leadership saw danger in too much interference in Far Eastern affairs.

Whatever its quality, the Truman approach to the world challenge was politically vulnerable. It was committed to living with danger and not to destroying it. It was defensive in posture in both Europe and the Far East. Five years after the costly victories of World War II, it was still engaged in a cold war with another antagonist far more formidable than the first. To many Americans accustomed to living in a world of absolute security the postwar position of the United States was both intolerable and inexcusable.

§ 4

For Republican nationalists there was an answer. Nothing less than domestic villainy could bear the responsibility for such failure. They denied that the Western position was crumbling before revolutionary forces in Asia and Africa. To them the American fiat was still potentially effective all over the world; any diplomatic defeat therefore must be self-inflicted. The real challenge to American security, as they viewed it, sprang from United States leadership which had invited the Russian occupation of Eastern Europe and delivered China to the Reds.

Such illusions of invincibility were not strange to the American scene, for they tapped emotions deeply rooted in the American experience. Until 1940 isolationism had furnished the ultimate promise of American security. Events abroad, it had argued, were inconsequential, because the vital interests of the United States could not be destroyed by occurrences beyond the seas. Herbert Hoover characterized this assumption with considerable precision: "The potential might of this nation is the strongest thing in this whole world. . . . That strength is always here in America. . . . America cannot be defeated." Geography added an element of logic to the isolationist dogma, for the Western Hemisphere was surrounded by a moat which supposedly constituted an almost insurmountable military barrier.

Isolationism had assured the American people a high standard of living in a world that was safe from revolution, challenge, or cost to the nation. It promised them that if the United States minded it own affairs it could achieve a world of its own choosing in which others would quietly accept their lasting status of inequality. It accepted the rewards of empire without acknowledging the responsibilities for its defense. It claimed the wisdom of the Founding Fathers without realizing that they had led a nation of little power, population, or security; and that they had recognized with humility the limitations of this nation's ability to benefit the continent of Europe. These men had rejected involvement in Europe as a misdirected use of the young Republic's limited energies.[14]

The record of American diplomacy in the nineteenth century merely affirmed the apparent validity of the isolationist program. Relying solely on its own resources and abstaining from interference in the affairs of the world, the United States had enjoyed astonishing success. It had secured what war and negotiation could bring and that right quickly and cheaply. It had removed the British and Spanish threat from the Mississippi Valley frontiers, the Mediterranean pirates from their grasp on American merchantmen, the French from Louisiana, the Spaniards from Florida, the Mexicans from Texas and the Southwest, the British from Oregon, the Russians from Alaska, the Spaniards from Cuba, Guam, Puerto Rico, and the Philippines, and the British from joint canal rights in Central America. Such success carried its penalty, for it gave credence to the illusion that this nation could always enjoy security without assuming any responsibility for the costs of security.

Militant isolationism in the twentieth century forgot that it was not its program that brought success to American diplomacy. What power was required to keep America secure—and it was considerable—was supplied by the British navy and the balance-of-power system in Europe. But decades of success without the normal obligations of success gradually destroyed the sense of reality in United States foreign affairs. Twentieth-century Americans tended to equate diplomacy and statesmanship with the mere declaration of utopian ends which perpetuated the isolationist illusion of omnipotence. Their inclination to attribute American success to virtue rather than to power culminated in the Kellogg-Briand Peace Pact which, as Foster Rhea Dulles has suggested, satisfied "the conscience of the American people without requiring of them any positive action, and also created an illusion of safety which seemed to obviate the need for any more direct participation in world affairs."[15] These illusions proceeded to deny what the past had tended to conceal: that a nation, however powerful, is a limited entity and its foreign relations must ever be conditioned by forces beyond its own ordaining.

At mid-century this mood of assurance was being challenged. For those who refused to concede that the nation's will was still not absolute over the globe, the American isolationist tradition still furnished an answer. The reactionary-nationalist foreign policy elite, as Gabriel Almond defines it, attributed American postwar insecurity to the gradual destruction of the traditional American free enterprise system.[16] Since the administration of Woodrow Wilson, they cried, socialism, New Dealism, heavy military expenditures, and high taxes had undermined the strength of the nation to go its own way in peace and security. Insecurity had come, wrote Dan Smoot, when "one generation of Americans faltered in faith and began to introduce the worn-out quackeries of Old World collectivism into the American system." If the United States would return to the economic and political system that existed before 1914, if it could return to the old Americanism, the nation's problems, foreign and domestic, would disappear.

Organizations of the extreme right, such as Merwin K. Hart's National Economic Council, had opposed the Marshall Plan as a scheme to "finance socialism in Europe," and the United Nations as an octopus leading to a "statist, collectivist world." It attacked the North Atlantic Treaty as an abandonment of the traditional American policy of avoiding permanent alliances; it opposed both heavy military commitments abroad and heavy taxes at home. The United States should clear the decks for action, it urged, "by reducing our government expense and rejecting the whole Truman program for a socialized welfare state." The American Coalition of Patriotic Societies—a merger of some 85 organizations such as the DAR, American War Mothers, the Dames of the Loyal Legion, and the Sons of the American Revolution—led by John B. Trevor, agreed that the danger to American security lay in the "national socialist planners." "It is they whom we must identify and defeat and remove from every post of authority and influence from which they make war upon our culture, our laws, our traditions and our freedom," ran its exhortation.

By 1950 this nationalist-isolationist rationale was clear. Whatever alterations of power had occurred in the world, they need comprise no threat to the United States. Under a program of economic and political orthodoxy this nation would require neither regimentation of man power nor excessive military expenditures. If it would destroy the paralysis of collectivism at home, it would be militarily and politically unassailable.

This deviation from the foreign policy mood of the nation was not extensive in 1950, but it had the support of the McCormick and Hearst press and several well-known columnists. What was more significant, it reflected the deepest isolationist traditions of suspicion, distrust, and withdrawal from the world, as well as the deep conviction that an isolated America could live securely without allies, overseas commitments, or military preparedness even at mid-century. It accepted past good fortune as something earned by intelligent policy and therefore an endowment that would last as long as the nation remained true to its ninetenth-century traditions.

Isolationism decried all reliance on diplomacy, for diplomacy presupposes a world of nations of some equality, none of which can have its way completely. In such a world, nations exist through the techniques of negotiation, bargaining, mutual concession, and compromise. Settlements are never regarded as permanent, but as reflecting merely the distribution of power as of the moment. But the American isolationist tradition assumed that the United

States was good enough and strong enough to do what it pleased. Any negotiation, therefore, which resulted in compromise was tantamount to appeasement, if not to weakness and vice. The United States with its moral dignity need ask nothing less than unconditional surrender. What such inflexibility in United States relations with the world promised besides total war or total isolation was not clear, for only realistic diplomacy could carve out successful policy between these absolutes.

American isolationism as reflected in the reactionary-nationalist elite confronted American thought with five clearly defined tendencies—a concern for the domestic economy, the overestimation of United States power, the underestimation of the enemy, a belief in the nation's moral superiority, and unilateralism in diplomacy. Despite its strength, this powerful heritage was not necessarily inherent in the American scene. At heart isolationism was a political program which had been perpetuated successfully through the years by editors and politicians, whether from conviction or from the desire to exploit its partisan potentialities, for the reason that no conceivable alternative could underbid it in the political arena. Isolationism would continue until it either tripped over its own inconsistencies or ceased to be an effective pawn in the political struggle for power in many areas of the United States.

§ 5

For the vast majority of Americans in 1950 this isolationist tradition was no longer relevant. World War II had demonstrated its obsolescence, but had not destroyed the emotions and traditions which underlay it. What remained was significant—a hatred of Europe, a belief in American purity which should not risk corruption by contact with other nations, and a wistful hope that America could live in seclusion while maintaining its traditional virtues. If these emotions were recessive, they continued to have a paralyzing effect on American policy. "More than anything else, perhaps," writes A. M. Schlesinger, Jr., "they have kept America a slumbering giant, unable to export its democratic faith to the peoples of other nations, unable to play a full and affirmative role in the world."[17]

Isolationism required a new formula by which the old emotions could come to terms with the new realities. Eventually a *new isolationism* evolved which appeared to accept the postwar American obligations abroad. Its proponents vigorously rejected the term "isolationism." "I don't know what they mean by isolationism," Taft said; "nobody is an isolationist today." Senator William F. Knowland of California agreed. "This nation," he added, "can no more return to isolation than an adult can return to childhood." Once established, there was much in the new isolationism that justified such denials. On the surface it had more in common with Truman's program than with the America First Committee of 1940-41. Taft's seven-point program, for example, called for rearmament, economic and military aid to anti-Communist countries, warning to the Soviet Union that aggression beyond certain lines would bring retaliation, committing American troops to nations threatened by attack, and ideological warfare against the Communist system. This, it would appear, was the Truman program.

Yet this apparent break from the older isolationism involved no psychological contradiction. The inconsistencies of Congressional debate and within Taft's own book, *A Foreign Policy for Americans* (1951), suggested an immense internal conflict within neo-isolationism between the acceptance of limited responsibility abroad and the tendency toward complete withdrawal. The new isolationism was prepared to support programs of some commitment to Europe, but with the apparent intent of an eventual withdrawal. Thus the new isolationism has been termed "an attempt to make the world safe for American retreat from it."[18]

Neo-isolationism revealed powerful ties to the past in its conviction that domestic policy was far more fateful than foreign affairs. In government spending it found the overriding threat to national security. Taft doubted that the Russians had military conquest of the world in mind. "I believe they know it is impossible," he wrote. "It would take them at least a hundred years to build up their sea power." General Douglas MacArthur brought additional prestige to this doctrine in 1951: "Talk of imminent threat to our national security through the application of external force is pure nonsense." From this estimate of the external challenge the General pinned down the real threat. It came, he said, from "the insidious forces working from within which have already so drastically altered the character of our free institutions . . . those institutions we proudly called the American way of life." The dangers to American survival were not external; they were internal.

W. Reed West, in defending Taft's program, admitted that it started "with our internal economy and the amount of taxation it will stand, and from this proposes that we arm ourselves in the way that our resources, capacities, and geographical position can be made most effective." Taft himself wrote with classic simplicity, "Just as our nation can be destroyed by war, it can also be destroyed by a political or economic policy at home which destroys liberty or breaks down the financial and economic structure of the United States." Foreign policy must not impose "such a tremendous burden on the individual American as, in effect, to destroy his initiative and his ability to increase production. . . . We cannot assume a financial burden in our foreign policy so great that it threatens liberty at home." High taxes, Taft observed, could produce socialism as easily as the government's commandeering of industry.[19]

If a major threat to American security lay in excessive government spending, then it seemed logical that the level of spending be reduced. The Chicago *Tribune* argued that "with far less money for defense than has been appropriated, and probably without resort to the draft, this country can feel secure. The North Atlantic Treaty Organization is not needed for our safety." Taft opposed the North Atlantic Pact as a commitment "so dangerous as to commit the United States to a course beyond its capacity," and he characterized the UN as "an utter failure as a means of preventing aggression." The new isolationism revealed the same contempt for collective security and the same affinity for unilateral action as did the reactionary-nationalist school.

Translated into military terms, the new isolationism still reflected the premises of the prewar isolationism of Hoover and Taft. The United States, ran the argument, could still find security within itself; air and sea power rendered large armies obsolete. In December, 1950, Hoover demanded that the United States send not another man or dollar to Europe until it manned its own defenses; instead, the United States should withdraw to the defenses of this continent. "The foundation of our national policies," he declared, "must be to preserve for the world this Western Hemisphere Gibraltar of Western civilization." The United States, he argued again, did not need Europe for its defense. Taft called this nation the citadel of the free world and demanded that its defense be the primary goal of American policy. Congressman Edgar A. Jonas of Illinois summarized the new isolationist program: "The Hoover-Taft policy is definitely confined to making America an impregnable fortress, and opposed to frittering away our American substance in man power and material by participating and meddling in the many quarrels that now prevail in European and Asiatic sectors."[20]

Whether the new isolationism varied from the policy of building strength and unity in the free world in degree or in principle depended on the specific issues. But in its claim that too much was being spent it tended to whittle down the appropriation bills for foreign aid and retract American military commitments to Europe, for its assumptions of a home-grown threat forced it to compromise with world realities of 1950. Taft clearly revealed the dichotomy in the new isolationism. "The policy on which all Republicans can unite," he said, "is one of all-out opposition to the spread of communism, recognizing that there is a limit beyond which we cannot go." This led the editor of the New York *Post* to dub it "The all-out, halfway policy."[21]

For the defense of Europe the neo-isolationist program was complete. Next it had to implement its more aggressive program toward the Far East (it had been said that a neo-isolationist was one who wanted to fight in China) without challenging its domestic program of reduced expenditures. China must be made safe for America through support of the Nationalist cause, but that safety must be obtained at minimum cost and without American responsibility or involvement. Here where the traditional American policy of the Open Door had been subverted by Communist success the United States must again be free to venture forth without suffering the costs of making the area safe for such venture.

In its expectations for China the new isolationism found its chief challenge. It assumed that Chiang was preferable to Mao Tse-tung and therefore must be returned to power, and, that communism was a direct threat to American democracy and must be driven from the Asiatic scene. But to accomplish such a result required a price, and this price might be so high that it would destroy the domestic program of reduced expenditures and perhaps American security everywhere. Therefore the new isolationism had to explain away the existence of Red Chinese power—that the defeat of Chiang, if against American interests, had not been beyond American power to prevent. If the United States did not have its way in China, the threat to American security in the Orient must lie at home.

Senator Joseph McCarthy of Wisconsin supplied the rhetoric which tied the Asia-first orientation of the new isolationism to the concept of limited expenditures. His sensational charges, beginning with the Wheeling, West Virginia, speech of February, 1950, gave the new isolationism its needed rationale. The State Department, especially the Far Eastern Division, he said, was "thoroughly infested" with Communists; Philip C. Jessup, the department's chief trouble-shooter, had an "unusual affinity for Communist causes," and Owen Lattimore, former department adviser, was the chief architect of Far Eastern policy and the chief Soviet espionage agent. McCarthy's argument rang the changes on America's deepest isolationist emotions. "How can we account for our present situation," he said, "unless we believe that men high in this government are concerting to deliver us to disaster? This must be the product of a great conspiracy on a scale so immense as to dwarf any previous venture in the history of man."[22] Such conclusions received additional credibility from the disclosures of Whittaker Chambers in 1949 which charged Alger Hiss, a government lawyer who had held important State Department posts, with giving confidential documents to the Communists in the thirties. Hiss was convicted on perjury charges in 1950.

Whatever the quality of the Senator's interpretation of American failure in China, its appeal to the new isolationists was magic. By raising the cry against the supposed danger of Communist subversion within the United States, McCarthy found the argument which would both cover the withdrawal from Europe and permit a show of aggressiveness in Asia without assuming an expensive military commitment. If the United States had found the task of subduing the revolution in Asia beyond its capabilities, it did not mean that Asia had unleased a new energy. It meant simply that the State Department was full of Communists. McCarthy had invented the scapegoat of collective treason and employed it, as Hans J. Morgenthau has written, "to reconcile the delusion of our omnipotence with the experience of limited power."[23]

Taft and much of the Republican party moved into line behind the Wisconsin Senator, for McCarthy had become indispensable to the new isolationism. Bertrand Russel, the British philosopher, has observed:

Average Americans were oppressed by two fears, fear of communism and fear of the income tax. So long as the Democrats remained in power these two fears worked in opposite directions. But McCarthy discovered how to reconcile them. The real enemy, he said, is the Communist in our midst, and it is very much cheaper to fight the Communist in our midst than to fight Russia. So long as Americans are loyal and united— so he told the nation—they are invincible and have no need to fear machinations of alien despotisms. If we purge our country of disloyal elements we shall be safe.[24]

Soon Taft was speaking of the "continuous sympathy toward communism . . . which inspired American policy." Whether Taft actually believed this or not, he encouraged McCarthy to "keep talking, and if one case doesn't work out," he added, "proceed with another." The Republican party shifted rapidly toward the endorsement of these attacks, and in the Republican Policy Committee statement of March, 1950, Taft admitted that the "reaction seems to be pretty good on the whole."[25] Senator Styles Bridges of New Hampshire informed reporters that some members of the Republican party would shortly initiate a series of public attacks on Secretary of State Dean Acheson and his department.

Neo-isolationism gave the ensuing discussion of Far Eastern policy a character unprecedented in American history. In the words of Henry Wriston, then president of Brown University, the political onslaught on foreign policy "turned discussion away from constructive criticism of errors in judgment toward sterile assaults upon personal integrity." There was a need for a rational evaluation of the means and ends of American purpose, but the ultimate assumptions of the new isolationism made a sober debate on foreign affairs all but impossible.

In Europe the fulfillment of neo-isolationist purpose would have assured little but the expansion of Russia until the United States either withdrew to the Western Hemisphere or struck back with total war. In Asia it promised little more, but at least it embodied a rationale that could quell the charge that its objective was ridiculous in its pretensions. Talk of returning Chiang Kai-shek to the mainland made sense only if the actuality of power in the Orient could be denied, for the new isolationism had no more interest in spending for Asia than it did for Europe. But Asia was in revolution, and the question of 1950 was sharp and clear: Where would the new isolationism turn when it discovered eventually that the Chinese could not be pushed around and that a dynamic Orient could not be controlled; and, secondly, where would it go when it discovered that Communist infiltration, to the extent that it existed at all, had not influenced policy or at least had not created the situation in the Far East which had come to plague American policy? But these questions were not immediately obvious and the great debate moved forward with the seeming assurance that such a dilemma would never arise.

2

The Great Debate

Not since Washington assumed the duties of office in 1789 has an event beyond the immediate involvement of the United States produced such extensive and vituperative debate as the fall of Chiang Kai-shek. A vigorous evaluation of past China policy was warranted in 1950. Chiang's exile on Formosa demanded an analysis of those forces which had undermined his regime so that future American policy in the Orient might prove more successful. What carried this needed discussion to the point of irrationality, however, was the charge by the Nationalist China bloc in the United States that errors in policy (to the extent that they could be demonstrated) stemmed from willful neglect and the purposeful acceptance of Communist objectives by the Truman administration.

From the mass of fact and opinion—some sober and some irresponsible—produced by the charges and counter-charges of politicians, journalists, students of American foreign policy and of Far Eastern affairs, only three patterns of thought stand out. As in all great discussions of public policy, the facts and ideas involved in this debate were limited; almost from the outset the utterances became repetitive. One essential question faced all elements in the discussion: What policies, in retrospect, could or should the United States have pursued after 1945 which might have rescued the floundering ship of Nationalist China?

1) Key spokesmen of the Truman administration moved quickly from the hope that the vessel might be repaired to the conclusion by 1948 that it was doomed. Thereafter they would have deserted the hull but for fear that their desertion would be interpreted as the cause of its final destruction. This conclusion of hopelessness enjoyed the support of the vast majority of Far Eastern experts in the United States. A second group, mostly students of United States diplomatic and military policy, conscious of the results of American policy, believed that the United States could have done better. By applying the rules of successful policy formulation, they agreed that the United States until 1945 broke sound principles of diplomacy and thus contributed to the breaking up of the Kuomintang. But none of them saw much alternative for American policy after the defeat of Japan and the outbreak of the Chinese civil war. Some have suggested that the United States might have abandoned Chiang's listing craft at that moment since it was obviously doomed. 3 A third group—this one the most unified intellectually of all—comprised the neo-isolationists who assumed not only that the ship could have been saved with a simple rescue operation, but also that American officials purposely stood aside with the hope that Communist waves would eventually engulf it.

For the Truman administration the problem of Chiang became acute as early as 1948. The Kuomintang was disintegrating rapidly, confronting the administration in Washington with the hard decision of extending further support or of terminating its commitments as rapidly as possible. By February, 1949, the collapse of Chiang's regime was immi-

nent. In this crisis the President called Secretary of State
Acheson, Senator Vandenberg, and Vice President Alben
Barkley to the White House to formulate a policy that
would forestall Congressional criticism. Vandenberg opposed desertion of the Nationalists for fear that the United
States could "never be able to shake the charge that we
[were] the ones who gave poor China the final push into
disaster." \He urged the administration to wait until the
fall of Chiang was "settled *by China* and *in China* and not
by the *American government in Washington.*" Vandenberg never evinced any hope for preventing the immediate Communist conquest of China, but he wanted the
United States to avoid the responsibility "for the *last push*
which makes it possible."[1] Truman and Barkley supported
Vandenberg; the United States continued to support the
Kuomintang officially while it waited "until the dust
settled."

Chiang's final collapse, whatever the cause, loomed so
large on the immediate diplomatic and political horizon
that the Truman administration felt compelled to explain
it to the American people. In August, 1949, it published
the famous China White Paper, a bulky document which
attempted to show that the upheaval in China was the
result of massive internal change over which the United
States had no control. Acheson once summarized the administration's defense in one terse statement: "Nothing
that this country did or could have done within the reasonable limits of its capabilities would have changed the result,
nothing that was left undone by this country has contributed to it."

Acheson's opinion that the problem of China was beyond this nation's capacity to influence had the support
of the most extensive body of thought relative to the Far
East in existence. This concept of internal upheaval stem-

med logically from the basic assumption that all Asia was submerged in a genuine revolution of rising expectations such as Europe had not witnessed. The struggle within Asia, therefore, was ideological at heart rather than military. Nor could it be explained by Communist imperialism emanating from Moscow, for this upheaval antedated the rise of Bolshevik power in Russia.

This quest of the Orient, said those who accepted its reality, had been aimed at equality with the West. But equality meant different goals to different nations. As Edwin Reischauer has suggested, for the Japanese it meant military equality so that Japan might defend herself against Western warships; for China it meant political equality so that the Chinese would no longer be the victims of unequal treaties; for the Indians and Burmese it meant national equality so that they would no longer be ruled by aliens.[2] More precisely, this massive effort of the Orient to enter the twentieth century has been the product of three basic principles of Western civilization—racial equality, self-determination of peoples, and social justice. These three have been combined into the intense nationalism that for the past half century has sought a new deal for all Asiatics.

Japan's successful invasion of southeast Asia in 1941 instilled new courage in native nationalist leaders and brought the underlying revolution to a new stage of insistence. As one Malay nationalist said, "Yes, I worked for the Japanese during the war. They did more to awaken my country than all the years of English rule. They showed us what Asians could accomplish." One month after the fall of Singapore the astute London *Economist* warned: "There can be no return to the old system once Japan has been defeated. . . . The need is for entirely new principles or rather the consistent application of principles to which lip service has long been paid." Edgar Ansel

Mowrer concluded after a tour of the Orient that Asians in the postwar world demanded above all the recognition of status.[3]

Asian leaders warned the West that the settlements following the war would embody the principle of Asiatic equality or there would be no security for the West in the Orient. E. H. Carr, the British historian, added his conviction that in an Asia struggling for recognition any white armies fighting against Asians on Asiatic soil, whatever the justice of their cause, would be regarded *ipso facto* the aggressors. And James Michener wrote in 1951: "Imperialism is absolutely finished. Any white men who try to re-establish it will be murdered ruthlessly."[4] The real challenge of Asia for the West, then, resulted from a deep resentment against past colonialism and Western pretensions of superiority that had been accumulating among Asiatic leaders for decades and had reached by 1945 a state of urgency beyond the comprehension of most Americans.

From this concept of revolution flowed one interpretation for Chiang's decline. During the immediate postwar years it was obvious that the Chinese Reds were drawing upon some power that transcended the force of peasant armies, although none would deny the latter's military effectiveness. During the Japanese occupation they had become well disciplined and unusually adept at guerrilla tactics. But the real source of strength that permitted the Reds to overthrow the Nationalist regime, said this school of thought, lay in the Chinese revolution which Mao Tse-tung, with his efficiency and promise of reform, appeared better able to fulfill than the regime of Chiang Kai-shek. In essence the concept of revolution attributed the great decisions within China between 1945 and 1949 to the Chinese masses.

Acheson summarized this concept of the China situation before the National Press Club in January, 1950: "The Communists did not create this condition. They did not create this revolutionary spirit. They did not create a great force which moved out from under Chiang Kai-shek. But they were shrewd and cunning to mount it, and to ride this thing into victory and into power." In similar terms Derk Bodde analyzed the transfer of power at the Chinese capital. "By its cupidity and corruption, cynicism and apathy, stupidity and inability to make contact with the common man," he wrote of the Kuomintang in *Peking Diary*, "it has irrevocably forfeited that mass support it once enjoyed, and by the same token the Communists, displaying the reverse of these qualities, have succeeded in capturing that support."[5]

For this large school of writers who have studied recent change in the Orient, American policy in China failed because it underestimated the economic, social, and ideological appeal of the Chinese Reds. Reform and not military aid was the answer to the Kuomintang's dilemma, for rightly or wrongly the Chinese people held Chiang responsible for the postwar disasters which had overtaken China. The final decision, therefore, lay with Chiang, and to that extent the decisions made in Washington, whatever their nature and wisdom, were not crucial. Such students of the Far East agree that the assumption that United States power was sufficient to control China's destiny flowed from an illusion of United States authority that did not exist. "It assumes," concluded John K. Fairbank in the November, 1950, issue of *Atlantic*, "that we Americans can really call the tune if we want to, even among 475 million people in the inaccessible rice paddies of a subcontinent 10,000 miles away."[6]

§ 2

Other scholars of equal reputation are not so sure. Such students of American diplomatic practice as Hanson W. Baldwin, Hans J. Morgenthau, Chester Wilmot, Herbert Feis, and even Winston Churchill represent an area of thought which lays much of the West's decline in power at the door of World War II military decisions. Baldwin, military expert of *The New York Times*, in his *Great Mistakes of the War* (1950), developed this theme with brevity and precision. In essence he believed that American strategic decisions of the war contributed to the augmentation of Communist power in Europe and Asia because of their single-minded pursuit of military victory. Baldwin charged Roosevelt with ignoring the repeated warnings that came from the State Department that his military decisions and his diplomacy would result in the loss of Eastern Europe. He held that the American failure to invade the Danube plain and the Balkans, plus the halting of American troops short of Berlin and Prague, helped to establish the Russian hegemony over the Slavic peoples. Similarly the Yalta agreement, with its territorial concessions to Russia to induce her to enter the Pacific war, brought Soviet influence into the Orient long after it was required.

This view that the quest of "unconditional surrender" of Germany and Japan went far toward creating two worlds has been developed in many other notable volumes. Chester Wilmot, in *The Struggle for Europe*, developed with great care this theme for the European phase of the war. Winston Churchill, in the concluding volume of his personal account of the war, *Triumph and Tragedy*, added some new arguments and perfected some of the old.

Yalta has borne the brunt of much of this criticism as one of the crucial decisions in the sequence that led to the

decline of American security in the postwar world. Wilmot
has been so critical of this conference that he termed it
"Stalin's greatest victory." Baldwin added that Churchill,
although he played only a secondary role in the Far Eastern arrangements, must share the responsibility "for the
moral, psychological, military, and political blunders of the
Yalta concessions."[7] Specifically, the Yalta agreements have
borne the responsibility for placing Poland behind the
Iron Curtain and weakening Nationalist China in its struggle with the Chinese Reds. Yet among historians and
journalists the Yalta debate, despite its vigor, has been conditioned by moderation and conflicting evidence.

Much attention has been centered on the Polish decisions
at Yalta. Yet here for academicians the debate has been
slight indeed, for the overwhelming reality of February,
1945, was the Russian military occupation of almost all of
Poland and the existence of the Soviet-created Lublin
Government for Poland. This reduced to narrow limits
the room for diplomatic maneuver at Yalta. Charles E.
Bohlen has insisted that the Red Army set the limits of
Russian expansion, not the Yalta agreement. The map of
Europe, he has declared, would look much the same had
there never been a meeting at Yalta. Roosevelt, Morgenthau suggests, had the choice of either forcing the Red
Army to retreat or persuading it to retreat. Unable to
exert military pressure against Russia, Roosevelt struck
back with a piece of paper based on the principles of cooperation and the idea of universal democracy. His only
hope was to use free elections as an entering wedge for
exerting some influence in Eastern Europe again. To
secure a free Poland at the time of Yalta no longer seemed
possible, for the Russians were already in possession of
whatever territory they desired.

Wartime decisions set the stage for the Russian advance, but wartime decisions based on political considerations do not always come easily. The United States and Britain were heavily committed as late as 1944. As Charles B. Marshall has argued, there were no great margins of choice that were frittered away. Had the invading armies of the West entered the mountainous morass of the Balkans, would not the Russians have pursued the Germans to the Rhine? What set the limits to the Russian advance, except for the arrangements made over Berlin and Prague, was the total quantity of Allied power and the force of the Russian army moving along the ground into the vacuum created by the collapse of Germany. Had the West penetrated deeper and faster at one point, the Russians might have countered at another.[8] In *Triumph and Tragedy*, Churchill has summarized the problem of halting the Red advance:

It is easy after the Germans were beaten to condemn those who did their best to hearten the Russian military effort and to keep in harmonious contact with our great Ally, who had suffered so frightfully. What would have happened if we had quarreled with Russia while the Germans still had two or three hundred divisions on the fighting front? Our hopeful assumptions were soon to be falsified. Still, they were the only ones possible at the time.[9]

Perhaps the gravest charge that such critics would make of the Yalta agreements on Poland was that they were hurriedly drawn by men who were not in basic agreement but who insisted on the appearance of unanimity. The leaders, acting much on their own, were trying, as Churchill later remarked, to organize the world in five days when even the Lord had taken seven.

Churchill and Roosevelt compromised on the Lublin Government by agreeing to its reorganization with a Com-

munist majority. Roosevelt did not even insist on the
British proposal that the promised "free and unfettered
elections" should be supervised by the American, British,
and Soviet ambassadors at Warsaw. The Polish agreement
was, in the words of Admiral William Leahy, "so elastic
that the Russians [could] stretch it all the way from Yalta
to Washington without ever technically breaking it."
Wilmot believed that the United States and Britain were
still strong enough to have stood firm on the principle of
the Atlantic Charter and to have forced a more cautious
Soviet policy. He concluded that it was "too much to say
that Yalta was a 'sell-out.' But it could have been made a
showdown."

In its Far Eastern provisions students of American
diplomacy have made a far stronger case against Yalta.
Here the Russian invasion of territory beyond her borders
not only occurred after the conference but actually was
bargained for with a series of extensive territorial concessions. These concessions, comprising South Sakhalin,
the Kuriles, and rights to Dairen, Port Arthur, and Manchuria, were made without the knowledge of Chiang Kai-
shek or the advice of the British.

Once the United States was committed to the destruction of Japanese power, American political and military
leaders, especially those representing the United States
Army, never deviated from the conviction that Russian
participation in the Pacific war would greatly simplify the
task of defeating Japan. By October, 1944, Stalin had informed Churchill and Ambassador Averell Harriman in
Moscow that he would launch an attack on the Japanese
three months after the defeat of Germany, and he stated
his price in territory. After the decision to invade Japan
was made, the military problem on the mainland consisted
of pinning down the Kwantung Army in Manchuria and

all Japanese forces in north China. The United States would conduct the actual invasion, first striking Kyushu and then Honshu. Military necessity dictated that Russia enter the war against Japan as soon as possible to prevent the transfer of Japanese troops from Manchuria to the home islands. Few Army officers questioned the need of a Russian invasion of Manchuria before the United States' invasion of Japan. In March, 1945, General MacArthur declared that this nation "should make every effort to get Russia into the Japanese war before we go into Japan, otherwise we will take the impact of the Japanese divisions [in Manchuria] and reap the losses. . . ."

Japan was closer to cave-in at the time of Yalta than the generals believed. And the Russians, having invaded Manchuria in 1945, prevented the Chinese Nationalists from using Dairen, the most available port in Manchuria, to send forces into the area. When the Russians shortly thereafter began their withdrawal from Manchuria, they carried with them machinery which might have aided China's economic recovery, and they left behind Japanese military equipment which fell into the hands of the Chinese Communists. This brief invasion of Manchuria by the Russians was an important factor in the successful struggle of the Reds for control of north China. Herein lies the most serious indictment that can be made of Yalta's Far Eastern provisions.

Baldwin has been most critical of what he terms "a mistaken political gesture based on a mistaken military analysis." Yalta, he was convinced, made a Pacific power of Russia. Wilmot agreed. Answering Edward Stettinius' oft-stated defense of Yalta that the Soviet Union received less than she might have taken without an agreement, Wilmot posed a counter question: "What did the Soviet Union receive that she could not have taken without flagrantly violating the principles of the Atlantic Charter. . . . ?" Yalta, he charged, "provided Stalin with a moral cloak for his aggressive designs in Asia and, more important, with almost a legal title enforceable at the Peace Conference to the territories and privileges he demanded."[10]

Herbert Feis, who has written a most scholarly and detailed analysis of American postwar policy in China, agreed that the Far Eastern provisions of the Yalta agreement were too hurriedly drawn. The first error, he believed, was the Cairo decision to reduce Japan to a dependent power in the Pacific; the second was the decision to allow Stalin to bargain directly with China at a time when China's power was at a low ebb. Still, many writers have argued that any criticism of the Yalta decision to invite the Russian invasion of Manchuria has the benefit of hindsight. Louis Morton suggests that it was not the atomic bomb alone which accomplished the Japanese surrender. He believes that Russia's declaration of war had an impact on Japan commensurate with that of Hiroshima.[11]

After civil war came to China, even the critics of Roosevelt's wartime policies agree that little could have been done to save the Kuomintang. Feis concluded in *The China Tangle* that by 1945 the problem had moved beyond the limited means and measures of American policy to resolve, for to become openly involved in the Chinese civil war would have been too large and endless a commitment. To crush the Chinese Reds would have necessitated the crushing of a popular revolution. This would have incurred an obligation of incalculable proportions and would not have been to the best interests of the United States. Yet, if this is a proper evaluation of the Chinese scene, then the alternative would have required the immediate recognition of the Chinese Reds as the future rulers of China. Morgenthau believes that the latter course offered some hope of success, for although the Chinese Communists were Marxists, they owed nothing to Moscow for their success. The Chinese, unlike the European satellites, were free to pursue their own diplomatic policy.[12]

United States policy toward China followed neither of the clear-cut courses available. Domestic politics forced the continuance of aid to Chiang, but not enough to save him. American policy failed in that it neither assured the success of Nationalist China nor prevented the building up of intense antagonism in the new Chinese leaders toward the United States as they slowly achieved power.

American policy did not maintain United States interests in China, but none of these critics of American wartime and postwar decisions would agree that Stalin's gains resulted from any conspiracy in the State Department or from Roosevelt's senility. Baldwin, as severe a critic of Roosevelt's policies as any, condemns as ridiculous and disgusting the efforts of those who would attribute treasonable purposes to American leaders for the policies which brought defeat. "This is not history, but politics," he wrote in the *Atlantic,*

a particularly reptilian form of politics which would have us believe that . . . our mistakes at Teheran, Yalta, and above all in our politico-strategic policies were part of a Great Conspiracy intended to hand the country over to Communism on a silver platter. The more quickly such drivel is dismissed the better; we should be able to recognize, pinpoint, and examine the mistakes of the past without indulging in generalized judgments condemnatory to the sincerity, patriotism, and integrity of all who played a role on the stage of history.[13]

American policy failed, agreed Feis. "That being so," he added, "we need not make excuses either to ourselves, the Chinese people, or the rest of the world for having pursued these purposes. Nor should we this soon conclude

that a better appreciation of what we sought to do with
and for China will not emerge out of the debris of hatred
and regret which have silted over it."[14]

§ 3

The powerful neo-isolationist rationale for postwar
American action in the Far East flowed logically from two
assumptions: that the decline of American security had
resulted from erroneous policy (Taft relied heavily on the
criticism of Baldwin); and that diplomatic defeats of such
magnitude could not have stemmed from conditions in the
Orient and therefore must have been self-inflicted. This
implied a complete rejection of the concept of revolutionary change in the Far East. In a bitter memorandum of
August, 1949, Senators Styles Bridges, William Knowland,
Kenneth Wherry, and Pat McCarran termed the China
White Paper "a 1,054-page whitewash of a wishful, do-
nothing policy which has succeeded only in placing Asia
in danger of Soviet conquest." United States policy failed,
in short, because it had pursued the goals, not of this
nation, but of the Soviet Union. Whereas it is true that
many neo-isolationists never accepted the extremism of
those writers who did most to perfect the doctrine of conspiracy, the variance in belief was one of degree and not of
basic assumptions.

Neo-isolationist dogma rested on a foundation that was
easily grasped. The United States had fought a long, bitter,
expensive war in the Pacific only to have its victory
jeopardized by Russian successes. With only five days of
fighting the Soviet Union had gained all of its objectives
in the Orient except a share in the occupation of Japan.
For such Russian triumphs John T. Flynn had only one
answer: "Stalin had to have people who would take an

influential part—indeed a decisive part—in making America's own decisions. And these had to be Americans. No others in any effective measure could get into those innermost spots where the great decisions on the war and on postwar policy would be made."[15] Stalin required control of the State Department. This was easily secured, wrote Flynn, for "America swarmed with spies."

To such new isolationists this betrayal of American purpose abroad required primarily a force outside the government which was equipped to propagandize the American people into an acceptance of its policy as well as to exploit a receptive attitude within the government itself. In her book, *The China Story*, Freda Utley acknowledged a "powerful combine," including the Institute of Pacific Relations and other groups and individuals who "exerted paramount influence on the press and radio and on lecture platforms . . . to spread the gospel according to Mao Tse-tung." In the more colorful rhetoric of *The Yalta Betrayal*, Felix Wittmer attributed American policy to "the pinks and reds of the alphabet group agencies and the legions of blueprint saviors of the world [who] outdid one another in proclaiming the glory of the Kremlin. . . ."[16] More specifically, he pointed to such "stout friends of the Soviet Union" as Dean Acheson, Philip C. Jessup, Archibald MacLeish, George C. Marshall, Henry A. Wallace, and Harry Dexter White.

This coalition which allegedly sold out American interests spread from the IPR through such writers and journalists as Lawrence K. Rosinger, Gunther Stein, Israel Epstein, Thomas A. Bisson, Blair Bolles, and Vera Micheles Dean, and such academicians as Owen Lattimore, John K. Fairbank, and Nathaniel Peffer. These writers were charged with controlling the book-review columns of *The New York Times*, the New York *Herald Tribune*, and *The*

Saturday Review of Literature, and with dominating the viewpoint of *Harper's* and *Atlantic Monthly*. Their numerous articles, continued the accusation, were little but Communist propaganda. Their influence reached out like ripples on a pool, diminishing in depth while they increased in extent, until most who were affected were not conscious of the influence that motivated them.

It is true that most Far Eastern experts in the United States during the war were associated with the Institute of Pacific Relations. Some such as Owen Lattimore were even engaged by the government as specialists. It was this factor that made the IPR vulnerable to the attack of Senator McCarthy in 1950 for allegedly influencing the United States government to adopt its "pro-Soviet" policy toward China. These charges were repeated and eventually built into a total pattern of alleged treason by the McCarran subcommittee of the Senate.

Much had been published through the years under IPR auspices, but there was little evidence that the organization acknowledged or advanced any coherent policy toward the Far East. Defending IPR in a letter to *The New York Times*, William W. Lockwood pointed out that the attack on the Institute was an attack on a whole generation of American scholarship on the Far East and had, therefore, serious implications for American democracy. "There are no easy answers to the problems of Asia," he admitted. "But the least we can do in our own interest is to encourage American officials, journalists, scholars, and businessmen to report freely and honestly their findings, without fear of being irresponsibly labeled as Communists, black reactionaries, or anything else. Otherwise we shall sacrifice one of the chief assets of democracy in its struggle against communism."

This alleged conspiracy penetrated the State Department and the Foreign Service. The immediate blame for the fall of Chiang was borne by John Carter Vincent of the Division of Far Eastern Affairs and by John Paton Davies and John Stewart Service, both foreign service officers in China. Miss Utley in her charges of subversion was never sure whether these men pursued their policy from personal ambition, misunderstanding of the Chinese Communists, or treasonable devotion to their cause. But she concluded: "Those who manipulated the policy of their own government consciously or unconsciously for the benefit of a foreign power by misinforming their own people are more dangerous than spies, even though legally they are not guilty of treason."[17]

McCarthy's original charges against the State Department in 1950 had pointed to individuals, but suggested no pattern of subversion. During the succeeding months and years such writings as those of Miss Utley, William Henry Chamberlin, Geraldine Fitch, and John T. Flynn, substantiated by information secured by the McCarran subcommittee's investigations of IPR, laid bare for the new isolationists an extensive plot to destroy American foreign policy in the interests of the Soviet Union. Flynn believed the case so clear and definitive that "there [could] be no question in any fair mind that Lattimore and his confederates in the IPR and the State Department were responsible for our defeat in China and the victory of Russia."

What gave credibility to this concept was the underlying unity of opinion expressed by most writers on Far Eastern affairs. Whatever their personal views toward communism, all of those condemned for their role in American China policy shared one common assumption—that Chiang Kai-shek's administration had neither the efficiency nor the integrity to hold power in postwar China.

The Nationalist China bloc accepted the thesis that since the Communist party of New York disapproved of Chiang, all Americans who were critical of him were either Communists or fellow travelers. This method of identification placed all but a small fringe of American writers on Far Eastern matters in one enormous pro-Communist camp.

There is little evidence that those who denounced Chiang as hopeless took any pleasure from the anticipation of the Communist victory. For them it was a matter of Chinese selection, and they hoped that future American diplomacy would again build a balance of power in the Orient that would alleviate any loss of American security which might emanate from the fall of Chiang. Whether their lack of confidence destroyed the morale of the Kuomintang or the apparent corruption of the Nationalist regime destroyed their confidence in Chiang is debatable, but the critical attitude toward the Generalissimo persisted. Davies' report of November 7, 1944, was quite typical: "The Communists are in China to stay and China's destiny is not Chiang's but theirs. . . . If the Generalissimo neither precipitates a civil war nor reaches an understanding with the Communists, he is still confronted with defeat. . . ."

Within these predictions of doom was the spirit of warning and the hope that Chiang would save himself by reform. Perhaps General Albert C. Wedemeyer in August, 1947, stated this view as succinctly as anyone:

I believe that the Chinese Communist movement cannot be defeated by the employment of force. Today China is being invaded by an idea instead of strong military forces from the outside. The only way in my opinion to combat this idea successfully is to do so with another idea that will have stronger appeal and win the support of the people. This means that politically and economically the Central Government will have to remove corruption and incompetence from its ranks in order to provide justice and equality and to protect the personal liberties of the Chinese people, particularly of the peasants. To recapitulate, the Central Government cannot defeat the Chinese Communists by the employment of force, but can only win the loyal, enthusiastic and realistic support of the masses of the people by improving the political and economic situation immediately.[18]

For those who saw betrayal in the failure of American diplomacy, each incident in the progression of futility which began in 1945 presented evidence to prove the case against United States leadership. Yalta was not the result of mistaken military intelligence. Rather it symbolized the complete betrayal of Nationalist China. The presence of Alger Hiss at the conference gave credence to this view. Senator Taft observed simply, "It is significant that Alger Hiss was also at the conference and evidently made his influence felt as one of the State Department experts who traveled with Stettinius to Yalta." That Bohlen and others who were present denied that Hiss advised Roosevelt on Far Eastern matters seemed unimportant. The attacks on Yalta continued to be as common as they were savage. Patrick Hurley termed it "immoral and cowardly," whereas William C. Bullitt declared that "no more unnecessary, disgraceful, and potentially disastrous document has ever been signed by a President of the United States." Stanley F. Hornbeck, recalling that Chiang was not present, concluded, "We bought, with Chinese coin, unneeded Russian action and worthless Russian pledges."

These critics agreed that, after Yalta, Chiang might still have been saved but for the weakness of American policy. What corruption had characterized his regime resulted from the enormity of the problems which he faced and from the lack of American support which alone could have made reforms possible. The Marshall mission, which,

Utley has written, forced Chiang to accept a truce at a moment when his troops were victorious, "could only shove China straight into the lap of Moscow."

They accepted the conclusion of General Wedemeyer (who can be quoted on all sides of this debate) that the United States after 1947 had no choice but to increase its resistance to Communist aggression "through the presently corrupt, reactionary, and inefficient Chinese National Government." Continued Wedemeyer, "If Chiang Kai-shek is a benevolent despot . . . or whether he is a Democrat or Republican, that is unimportant. The relevant and important facts are that the man has opposed Communism throughout his history. . . ."

Final success in the struggle for China, then, lay not in the relative support enjoyed by the two antagonists within China, but rather in the extent of their foreign support. The Nationalist Chinese bloc persisted in the charge that the Chinese Reds received continued aid from Moscow (although this is denied by such students of the question as Robert C. North, Max Beloff, and Benjamin I. Schwartz) whereas the United States supported the Kuomintang so meagerly that it fought the crucial battles short of ammunition. Geraldine Fitch concluded in her *Formosa Beachhead:* "There is no doubt of it: *ammunition tipped the scales.* All the guns in the world will not win wars without bullets." The Communist conquest of China was, in simplest terms, a matter of armed aggression, backed by Moscow, which the United States from weakness, stupidity, or treason refused to halt. What delivered China to the Reds, wrote Utley, was "ignorance, refusal to face facts, romanticism, and political immaturity or a misguided humanitarianism, and the influence of Communist sympathizers and the careerists who staked their reputation on a pro-Soviet policy."[19]

§ 4

Not all Republican spokesmen accepted this extremism, but increasingly in 1950 and 1951 the underlying neo-isolationist assumption of internal subversion penetrated G.O.P. thought, oratory, and newspaper editorials. Under this impact the words Tehran, Yalta, and Potsdam became the most powerful political stereotypes of this generation. All three became symbolic of United States defeat which had been engineered in the State Department and Foreign Service. This denial of any competing force in China strengthened the Asia-first orientation of foreign policy which placed its emphasis on rectifying the American position in the Far East rather than on implementing the policy of containment in Europe. "Put in simplest terms," wrote Richard W. Van Alstyne in 1952, "American foreign policy faces the paradox of two dangers: In Asia the danger is that it will meddle too much, in Europe that it will not meddle enough."[20]

Eventually the new isolationism, with the prestige it derived from its grasp on American politics, became a primary determinant in American Far Eastern policy. In its initial stages the new dogma offered no specific solution for the challenge to American security other than the freeing of government from the clutches of those who had served the Kremlin. Even such purpose, however, was sufficient to alter completely the acceptable requirements for successful policy in the Orient. Since the threat to American interests supposedly lay at home rather than in Asia, only a substitution of personnel, provided they were patriotic, would be required to compensate for American losses in China. Secondly, since Chiang had not been deprived of power by any decision within continental China, but rather by indecision within the State Department, future American policy should be devoted primarily to securing his return to the mainland where he would again be welcomed by the Chinese people and would again bring stability to the Orient. And, lastly, since the Communist success in China was the result of military aggression alone, military power properly applied would answer the American purpose in the Far East. After 1950 these three assumptions comprised the foundation of neo-isolationist foreign policy.

But more was required. The furious despair of 1950 explained past failure, but it offered no specific formula to guide future policy nor any assurance of ultimate success. It was General MacArthur who gave the new isolationism its first forward impulse without destroying its previous foundations. In his program was a scheme of analysis by which the United States, without challenging its freedom at home through vast military expenditures, could puncture the Bamboo Curtain and recapture the security which this nation had once enjoyed in the Orient. Its reliance on unilateral action required neither allies in Asia and Europe nor costly economic and psychological programs that promised only intangible results.

President Truman's decision to commit American troops to Korea in June, 1950, produced no immediate reaction on the domestic political scene. Such Republican leaders as Senator Vandenberg attributed the attack to both an over-all American military weakness which had created a power vacuum in the Far East and to the aggressive tendencies of Communist leadership. In a letter of July 3, he lauded the President's action: "When the time came for you to act in behalf of free men and a free world, you did so with a spectacular courage which has revived the relentless purpose of all peaceful nations to deny aggression." General MacArthur who was close to the scene of action added: "The decision of President Truman on June 27 lighted into flame a lamp of hope throughout Asia that was burning dimly toward extinction. It marked for the Far East the focal and turning point in this area struggling for freedom.".

Whatever bipartisanship had characterized the early months of the conflict, it quickly disintegrated after the Red Chinese entered the fray. Months of stalemate in Korea, followed hard by the dismissal of MacArthur in April, 1951, carried the Far Eastern debate to a new stage of intensity and bitterness. Capitalizing on the war's unpopularity, the new isolationists found the argument which rendered the war the unnecessary consequence of faulty policy. The United States had invited the aggression in Korea by failing to create an army in South Korea that would have matched the power of the Communist-led forces of North Korea. Then to make matters worse, in June, 1949, the United States had withdrawn its own troops from South Korea, leaving behind no force sufficient to discourage an invasion from the north. And finally in January, 1950, Secretary Acheson, defining publicly the defense perimeter which this nation would maintain in the Pacific, excluded pointedly both Korea and Formosa. These two areas, said Acheson, could not be guaranteed against military attack.

Neo-isolationists detected in American policy toward Korea in 1951 the same pattern of weakness to which they had attributed United States failure in China. Taft declared that without doubt the administration's vacillation toward Korea invited the Communist attack. The North Koreans had merely taken the Secretary of State at his word. "They knew that we had permitted the taking over of China by the Communists," said Taft, "and saw no reason why we should seriously object to the taking over of Korea. The Korean War and the problems which arise from it are the final result of the continuous sympathy toward communism which inspired American policy." In Korea, declared Miss Utley, "the first payment in American lives was demanded for the blunders of our policy makers in the Far East."[21] For both these spokesmen of the new isolationism the challenges of China and Korea were identical. In each crisis the United States had failed because it refused to apply the requisite military power.

General MacArthur's military program for Korea was hammered into the American consciousness during the noted Congressional hearings at which he appeared early in May, 1951. Throughout the hours of questioning he recognized only one acceptable goal for American policy: the termination of what he described as the weekly and monthly slaughter of American men. The Truman administration, he charged, was wasting human life by its refusal to fight with a will to win. MacArthur's formula for victory was clear, and he assured members of Congress that it could be achieved on Korean soil. First, he insisted that the United States bring needed pressure to bear on the continental Chinese by taking the wraps off Chiang Kai-shek through removal of the Seventh Fleet from Formosan waters where Truman had placed it, by giving him logistical support, and by granting him the freedom to follow his own judgment in launching an offensive against the Reds. Second, he demanded that this nation lift the restrictions on American naval and air forces, blockade the China coast, and warn the Chinese Reds that additional fighting would bring an air assault above the Yalu.

Victory would require no additional ground forces. "Our chief strength is the Air and the Navy, as compared to the Chinese," he said. "That is where we should apply the pressure. . . . They are wide open. And by using those scientific methods which are at our disposal you will obviate the necessity of putting in ground troops and losing them by the thousands as we are doing now."[22]

For MacArthur the Korean War was a challenge that demanded the full attention and strength of the United States. He criticized the administration for not shifting its emphasis to Asia. In his letter to Congressman Joseph Martin in March, 1951, he had written: "It seems strangely difficult for some to realize that here in Asia is where the Communist conspirators have elected to make their play for global conquest; that here we fight Europe's war with arms while the diplomats there still fight it with words. . . ." The General hoped that the European allies eventually would endorse his program, but if they did not, he added, the United States should pursue victory alone.

During the hearings MacArthur recognized no mitigating circumstances in the world-wide nature of American commitments which stemmed quite naturally from the nation's position of world leadership. He admitted no direct concern over the pledges which the United States had given to the United Nations, to NATO, or to the defense of Europe. Nor did he reveal any great interest in matters of atomic preparedness or civil defense. Great nations of the past, always conscious of their far-flung obligations as well as their limited power, had attempted to keep all conflicts as limited and peripheral as possible. Great Britain, for example, followed this principle in her days of greatness in the nineteenth century. Her wars were limited wars—to stop aggression or protect a boundary. Like the famed Crimean War, they did not terminate in total victory. But MacArthur would accept no concept of limited war. Never before in history, he declared, had war been waged piecemeal or available military power held in leash in the interest of political considerations.

MacArthur's critics in Congress feared that his program underestimated the enemy and the danger of general war. Senator J. William Fulbright wondered how air attacks alone on China proper (MacArthur had said that any invasion of China by United States troops would be ridiculous) could terminate the war when the Chinese people had resisted a Japanese invasion in force for thirteen years. He feared that once the United States became committed to victory there was no telling where and when the war against China would end. What magnified the danger of a hard commitment against China was the conviction that Russia, not China, comprised the ultimate threat to American security. Senator Brien MacMahon, stressing the global nature of the struggle between the United States and the Soviet Union, reminded the General that an all-out war against Red China would in no way impair the strength of Russia's divisions, air power, or the size of her atomic stockpile. But MacArthur would not agree that Russian might was the real danger. Rather, he said, it was communism everywhere, even in the United States.

Nor did he believe that expanded war in Korea would bring Russia into the struggle. He felt rather that Russia's military plans were pitched on a broader base than war in Korea, and therefore United States military policy in Korea would have no crucial effect on Soviet moves. He declared that it was more important to end the war than to speculate on what Russia would do. Russia's entry was a normal risk that had to be assumed, and he reminded his critics that the United States had undertaken such broad risks when it entered the Korean War in 1950. MacMahon agreed, but added that the changed nature of the war had vastly magnified the Soviet threat. It was now time, he said, "to stop, look, and listen and see where we are before we plunge into a course that may take us over the precipice before we are ready."[23]

MacArthur's new program for victory fitted the neo-isolationist assumptions precisely. The United States could recover its former position in Asia, while reducing its ground commitments and military expenditures, if it would build future policy around Chiang Kai-shek and United States air and sea power. This was a policy both clear and easily grasped, and the General offered it with a sense of urgency and passion that could not be ignored. He charged that any administration policy which would settle for less than total military victory was guilty of "appeasement." He called past policy weak and "ignominious"—a "callous" policy of "timidity." He attributed it to European dictation which prevented American leadership from defending American interests. "Never before have we geared national policy to [such] timidity and fear," ran his conclusion. His hope for the nation lay in a policy of "spiritual recrudescence."

MacArthur's identification with the new isolationism appeared to give it a deep concern for the outside world which McCarthy with his attention to the State Department and Taft with his program of withdrawal from Europe had not given it. MacArthur, moreover, gave meaning to the Asia-first orientation of the new isolationism. His program appealed to those who disliked Europe but had no animus against involvement in Asia where the challenge was immediate and the military threat less severe. The General, long a national hero, added immeasurably to the political capital which the Republican party could exploit in attacking the Korean policy of the Truman administration.

Although the force of this assault did not reverse the Far Eastern policy of the United States, it did eventually produce a shift in American policy toward two significant neo-isolationist goals. First, it forced the administration to take a more rigid posture toward Chiang and to speed its aid to his Nationalists on Formosa. Second, it strengthened the movement toward an Asia-first policy by increasing Congressional appropriations for the Far East at the expense of the European program.[24] In Korea, however, President Truman continued to hold the line militarily while preventing a general war. General Omar Bradley summarized the administration's position when he declared that any expansion of the Korean conflict would "involve us in the wrong war at the wrong place at the wrong time and with the wrong enemy." Whatever the quality of this concept of limited war, it was one that appeared unequal to the task of capturing the American imagination.

3

The Price of Partisanship

§ 1

To what extent American policy had contributed to the collapse of Nationalist China between 1945 and 1949 was not resolved by the Great Debate. Yet the remorseless subtlety of the neo-isolationist argument burst like a thunderclap over the nation. For those who accepted the conclusion that Chiang Kai-shek had been deprived of power by a combination of Russian aggression and American subversion, the expectation of his eventual return to the mainland was not beyond the American will to achieve. Policy anchored to American sea-air-atomic supremacy might deny the revolutionary content in the Asiatic upheaval, but it promised the re-establishment of the balance of power in the Orient that had existed in 1945. And it promised to effect this illusive object with limited American financial and military commitments.

Within this framework the new isolationism's appeal was magic. It ruled out the need for refined thought and the careful evaluation of world conditions. Since there appeared to be no real threat from abroad, it no longer seemed essential for American citizens or even members of Congress to study Russian policy or attempt to fathom the wellsprings of change in Asia. In fact, the new doctrines

60

logically denied the very existence of the latter challenge. This judgment was not without irony, for those who spoke with the gravest apprehension of the nation's loss of security had the least interest in communism where it existed. The more rampant became the search at home, the less concern its proponents manifested for the 800 million people under Marxist domination residing outside the United States.

Neo-isolationism did not flinch from this apparent absurdity. It continued to speak of the inexorable danger confronting the nation while it neither prepared to meet it with superior force nor to resolve it with negotiation. The frantic search for security at home from those who supposedly had rendered America's position unsafe in the world gave evidence of a hopeless intellectual confusion. George F. Kennan at a Notre Dame University convocation in the spring of 1953 observed of those who promoted it:

They distort and exaggerate the dimensions of the problems with which they profess to deal. They confuse internal and external aspects of the Communist threat. They insist on portraying as contemporary realities things that had their actuality years ago. They insist on ascribing to the works of domestic Communism evils and frustrations which, in so far as they were not part of the normal and unavoidable burden of complexity in our life, were the product of our behavior generally as a nation. . . .[1]

Such a response to the challenge of Communist imperialism in Europe and Asia seemed to assure little but the indefinite perpetuation of tension and insecurity abroad. But it satisfied the underlying insistence that there was an inexpensive way to accomplish the disagreeable and expensive task of maintaining American security in a dangerous world. The price exacted from the performance of

American diplomacy by this illusion of cheap success was enormous. What made the burden even heavier was the resultant creation of illimitable expectations in the minds of the American people.

Whatever the sincerity of those who minimized the external threat to American security, their acceptance of the new isolationism's rationale tolerated no alternative course. To assent to the doctrine that the danger to the nation lay in communism as an agency in the foreign policies of Russia and Red China rather than in communism as a domestic economic and social system would have endangered the intellectual foundations of their position. Only by insisting that the challenge was home-grown could the crusaders give meaning to the broad search for subversives through Congressional investigations rather than through the quiet, continuous, scientific, and necessary search for foreign agents pursued by the Federal Bureau of Investigation. For that reason Congressional action and public discussion, in the words of publisher Arthur Hays Sulzberger of *The New York Times*, made "little distinction between the people who were led into such a system as an academic exercise a decade or two ago and the people who at that time or since became and remained part of an international conspiracy in the interests of Soviet Russia."[2]

Public reaction was intense. Sincere, but bewildered, Americans, moved by the intensity of the accusations, were made aware suddenly of an imminent danger to national security. Their conviction that the United States was threatened by a Communist danger which no one had discovered before led to an air of alarm and anxiety. Its effect on American thought was electric. The illusion of a domestic threat to American purpose abroad, especially in Asia, no longer permitted many American citizens to distinguish between the normal hazards of diplomatic activity and the question of espionage. Convinced that they need not accept the normal burdens of world leadership and the expense and frustration which it entails, they were stampeded into dangerous attitudes which injured their capacity to recognize the real challenges which the United States was facing in the world.

From the repeated denial of any major threat from abroad flowed an impatience urging that anything short of absolute security was utterly intolerable. For many this impatience with living in a dangerous world tended toward a conclusion that there was no solution except the extreme one of atomic war. The persistent reiteration of American invincibility made anything less than the total fulfillment of the nation's will abroad unnecessary and obscured the ultimate costs and penalties that such policy might involve. Some Americans seemed to forget that two world wars had not created a perfect world and that it was doubtful if a third would serve mankind any better.

For students of United States foreign policy this state of mind among many citizens, some in positions of authority, became alarming in its growing instability. In an address at Radcliffe College in June, 1954, Kennan observed: "The lack of flexibility in outlook, the stubborn complacency about ourselves and our society, the frequent compulsion to extremism, the persistent demand for absolute solutions, the unwillingness to accept the normal long-term hazards and inconvenience of great power—it is these things in the American character that seem to me to give added gravity to a situation which would in any case be grave enough. . . ."[3]

§ 2

This concept that perfect security was obtainable exposed the State Department and the Foreign Service to

unlimited attack. For such extremism created a gap between what *was held* to be possible and what actually *was*
possible. This was an area in which the national performance of necessity was inadequate, but one in which the
resulting discrepancy created a field of doubt and suspicion
for partisan exploitation.

From the beginning thoughtful Americans who understood something of the mechanism of policy formulation
in the United States considered the charges leveled at the
State Department unreasonable. As Morgenthau wrote
recently, "The formulation of American foreign policy is
characterized by a diffusion so extreme as to border on
chaos."[4] To subvert American policy another nation would
have required a complete network of agents which would
have penetrated not only the key policy-making posts of
the State Department, but also the National Security Council and the White House. It seemed doubtful in 1950 or
1951 that any foreign power could have established such
a network.

Gradually the attack on the State Department simmered
down to a persistent flaying of Dean Acheson, although
singling out the Secretary of State revealed a certain irrationality in the neo-isolationist position. Before 1950
Acheson had done more to check the Russian advance than
any other public official. He had been an astonishingly
successful Secretary of State; he deserved much of the
credit for the Truman Doctrine, the Marshall Plan, and
the successful establishment of the North Atlantic Treaty
Organization. These achievements, noted the London
Economist, caused Acheson to be "regarded in the outside
world not merely as a good Secretary of State, but as the
best the United States has had in modern times."[5]

Despite their achievements, Acheson's European policies
were too costly to be popular. Then in 1949 came his failure

to save the situation in the Far East. His continued insistence after the opening rounds of the China debate that the problem lay in vast revolutionary changes taking place in the Orient and not at home made him suspect. To men who believed China more important to American security than England, and Chiang's cooperation more essential than that of Clement Attlee or Winston Churchill, the Europe-first policy which Acheson advocated appeared weak and un-American.

After 1950 the search for a scapegoat centered on Acheson, for he was the easiest target in sight. His personality, his genteel New England background, his faultless grooming (one Congressman habitually referred to him as "that goddam floorwalker"), his air of aristocratic detachment, and his intellectual superiority made him superbly vulnerable. As Lester Markel observed early in the fray: "You soon discover in the Secretary his quick intelligence. You suspect this gets him into trouble, because though he may not mean to condescend, he seems often to be condescending."[6]

Acheson became symbolic of that officialdom whose culpability had to be established to prove the soundness of the new isolationist rationale. Consequently, the assault on him reached a virulence seldom equalled in American history. To the British, whose interpretation of the world coincided with his, the charges were unbelievable. John Duncan Miller of the London *Times* interpreted the attack as essentially "a revolt of the primitives against intelligence."[7] The Republican caucuses of both houses demanded his dismissal, and the Nevada Democrat, Senator McCarran, chimed in, "Whether what has been said about him is either proper or correct doesn't matter now." Acheson had been made a political liability and had to go.

Whatever errors were made in American policy, it appears that they were the result of misunderstanding and not treachery. Misconceptions regarding China were held at all levels of American officialdom. It was, Herbert Feis has observed, "The tale of the wearing out of a conception that was not well enough aligned with reality."[8] Yet the expectations that flowed from charges of disloyalty were almost beyond calculation, for it meant that failure in Asia would be remedied by placing wiser and more trustworthy men in charge of American policy.

In essence, the attack on the State Department was not generated by knowledge or proof of subversion, but by the doubt created through a specific interpretation of the recent Chinese past. The reading of history came first. But once it was determined that the United States might have had its way and that Chiang was the recipient of foul play, any American officer who appeared responsible had to be pursued. Whether a huge conspiracy actually existed was not material. The charges had to be made and repeated to substantiate the neo-isolationist analysis of American policy failures in China.

This dogged pursuit of the State Department to validate previous assumptions of subversion placed a burden on it as grave as it was unnecessary. Security became a political football, for the investigations eventually had to prove to the American people that the government was dominated by subversives. No longer would the security system distinguish between the enemies of the United States and those who deserved the encouragement and protection of the American government. Nor was there any method of getting a pursuer off the trail. Men accused of disloyalty could be forced to go before boards time after time. Normally when a man is cleared, he remains cleared. But that was not true as members of Congress after 1950 combed the State Department and Foreign Service for traitors. Critics assumed perhaps that if all important officials in the department were treated as such the nation could free itself of treason. One notable casualty to the United States was the prodigal waste of the talents of many of its trained citizens. As late as 1952 the end was not in sight, but these attacks would not last forever. As Vannevar Bush later observed, their purpose was political and there would be no point in pursuing them beyond their political effectiveness.[9]

§ 3

Under partisan pressure American diplomacy soon lost its flexibility. The immediate issue which confronted Executive judgment in 1950 was the question of the Chinese civil war. Would the President join some twenty-five other nations, including the United Kingdom, and formally terminate the American role in the war by recognizing the new regime? Or would he ignore the new regime and officially permit the war to continue? Americans who believed that the Chinese people had rejected Chiang with finality and could anticipate no loss of American power in recognition, hoped that the President would quietly extricate the United States from an exposed and dangerous position. The Reds would want Formosa, observed Joseph C. Harsch of *The Christian Science Monitor*, for the same reason that Queen Elizabeth beheaded Mary, Queen of Scots, that the French revolutionaries beheaded Louis XVI, and the Russian Bolsheviks, Czar Nicholas. A lost cause is never dead as long as the deposed head lives in exile with powerful foreign support.[10] Such reasoning the Truman administration seemed to accept.

On January 2, 1950, Senator Knowland of California released a letter from former President Herbert Hoover which declared that the United States should continue to support the Kuomintang and, if necessary, extend naval protection to Formosa and the Pescadores. Truman countered three days later with the statement that the United States had no intention of becoming involved in China's civil war by establishing military bases on Formosa or by utilizing American armed forces to protect the Nationalist government. Economic aid would continue, but no "military aid or advice." Also in January, before the National Press Club, Acheson expressed the same attitude toward the future of the Kuomintang and placed Formosa outside the immediate defense perimeter of the United States. But this terminated the Truman administration's "calm reappraisal" of American policy toward China.

Throughout 1950 the new isolationist pressure against accepting the existence of the Red regime in China mounted. In November Knowland warned that if Formosa fell the American defense line would retreat to the Pacific coast. Appeasement, he asserted, is surrender on the installment plan. And he defined appeasement in terms that all could understand:

Talk of seating the Reds in the UN is appeasement. Talk of establishing a neutral zone in Korea is appeasement. Waiting around for Mao Tse-tung to become a Tito is appeasement. The same people who told the United States Mao was only an agrarian reformer are now telling us Mao is a Tito. They are either badly misinformed or deliberately misinforming the American people. They are as wrong now as they were before.

Such intemperate accusations smothered impartial inquiry and made a reasoned discussion of Far Eastern policy almost impossible. The atmosphere of suspicion and fear narrowed the scope of official thought. The administration was forced to uphold its patriotism rather than its policies; no longer did it think seriously of alternatives or their consequences. The President was shortly walking the tightrope between the nonrecognition of Red China and the limiting of war in Korea. He assumed the lead in opposing the Russian move to unseat Nationalist China in the UN. Yet his stand appeared ambiguous to his opponents. He would oppose recognition, he declared, but he would abide by the decision of the majority. Nor did Acheson give any assurance that he would exercise the veto power in the Security Council to block such a move. Meanwhile the Truman administration tacitly agreed to defend Formosa and began the build-up of Chiang's forces.

Gradually the hold of neo-isolationism on American Far Eastern policy tightened. Acheson's ambiguity on recognition intensified the opposition to him. Congressional attacks gradually froze many officials in a position of terror whenever they were confronted with an Asian problem. Finally during the MacArthur hearings of May, 1951, the Republican leadership extracted a promise from Acheson that he would never recognize Red China nor permit the UN to do so. One official even insisted under questioning that the State Department had never contemplated any other course. To bind American diplomacy to an inflexible posture in perpetuity Richard H. Rovere considered absurd, to say nothing of impossible. To discard a potential bargaining point in advance of bargaining, he warned, was a political extravagance that the nation could not afford.[11] At any rate, American diplomatic policy toward the Orient had congealed.

This inflexibility toward China created a serious diplomatic burden for the United States, for the American decision not only appeared to be out of harmony with Western diplomatic tradition, but also it was one shared by no other major power in the world. The question of Red China's admission to the UN was not involved. The

Chinese nation was a charter member of the organization and held a seat in the Security Council. The question was, which regime represented China, the government on Formosa or the Peiping regime? John Foster Dulles had warned in 1950 that the Assembly of the United Nations, if it would serve the cause of peace, must be representative of the world as it is and not include only those portions of which the United States approved. He suggested that this nation accept all others without attempting to separate the "good" from the "bad." Then he added: "If the Communist government of China in fact proves its ability to govern China without serious domestic resistance, then it, too, should be admitted to the United Nations."

But the new isolationists, in their devotion to Chiang's cause, recalled the seldom-applied doctrine that recognition implies approval. They believed that the Chinese Reds, since they were the consequence of treason in our own government, had neither the capacity nor the morality to rule China and therefore wielded no authority which demanded recognition or respect. They believed that the United States had a moral obligation to support Chiang. George Sokolsky stated this thesis succinctly, "The errors which brought on his defeat were not Chiang's; they were Marshall's. They were not China's; they were America's."

This insistence that Chiang's was the actual government of China presented a challenge of broad ramifications to American foreign policy. First, it denied the validity of the classical diplomatic practice that nations recognize *de facto* governments. A justice of the United States Supreme Court reaffirmed in the twenties the standard American tradition that recognition is a matter of observing. Any regime that is obviously in control of another nation's organized government should be recognized. Thomas Jefferson, recalling the recent revolutionary past of the United

States, clearly recognized this principle in his instructions to the American minister at Paris in 1793:

We surely cannot deny to any nation that right whereon our own government is founded—that every one may govern itself according to whatever form it pleases, and change these forms at its own will; and that it may transact its business with foreign nations through whatever organ it thinks proper, whether king, convention, assembly, committee, president, or anything else it may choose. The will of the nation is the only thing essential to be regarded.[12]

Not often has the United States digressed from this principle. Notable exceptions were Wilson's refusal to recognize Latin American regimes of which he disapproved and the prolonged reticence of American presidents before Roosevelt to recognize the Soviet regime of Russia. What was relevant in the issue of Red China was whether the totalitarian aspects of its regime, its disregard for civil rights, and its troublesome foreign policy should deny to it the right to negotiate with other nations and with the UN. Neo-isolationists denied that Red China had any voice outside Moscow. Ran Sokolsky's argument: "It can . . . be regarded as safely within precedent and reason for the United States not to recognize Communist China or any other new Communist country as long as that country's foreign policy is controlled by the Kremlin."

British policy toward China brought the American diplomatic dilemma into focus. Britain from the beginning adopted an attitude of tolerance toward the Peiping regime. Clement Attlee's outspoken friendliness, for example, was designed to please, not offend, the British people. Actually British statesmen and the British press had been at odds with United States policy toward China since the close of the war.

The British distrust for the new American diplomacy

stemmed from three sources. First, the British, having experienced the force of nationalism in India, entertained no illusions about the power being exerted in the current upheaval in the Orient. Thus they disagreed violently with the American neo-isolationist reading of recent Chinese history. Second, the leading British interests in the Orient, unlike those of the United States, never focused on China. To Britain, Malaya and India were of greater importance. Third, the British never shared in the American expectations for the Nationalist regime of China. The Rooseveltian policy of elevating China to a big power status was regarded by England as an American illusion. Since Britain had no special diplomatic or emotional ties to Chiang, his isolation from the mainland in 1949 appeared of minor significance and no major threat to British security.

Always assuming that American policy of supporting Chiang would fail, the British had no desire to back a loser. They had no animus against Red leadership and were ready to offer recognition as early as 1950. Since they accepted Asiatic nationalism as a potent reality, they believed recognition the only realistic China policy available to England. British Foreign Secretary Bevin assumed in 1950 that the Truman administration would agree and shortly extend recognition also.

During the summer of 1950 Britain became alarmed at the continued American commitment to Chiang on Formosa. In August the *Manchester Guardian Weekly* observed: "The Western world is horrified at the thought that by the President's declaration about Formosa the United States may have laid herself open to possible war with Communist China, the very thing the Russians most want to provoke."[13] What the British feared was that the President's effort to neutralize Formosa with the Seventh

Fleet would make the United States appear as the champion of Nationalist China.

Britain feared that American policy, if continued, would one day bring a major conflict to the Far East. "There was a virtually unanimous feeling even in mid-1950," writes Leon Epstein of the British, "that the United States had already alarmed the Chinese Communists by its non-recognition, by its continued attachment to Chiang, by its ambiguous attitude about Formosa, and by MacArthur's apparent intentions [in Korea]. The only point in British dispute," he continued, "was whether America's China policy resulted from honest error or deliberate malice."[14] For Britain, American policy seemed to reveal the petulance of the weak rather than the tolerance of the strong. Only the desire of the British to avoid a sharp break with the United States caused them to refrain from a vigorous challenge to American policy toward China as it evolved in 1950 and 1951.

Nor did the members of Asia's neutral bloc entertain any greater sympathy for the new American diplomacy. Asian leaders, like the British, viewed Mao's success as a matter of Chinese choice and therefore saw no hope for Chiang. They shared neither America's fear of communism nor its hatred of Red China. In fact, since Mao Tsetung represented the most powerful nonwhite nation on earth, they took some pleasure from his success. Being devoid of military power themselves and therefore totally devoted to peace, they resented the American refusal to enter into any negotiations with Red China. Such Asiatic leaders as Carlos P. Romulo of the Philippines, like the British, wondered whether American policy toward China was the result of conviction or the quest for domestic votes.[15]

American neo-isolationist purpose in Asia had one primary goal: to bolster the Chiang regime with the expectation of its return to the mainland. If it did not contemplate this object, then the devotion to his regime was largely without meaning (except for its impact on American politics). Since neither the NATO states of Europe nor the leading nations of Asia would support this goal, the immediate result of American China policy was almost total diplomatic isolation for the United States in this primary objective. United States policy of "going it alone" in the Orient was not the product of an intellectual choice; it was the recognition of a reality.

§ 4

Korea magnified the intellectual confusion created by the appealing assumption that the goal of diminishing Red Chinese power and prestige lay within the immediate capability of the United States. General MacArthur had spelled out the means—the unleashing of Chiang in the Formosan Straits and the more vigorous employment of United States air and sea power in Korea and along the China coast. For those who believed that domestic treason or stupidity had placed Chiang on Formosa this program seemed highly reasonable. During 1951 Senator Taft revealed great indignation that the United States refused to fight with all the means at her command. As early as January he demanded the use of Chiang's troops to relieve the pressure in Korea. The operation, he predicted hopefully, "should be a real hindrance to the occupation of Southeast Asia by Communist armies. In fact, it would seem to be the only hope." In a singular speech in April he gave evidence of his unlimited faith in American power when he demanded a cut in the projected size of the military forces, a reduction in the military budget, and more aggressive war in Asia. He explained his position further in *A Foreign Policy for Americans* when he suggested that the United States stop going beyond its capacity in Europe and increase its aid to friendly regimes in the Far East.

Gradually he became more emphatic. At a University of Chicago Roundtable he said it was "ridiculous to permit American boys to be attacked in an all-out war by Chinese Communists and not to use weapons which are immediately at our command." He would release Chiang and let him engage in raids on the mainland—at least for diversionary purposes. Thomas E. Dewey, returning from the Orient, bolstered Taft's position. "The time for greatness is overdue," he charged. "The time for action is running out. With action on the whole broad front we can, within the reasonable limits of our resources, save the critical Pacific area."[16]

Such views did not go unchallenged. Hanson W. Baldwin charged Taft with oversimplifying the Chinese issue. In his repeated analyses of Chiang's army in *The New York Times* he stressed its lack of immediate effectiveness. "There is a potential on Formosa," he admitted, but he added, "So far it is only potential. There are many things remaining to be done." He agreed that months of training and additional equipment together could make it effective. Taft's critics believed that Chiang's troops would have difficulty in defending Formosa itself and that perhaps a few hit-and-run raids along the coast with naval support from the United States would be the limit of their offensive power. They clung to the conviction that, whatever its quality on Formosa, the Nationalist regime had no political appeal on the mainland. They predicted that if the United States should attempt to place it there, the nation would soon discover the fallacy of Chiang's popularity.

By 1952 the conflict between ends and means in Taft's demands for the Far East had become troublesome, for certain factors in the Asiatic situation seemed to destroy a consistent scheme of implementation. At a Lincoln Day banquet in Seattle, Washington, Taft again called for a Chinese Nationalist invasion of the mainland. "An invasion, well organized," he said, "might snowball rapidly." Now Taft's strategy began to alarm certain fellow Republicans. Senator Wayne Morse of Oregon denounced it as an "ugly proposal on the part of the growing war clique in the United States that we commit an act which constitutes for the first time in American history an aggressive act of war." Then Taft began to demur. He had not meant an invasion of the mainland; he had meant only raids against such Communist-held territory as the island of Hainan. At Pocatello, Idaho, he "would not advocate an invasion of China unless the Communist Chinese move into Indo-China." At Denver the Senator said he favored sending arms to the states of southeast Asia, but not American troops—unless the United States was sure of victory. And if victory was not certain, then these nations "would just have to fall."[17]

Those new isolationists who favored the expanded use of air and sea power to deflate the Red Chinese empire also found their program challenged. Many observers in the United States agreed with the critics of the Truman administration that the acceptance of MacArthur's program would win the undying approval of Syngman Rhee, President of the South Korean Republic, and Chiang Kai-shek, but they believed that continued accession to the wishes of the European allies might better serve the security interests of the United States. Western Europeans feared that the bombing of Manchurian bases and the launching of total war against China would bring retaliatory bombing in

Japan and eventually threaten the world with a general atomic war. Many American military and civil leaders agreed.

In Britain the London *Economist* had no desire to pardon "the clearcut aggression of the Chinese Communists," but it wondered whether the American-led Korean campaign was keeping in view its limited purpose. The British, harboring no legacy of antagonism toward the Chinese Reds, had little interest in any strong declaration against Chinese aggression in the United Nations. Sir Gladwyn Jebb summarized the British attitude, "Let us continue to explore." And Prime Minister Attlee added: "For our part, we have not lost hope of a negotiated settlement of the Korean war. . . . We are, therefore, of the opinion that the UN should not at this stage take a new and important decision." Some loose references by Truman to the atomic bomb brought Attlee to Washington to urge moderation in American policy. By 1952 it was obvious that MacArthur and his supporters were not going to alter appreciably the Far Eastern policy of the United States, but British writers continued to reveal distrust of those Americans who demanded victory in Korea.[18]

Asian attitudes toward the Korean War presented a similar problem. Nehru of India had insisted from the beginning that the Chinese moved from deep-rooted fear of American designs in the Orient. He had warned repeatedly that the United States resolution branding China an aggressor in the UN would not to lead to peace, but only "to an intensification of the conflict." Asia, like Europe, could visualize the destruction of all postwar achievement in another great war. If the nations of western Europe were hesitant because China was so far away, those of Asia were alarmed because China was so close. In the United Nations it was the Asiatic and Arab states, led by

Sir Benegal Rau of India, that assumed the lead in search-
ing for a cease-fire in Korea.

Perhaps a broadened war against China through air and
sea power would not have disintegrated into another world
war. But the danger was never so remote that many noted
American writers would ignore the underlying Russian
threat. War against the Soviet Union appeared hopeless
without allies. Walter Lippmann warned those who would
go it alone in pursuit of victory. "American strategic air
power," he wrote, "cannot be brought to bear effectively
against the vital centers of the Soviet Union . . . except
from bases under British and French sovereignty. . . . We
must not count upon their support if, against their strong
objections, we involve ourselves in a general Asian war. . . ."
Leading journalists in the United States continued to support the concept of limited war, for the new isolationist
quest for total security appeared to be forcing destiny.
James Reston of *The New York Times* captured with precision the real issue in the Korean debate:

The government that extends the war and produces a world-
wide clash is in a much more serious position than the government that moves cautiously in concert with its allies. For if
the government is wrong now in its limited-war policy, it
must merely answer to General MacArthur and its other
critics at home. But if it adopts the MacArthur policy and
fails, then it must answer to the whole world and to history.[19]

§ 5

Finally, neo-isolationism destroyed the liaison between
the student and the politician on matters of Far Eastern
policy. Herein lay perhaps the most serious tragedy which
emanated from the China debate. The Truman administration had accepted the rationale of the academicians that
revolutionary change was sweeping the Far East and that

time-honored principles would no longer succeed in that portion of the world. Acheson had concluded his noted speech before the National Press Club in January, 1950, with the warning that a new day had dawned in Asia. "It is a day," he said,

in which the Asian peoples are on their own, and know it, and intend to continue on their own. It is a day in which the old relationships between east and west are gone, relationships which at their worst were exploitation, and which at their best were paternalism. That relationship is over, and the relationship of east and west must now be in the Far East one of mutual respect and mutual helpfulness. We are their friends. Others are their friends. We and those others are willing to help, but we can help only where we are wanted and only where the conditions of help are really sensible and possible. So what we can see is that this new day in Asia, this new day which is dawning, may go on to a glorious noon or it may darken and it may drizzle out. But that decision lies within the countries of Asia and within the power of the Asian people. It is not a decision which a friend or even an enemy from the outside can decide for them.[20]

After mid-1950 the Truman administration never again followed a policy based wholly on these assumptions.

Yet this concept of change appears to be so patently correct that it has been the theme of almost all books and articles that have been published on postwar Asia in the United States. Recently George F. Kennan, Adlai Stevenson, Edwin Reischauer, and Chester Bowles have developed it again. Few American experts on the Far East—and Stanley F. Hornbeck is a notable exception—have ever accepted the doctrine that Chiang's fall was produced by anything other than the expectations of the Chinese people. To them the great imponderables in the Chinese story were the role of Chinese public opinion, the cost in American lives and financial resources that would have been required to maintain Chiang in power, and the deeper issue of the possible response to such policy in China and throughout Asia. Some would deny that it was the proper function of the United States government to maintain a regime in power that could not maintain itself.

Nationalism's achievements in Asia already have been so enormous that they might well challenge the neo-isolationist reading of Chinese history. Since 1945, 570 million Indians, Pakistanis, Ceylonese, Burmese, Indonesians, Israelis, Filipinos, and South Koreans have attained their sovereignty. An additional 25 million people have become independent who until recently were still under the political dominance of some non-Asiatic power. Over a billion people in the world have changed their form of government since 1945, and in almost all cases the preponderance of military power was against them. How can one deny the force of revolutionary change in China and still account for the upheaval elsewhere in Asia and Africa? Certainly no one would accuse John Paton Davies or Owen Lattimore for the independence of India, Pakistan, Ceylon, Burma, or Indonesia, or for the civil war which in 1950 was already rocking Indochina. Yet all of these changes were the consequence of one force—nationalism—blanketing the region from Morocco to the China Sea.

To attribute recent changes in China which involve a half billion people to a few American personalities is to bestow power upon them which they never had. The insistence that the United States could have determined the course of Chinese history—and that at little cost—assumes that America's will is absolute. It assumes that the United States can demand perfect performance from its Asian policy, not from a balance of commitments and power, but from concepts of morality and legality alone.

Nationalism—the ardent quest for racial, political, and economic equality—has determined the success of all recent political movements in the Orient. It has unleashed such force that alone it would have produced the recent Asiatic upheaval had communism never existed. Wherever in Asia Communist regimes have triumphed or threatened to do so, their leaders have been forced to speak as nationalists and not as Communists. "Communism everywhere," Adlai Stevenson has written, "seeks to ally itself with this vast revolution as its friend and convert it to its ends. And this is a threat at least as great as the long, red shadow of the military might of the Soviet Union with which we are more familiar."[21] These are simple, widely recognized realities, but since 1950 they have baffled those new isolationists who persist in the belief that military force is the only solution for Communist advance. These citizens apparently cannot distinguish between the challenge of Europe which is Russian imperialism and the challenge of Asia which is a revolution of rising expectations.

It is strange that Americans should have so much difficulty in comprehending or appreciating the nature of the Asiatic upheaval. It has been little but the twentieth-century version of this nation's quest for freedom and national equality in the days of the American Revolution. Everywhere American spokesmen have flaunted such words as self-determination, sovereignty, constitutional systems, and individual freedom, and have publicized the desire of the United States to ameliorate the lot of downtrodden peoples. Everywhere colonial nations have been inspired by American experience and pronouncements. Yet those Americans who talk so glibly about freedom are confused by the insistence for something better which now grips people who live in squalor and poverty. They view Asian nationalism, not as a quest for objectives long held dear by the West, but as a source of embarrassment and expense. These attitudes are tragic, for it is difficult to understand how a solid Far Eastern program can be constructed on such foundations of misunderstanding.

Nowhere in Asia after 1950 was American policy anchored to the Asian struggle for equality. With an iron logic, the American posture toward China had forced American leadership, from fear or from conviction, to ignore the tides of nationalism in the Orient. The problem stemmed not from indifference, but from intellectual confusion. Changes which have affected the American people most seriously could not have come from revolution and from treason simultaneously. If one accepted the latter interpretation (or at least performed in office as if he did), then he had logically to reject the former. If one rejected nationalism in China, how could he accept it elsewhere in Asia?

This refusal to recognize the real wellsprings of change in Asia soon became the basic ingredient in the ineffectiveness of American policy. The serious conflict that seemed to exist between American purpose and Asia's nationalistic aspirations caused millions of Asians to be genuinely distrustful of the United States. Many of them, Reischauer has written, actually believed that the United States, with its emphasis on military force, was a greater threat to their independence than the Communist system.[22] The American reliance on military power rather than on popular support convinced them that the United States was bent on pursuing the *status quo* in a continent that is dedicated to change. The bitter resentment of Indian leaders toward American resistance to change in Asia led one to observe that if India had achieved her independence after 1950, she would have faced the opposition of the United States. But it is difficult to support the nationalistic aspirations of a continent when their existence cannot be fully acknowledged.

This intellectual reliance on military policy raises further questions of strategy and understanding. For Americans, it is true, the concept of military force is precise, and it appears reasonable that the United States should use its military might to defend as much of Asia as possible from direct Communist aggression. In practice, however, the area of its employment, even for air and sea power, is narrow indeed. Korea presented an untypical case, because here two conditions for the use of military power existed that have not appeared elsewhere and may not appear again. First, the campaign there was like fighting in one's own back yard because of its proximity to Japan, and both extremities of the defense line were anchored to the sea. Second, since the war there was one of pure aggression, the United States had the local populace fanatically on its side.

Beyond Korea in Asia the problem of military defense becomes more difficult. In Indochina, for example, a war similar to that of Korea would confront the United States with problems of transporting men and matériel two thousand miles, fighting in a more rugged terrain and climate, and maintaining a military line with one extremity melting into the jungle. To the west of Indochina the burdens involved in bringing United States military power to bear would become even heavier. And since the threat to the *status quo* in such regions, as in Indochina, probably would stem from internal revolt rather than external aggression, the United States would find itself in a welter of public apathy or outright resistance. Even the Indochinese Communists, sometimes amazed at their own success, admitted that an army fighting without the support of the indigenous population is like a fish fighting on dry land. Whether the employment or threatened employment of American military power in 1951 presented a realistic answer to the challenge of Asia was subject to doubt.

To the extent that the consequences to American diplomacy which flowed from the China debate were harmful there was nothing unique in them. Partisanship in foreign policy has never been constructive. Those tumultuous months of discussion and accusation in 1950 and 1951 succeeded in producing stereotypes of unquestioned political appeal. They also created new foreign policy illusions which would become the bases of future action. Under the new assumptions the demand for perfection seemed so reasonable because it appeared so attainable. Somewhere in the modern offices of the State Department lay the major threat to American security. To resolve this challenge required little but patriotic leadership. Abroad, especially in the Orient where any genuine strength in the adversary was denied, a limited application of military power would resolve any crisis also. If policy adjustments confused and excited the public, crippled the State Department, threatened to break the alliance, and ignored the challenges of Asia, these were the penalties that had to be paid in bringing American policy into conformity with the new dogma.

Only in the extent of the damage was this political venture into foreign policy unique. Previously such executives as Alexander Hamilton in the 1790's, Polk in his Mexican War policy, and Lincoln during the Civil War, or such leading members of the party responsible, as John C. Calhoun and Thomas Hart Benton in the Oregon crisis, were successful in defending traditional policies against partisan assault. But after 1950 the emotional impact in the United States became so intense that neither the Executive nor such previously bipartisan leaders of the Republican party as Margaret Chase Smith, John Foster

Dulles, John Sherman Cooper, or Henry Cabot Lodge, Jr., could prevent the assimilation of neo-isolationist illusions into official American policy. Nor could they defend successfully the State Department and the Foreign Service against unwarranted attack.

Three factors, it seemed, might eventually destroy the foreign policy symbols of the new isolationism and re-establish some moderation in American Far Eastern policy. These symbols might disintegrate from the weight of their own contradictions. Or new issues might come to the fore on which the Republican leadership might capitalize and thus retain its augmented strength while permitting the stereotypes to die. Lastly, a national Republican admin-istration, against which no charge of subversion could be made effective, might openly challenge the neo-isolationist assumptions, thereby halt the attack on the past, and recover the will to build a new foreign policy toward Asia. Mean-while American diplomacy would continue to grope for answers to the successive challenges of the Far East, isolated from the views of Western and Asiatic statesmen as well as from those of American students of Far Eastern affairs.

4

Foreign Policy In '52

John Foster Dulles, in the bipartisan mood of *War or
Peace,* analyzed succinctly the dangers of submerging
foreign policy in a national political campaign. "If, at a
time of national peril," he wrote, "two presidential can-
didates should compete in making novel and unreasonable
proposals, designed primarily to win votes, the end of the
campaign would leave our foreign policy in a shambles."
His reasoning was acute. In an age of unceasing Communist pressure, American diplomacy, carrying in trust
the future of Western civilization, required the dependability and consistency which would allow it to speak for
many nations and many peoples. It was essential, therefore,
that the United States give assurance to the nations of the
world that its people were "solidly united on the main line
of its foreign policy."[1]

Such observations flowed naturally from the pen of
Mr. Dulles in 1950, for he, with Senator Vandenberg of
Michigan, was a key figure on the bipartisan team of
President Harry Truman. But the foreign policy mood of
the nation was changing precipitously. Republican leaders
after 1950 had conducted a consistent and well-disciplined
campaign to discredit past American policy and to turn it

into a serious political liability for the Truman administration. The new isolationism, taking strength from this bitter controversy, was giving evidence of becoming a decisive force in the domestic struggle for power. By 1952 Senate and House Republicans, determined to capitalize on the issues they had raised, were calculating every move to increase their strength in the coming presidential campaign.

Neo-isolationism in early 1952 had not developed as an integrated program of action. Rather it had evolved from a series of concepts, thoroughly compatible in their basic premises, which together created the appearance of an acceptable alternative to Truman-Acheson policy. Whatever the individual emphasis, the new dogma embraced a primary concern for domestic freedom, a supreme confidence in the nation's power to recreate a world of its own choosing without additional military expenditures, and rejection of compromise with either Russia or China. Upon these premises Herbert Hoover had rationalized his Gibraltarism; Joseph McCarthy, his search for internal subversion; William Knowland, his fervent crusade for Chiang Kai-shek; and General Douglas MacArthur, his proposal for total victory in the Pacific. Each of these specific answers to the problem of American security was anchored to emotional and intellectual foundations which resided deeply in the American isolationist tradition.

This evolving program had promised security in Asia as early as 1951. But its ultimate challenge lay in the necessity of formulating an alternative policy to "containment" of Russia in Europe. United States insecurity, in a sense, stemmed from a swollen and aggressive Russian empire. Democratic policy, with its defensive posture, advanced no alternative to living with this Communist world under conditions of half-war and half-peace. Whatever security was still obtainable it sought in allies and military preparedness. Truman policy, in offering no immediate solutions, was politically vulnerable on three counts: it promised no recession of Soviet influence, it appeared to concede strategic initiative to the Kremlin, and it relied too heavily on ground troops to guard the military sectors in Europe. What was even more serious, it challenged the nation's patience in demanding that it hold a defensive position indefinitely. Such policy seemed to deny the power and resources of a great nation. American policy had become, wrote William Henry Chamberlin, "short on ideas, short on understanding of the nature and methods of the enemy, short on fighting will to win the cold war."[2]

Neo-isolationism required a formula that would give meaning to its postulate of American invincibility in Europe. Nor did this object prove illusive. If, as Senator William Jenner of Indiana had charged, the conflict between freedom and slavery had been lost, not in Europe or Asia, but in Washington, then little would be required but a clean break from the Yalta and Potsdam decisions which had allegedly consigned so many millions to the Russian empire. Not all Republicans agreed that the solution was that simple, but the assumption that the United States could right the balance of world power in its favor without war, increased expenditures, or allies, soon became general among the party leadership.

This rapid evolvement of a policy that guaranteed to re-establish prewar American security within the expectations of the new isolationism reached its ultimate formula in the writings of John Foster Dulles. In his article, "A Policy of Boldness," which appeared in *Life*, May 19, 1952, Dulles quickly came to grips with the dual dilemma of the Truman-Acheson concept of limited power and containment. American military policy, he charged, was so far-

flung and extravagant that it was encroaching on American
civil rights and liberty. Taxes were discouraging incentive.
The burden of American policy was "perilously high in
money, in freedom and in friendships." What was even
worse, American policies were "not designed to win a
victory conclusively."[3] They were based rather on frag-
mentary actions formulated to contain Soviet expansion
"by checking it here or blocking it there." Such policy
appeared designed not to eliminate peril, but to live with it
"presumably forever." Such negative purpose would never
bring security or relief from the exertions which "devour
our economic, political, and moral vitals." "Ours are tread-
mill policies," he said, "which, at best, might perhaps keep
us in the same place until we drop exhausted."

Dulles believed that such policies would eventually
produce either bankruptcy or militarism. To him the free
nations required a better choice than that of "murder from
without or suicide from within." There was, fortunately,
such an alternative available which would stop aggression
and reduce, to the vanishing point, the threat of war.
"There is one solution and only one," he insisted; *"that is
for the free world to develop the will to organize the means
to retaliate instantly against open aggression by Red armies,
so that if it occurred anywhere, we could and would strike
back where it hurts, by means of our own choosing."*[4]

But Dulles promised more. The free world, he believed,
could do far better than merely hold the line against
Russian pressure with the extensive military commitments
of 1952; it could turn also to the political offensive. The
time had come to develop a *dynamic* foreign policy based
on ideas that conform to *moral* principles. American
policy, to succeed, had to move beyond "containment";
it had to seek the "liberation" of those who lived under
compulsion behind the Iron Curtain. No longer dared the

United States shackle freedom and prevent it from threatening the hold of despotism. "We now sponsor the Iron Curtain to cut off our attracting power," ran his accusation, "and thus we help to give depotism a lease on life." American policy, therefore, would achieve its expectations only if it made *"it publicly known that it wants and expects liberation to occur."*

Dulles' policy of liberation demanded above all that the United States not recognize the existence of the Iron Curtain.[5] It should shun any "deals" that would recognize Soviet control over alien peoples. On the other hand, it should encourage the development of "task forces" to develop freedom programs for the satellite nations, gird the Voice of America for this new task, and invite other nations to join the United States in a Declaration of Independence for all captive peoples. The United States must liberate the satellites, not with heavy military expenditures, "but by intelligent care."

Dulles outlined a similar program for the Far East. His views toward the China civil war had shifted markedly from those expressed in *War or Peace*. Now he wrote that the United States should make it clear that it did not regard the Red regime of China as permanent. Rather it should extend moral aid and comfort to Chiang Kai-shek and all who had been resisting Communist expansion. In Asia also, he promised, this nation could right the balance with "more of a hopeful, purposeful, spirited dynamism."[6] A declaration that the United States had assumed a moral position to help the cause of freedom throughout the world, he predicted, would increase American confidence and place American policy again on the offensive. Bipartisanship, Dulles admitted, was no longer possible as long as the administration maintained its primarily defensive concept of foreign policy. "This," he warned, "is not good enough to stand the stresses and strains of these dangerous days."

In Dulles' dual proposal of massive retaliation and liberation the new isolationism reached its final and most perfect expression. Like MacArthur's program for victory in Korea, the Dulles doctrine appeared to have little in common with traditional isolationism. It was positive and forward-looking; it revealed no apparent concern for past failures and therefore required no deep preoccupation with the question of subversion. Yet all the basic assumptions of Dulles' program regarding this nation's will and the power to achieve it were shared by Hoover, Taft, McCarthy, Knowland, and MacArthur. He agreed with all the builders of neo-isolationist doctrine that the chief threat to American security lay in the challenges to domestic freedom in huge government expenditures and large, permanent military establishments. Nor did the concept either of massive retaliation or liberation prepare him to compromise this nation's moral purpose with negotiation. The program of massive retaliation, in fact, could well become a substitute for all diplomacy.

Dulles' devotion to the purpose of liberation illustrated clearly his deep attachment to the limitless expectations of the new isolationism. Critics immediately charged that such policy of inciting rebellion behind the Iron Curtain would lead ultimately to war or to the suicide of the most courageous friends of the West within the Russian empire. But what made the liberation policy even more significant were the apparent assumptions on which it was built. Dulles, in creating such extensive goals for American policy without the anticipated employment of military force, seemed to ignore the role of power in the creation and maintenance of the Russian hegemony over Eastern Europe.

Whether Dulles wanted this or not, it was his denial of power in Eastern Europe that permitted him to give the new isolationism its supreme goal and its ultimate rationale that treason and not the Red Army had created the Iron Curtain. His program permitted Americans to overlook the simple realities of 1945: that in the closing months of the war against Germany the West was still heavily dependent on the power of the Red Army and feared above all a separate Russian peace; and that the major source of Soviet strength at the close of the war lay in the shortage of opposing military power as the Red Army poured into the vacuum created by the retreating German army. At Yalta the heavy price was extracted from the West primarily because it had refused to stop Hitler in the thirties and as a consequence, after 1941, had to rely on Russian power. These facts seemed to be ignored by Dulles' expectations of liberation.

Dulles accepted completely the legalistic insistence of the new isolationists that the United States could have its way in the satellites if it would only stand firm in its moral indignation and persist in the demand that Russia comply with the provisions of Yalta. Here the policy of liberation was building a bridge between the utopian ideals of neo-isolationism and the unpleasant reality of power politics. It gave meaning to the charge of treason as the sole cause of the absolute decline of American security in postwar Europe. It permitted the American people to cling to the myth that United States postwar diplomacy with Russia need have conceded nothing.

Finally, Dulles carried the assumptions of invincibility far beyond those of his predecessors. Hoover and Taft had anticipated little more than the withdrawing of American commitments to the Western Hemisphere. In their retreat from Europe and high taxes they did not foresee the destruction of the Russian threat. They merely ignored it as of no immediate danger to the American way of life.

But Dulles, while rejecting none of the domestic concerns of the new isolationism, would settle for nothing less than the contraction of Russian power. In his formula of limitless expectations he found nothing incompatible between tax reduction and the actual rolling back of the Iron Curtain. Never before had the illusion of American omnipotence demanded so much of American diplomacy.

§ 2

Neo-isolationism was far more than an issue separating the Republican from the Democratic party in 1952. It had become a catalyst whereby powerful Republican politicians, centering largely in the Midwest, hoped to forestall the nomination of a liberal, internationalist G.O.P. candidate, place their favorite, Senator Robert A. Taft of Ohio, in nomination, and strengthen their hold on the Republican party.

Taft in 1952 had reached the acme of his power and influence.[7] His vigorous attacks on the Truman-Acheson foreign policy had made him a world figure. Moreover, they had elevated him to the position of Vandenberg's successor as the key Republican spokesman on foreign affairs. For those who were bent on making the most of the foreign policy issue he loomed as the natural candidate. His basic distrust of the European allies, his staunch support of Chiang Kai-shek, his insistence on tax reduction, his emphasis on air and sea power, and his acceptance of the charge of subversion in the Truman administration made him eminently acceptable to the Republican right wing.

This political element faced its chief barrier to party control in the concerted movement of such liberal Republicans as Henry Cabot Lodge, Jr., of Massachusetts, Thomas E. Dewey of New York, Wayne Morse of Oregon,

James Duff of Pensylvania, George Aiken of Vermont, and Paul Hoffman to seek the nomination of General Dwight D. Eisenhower, then head of NATO in Europe. To the Republican Old Guard this group comprised the urban, industrial, internationalist wing of the party which would perpetuate the Truman policies of "taxation and government spending on the road to socialism."[8]

Neo-isolationism, if it would reach its full potential as a political force, demanded a candidate who would mount the attack against the Truman policies with enthusiasm. The Taftites opposed Eisenhower's nomination, therefore, on two counts: he was committed to what they termed the discredited foreign policy of "tax and spend," and his identification with Truman-Acheson policy would prevent him from assuming the offensive against past policies with sufficient vigor. McCarthy had sought to identify Eisenhower with the actions of General George C. Marshall, which he held responsible for the failure of American policy. Wrote McCarthy concerning Marshall's wartime decisions: "In all these attitudes Eisenhower, who had been Commander-in-Chief in North Africa, was Marshall's firm supporter." Should Eisenhower be elected to the Presidency, warned Usher L. Burdick of North Dakota, it would be safe to predict that he would pursue the same concepts with which he had so long been identified.

Others noted that Eisenhower was strangely silent on matters of foreign policy. "He has gagged himself," complained Thomas H. Werdel of California in the House, "so that he will not discuss the issue until he is nominated at the Republican convention. . . ."[9] Werdel wondered how the General could attack the past "when he has been such a willing and active party to it." Such fears struck deep, but they could not prevent the nomination of Eisenhower at Chicago.

Eisenhower's supporters openly declared his selection a victory for those who believed that American foreign policy, despite the problems it had encountered, was sound in its assumptions of limited power. Lodge had predicted that the General would wield strength, fortify the alliance, and lead the world through the crisis by creating the type of leadership which the nation and the world required. Dulles pointed to his experience in Europe during and after the war which would enable him better to organize a durable and lasting peace. The choice came to Eisenhower, in short, because he could "most nearly solve the great central problem of our time."[10] Those who supported Eisenhower had been critical of American policy, but they had never accepted the new isolationist assumptions that the challenge to American security lay within the United States. Their accent on military preparedness and allies suggested little but new leadership for established policy.

Eisenhower's nomination aggravated rather than relieved the dichotomy within the Republican Party on matters of foreign policy. For the Republican platform, written largely by Dulles, proposed a foreign policy program totally at variance with that associated with Eisenhower. Every charge that had been leveled at the Truman administration and every premise of purposeful failure was written into the document. The Truman administration, it charged, had lost the peace so dearly earned in World War II. Tehran, Yalta, and Potsdam were termed scenes of "tragic blunders" which abandoned friendly nations such as Latvia, Lithuania, Estonia, Poland, and Czechoslovakia to fend for themselves against overwhelming Communist aggression. In Asia the administration had forced Chiang to the wall by denying him necessary support and thus had "subsituted on our Pacific flank a murderous enemy for an ally and friend."[11] Then it had invited the

Korean aggression and "invoked the patriotic and sacrificial support of the American people." But it had conducted the war "without will to victory." The platform scorned the concept of "Europe first." Allied morale in Asia was crumbling, it charged, because Russia's "Asia first" policy contrasted so markedly with the American policy of "Asia last."

Dulles charted the course for the future. He condemned the defensive policy of "containment." A Republican administration, he said, would "repudiate all commitments contained in secret understandings, such as those of Yalta, which aid communist enslavements." It would anticipate the independence of captive peoples. Dulles promised a program that would "mark the end of the negative, futile and immoral policy of 'containment' which abandons countless human beings to a despotism and Godless terrorism which in turn enables the rulers to forge the captives into a weapon for our destruction."

Lastly, Dulles promised to "sever from the public payroll the hordes of loafers, incompetents and unnecessary employees who clutter the administration of our foreign affairs." Instead, he promised to "substitute a compact and efficient organization where men of proven loyalty and ability shall have responsibility for reaching our objectives. They will reflect a dynamic initiative. Thus we can win the support and confidence which go only to those who demonstrate a capacity to define and get results." The new policy, moreover, would be achieved under the goal of a "balanced budget, a reduced national debt, an economical administration and a cut in taxes."

That the Republican high command selected Dulles to write the foreign-policy plank in the Republican platform suggests that he was acceptable to the Taft as well as the Eisenhower wing of the party. Actually by 1952 Dulles, with a long, impressive career in diplomacy, was becoming a leading Republican spokesman in foreign affairs. He was the grandson of John Watson Foster, Secretary of State under Benjamin Harrison, and the nephew of Robert Lansing, Secretary of State under Woodrow Wilson. As a young man Dulles had been secretary to The Hague Peace Conference of 1907 and an adviser to the American delegation at Versailles in 1919. Through his many foreign missions under Roosevelt and Truman and his writings on foreign affairs his prestige had mounted to the point where he had become by 1952 the inevitable choice for Republican Secretary of State.

In the Republican platform, neo-isolationist assumptions of American invincibility had become official Republican policy. American will was fiat all over the globe. For those who took this fiery rhetoric seriously (and one powerful wing of the party did), this platform could expose any future Republican administration that failed to achieve its purposes to endless internal attack and ridicule.

§ 3

Eisenhower's early determination to make foreign policy the key issue in the 1952 campaign produced consternation among those who believed that the growing partisanship of the previous two years was rushing toward extremism and destructiveness. Nor did this decision appear logical. Both Eisenhower and Dulles had been more closely identified with the Truman-Acheson foreign policy than had Adlai Stevenson, the Democratic nominee. Since Eisenhower had been the architect of the NATO defenses, it was assumed that he favored the Europe-first orientation of American policy. He had been Chief of Staff between 1946 and 1948 when the key decisions were made regarding China. Dulles had been a member of several important bipartisan commissions between 1945 and 1949 and had even drafted the Japanese treaty of 1951. The real quarrel of these two men, many observers were convinced, was with the isolationists of their own party. Both Eisenhower and Dulles, noted Ernest K. Lindley in *Newsweek*, were in the worst possible position to use the foreign policy issue.[12]

Yet political necessity drove Eisenhower relentlessly toward the exploitation of the question of foreign affairs. First of all, his views on domestic issues were unknown and appeared unimportant. As one adviser said: "Let's face it: The only excuse for Ike's candidacy is that he's the man best qualified to deal with Stalin." Second, in foreign affairs—high taxes, China, the Korean War, and the possibility of another general war—lay the issues that by 1952 had gripped the American people. Without embracing such issues it was doubtful whether Eisenhower could get his campaign off the ground. (On domestic policy his program seemed to differ little from that of the Democratic party.) Early in the canvass the Scripps-Howard newspapers, in a front-page editorial, reminded Eisenhower that he was "running like a dry creek." That another debate on foreign policy would enliven the campaign was obvious. What mattered was the nature of the alternative that Eisenhower would offer the American people.

That alternative became obvious when Eisenhower made his *rapprochement* with Taft at Morningside Heights in September, endorsed McCarthy and Jenner in the Midwest, refused to defend General Marshall in Wisconsin, and began to accuse the Truman administration of being duped by Communist propaganda. Soon it was noted that the Taft element in the Republican National Committee was playing a larger role in campaign strategy and was gradually pushing Eisenhower's foreign policy statements to the right. So marked was Eisenhower's drift toward the new isolationism, with which Taft had been identified, that early in October Senator Homer Capehart of Indiana prophesied, "In another two weeks, General Eisenhower will be thinking and talking on foreign policy just like Senator Taft."

This new orientation posed a serious intellectual problem for both Eisenhower and the American people. Either the General had never agreed with the Truman policies with which he had been involved, or in the interest of party unity or party victory he agreed to make the most of past failures in foreign policy and secure neo-isolationist support. Before the convention Eisenhower had insisted that he sought the Republican nomination to save the country from Taft and Truman.[13] When he embraced Taft during the campaign, however, his purpose was to elect Eisenhower. For the moment the question of alternatives was sealed. How Eisenhower could avoid accepting premises which would jeopardize future presidential policy was far less apparent. Some observers were willing to write off this new flirtation as a temporary expedient, and many historians have agreed that Eisenhower's decision had no influence on policy formulation; for others the growing commitment of the Republican leadership to new isolationist doctrine would embarrass future United States diplomacy in case of a G.O.P. victory.

At the prodding of Dulles the Republican leadership quickly accepted his "liberation" policy. Before the American Legion Convention on August 25, Eisenhower called attention to those nations which had been forcibly included within the Iron Curtain. "The American conscience can never know peace until these people are restored again to being masters of their own fate," he said. "We can never rest—and we must so inform all the world, including the Kremlin—that until the enslaved nations of the world have in the fullness of freedom the right to choose their own paths, that then and then only can we say that there is a possible way of living peacefully and permanently with communism in the world." In September Eisenhower repeated his conviction that there was no need for the United States to write off the satellites. "The containing of Communism," he charged, "is largely physical and by itself an inadequate approach to our task. There is also need to bring hope . . . to the world's enslaved peoples. . . ."[14] And at Denver in October he declared that the Republican party "pledged repudiation of the Yalta agreement which . . . has resulted in the enslavement of Poland."

Korea was the key issue of the campaign and Eisenhower exploited it in full measure. At Abilene, Kansas, shortly after his return from Europe in June, he admitted that there was no clear-cut solution to the problem. His conclusion was surprisingly candid: "We have got to stand firm and take every possible step we can to reduce our losses and stand right there and try to get a decent armistice." By late August he was becoming ambiguous on events leading up to Korea. He now spoke of the "really terrible blunders," although he did not specify them. Soon he was reaping political capital from the stalemate. By October he declared his conviction that it was a "useless War." Truman and Acheson, he declared, had "made a mess in foreign affairs," had "bungled" the nation into the "seemingly endless" Korean War with its ever-mounting "tragic toll" of American lives. In June he had opposed bombing across the Yalu, but in September he said: "I have always stood behind General MacArthur in bombing those bases on the Yalu from which fighter planes are coming. . . ." The nation, he continued, was right in distrusting leadership that had "allowed the godless Red tide . . . engulf millions . . . [and] failed to see the Red stain seeping into the most vital offices of our Government."[15]

Eisenhower's final dramatic declaration on Korean policy came at Detroit on October 25 in response to Truman's query that he produce an answer to the Korean stalemate if he had one. Eisenhower warmed to the challenge. "The biggest fact about the Korean War," he began, "is this: It was never inevitable, it was never inescapable. . . . There is no other reason than this: We failed to read and outwit the totalitarian mind." Terminating the war was the question which remained, and for that Eisenhower had an answer. He would "forego the diversion of politics . . . to concentrate on the job of ending the Korean war. . . . That job," he continued, "requires a personal trip to Korea. I shall make that trip. . . . I shall go to Korea."

On the actual solution he remained vague and unassuring. He promised to step up the program of arming and training South Korean forces, but he admitted that UN forces would remain of necessity. He would accelerate the program of psychological warfare to crack the Communist front, he would confer with the associated nations of free Asia, and he would always reject "appeasement."

§ 4

Adlai Stevenson's foreign policy statements of the 1952 campaign had no great significance, especially when compared to those of Mr. Eisenhower. But they illustrated a clearly defined body of diplomatic doctrine based on the concept of limited power. As such they revealed the enormous variation which two years of vigorous debate had created in the expectations of leading Americans regarding the nation's purpose abroad. But Stevenson's views, like those of Eisenhower, were partisan, for he could detect little fault in past Democratic policy. He laid claims to Democratic success that were not always warranted.

Repeatedly Stevenson stressed his devotion to the essential direction of past policy. "I think the Soviet Union," he declared, "will be influenced only by a steady, serious undeviating determination to build up the strength of the free world—not with a view toward war but with a view toward preventing war and negotiating the conditions of peace."[16] He foresaw no alternative to diplomacy in achieving any eventual settlement of the cold war. This he would not avoid, he promised, "for to close the door to the conference room is to open a door to war." Meanwhile vis-à-vis Russia he promised only a continuation of the same slow, costly policy of "containment." He promised no tax reduction, for, he said, freedom would remain expensive. During the century from Waterloo to the Marne the British fleet had protected the United States. Now it was this nation's turn to carry the burden of military expenditures.

In his defense of United States policy on China Stevenson revealed the greatest cleavage between his premises and those of Eisenhower. Nationalism, he charged, characterized by the determination of Asia to end legalized inferiority, had produced the upheaval that overthrew Chiang Kai-shek and challenged American complacency elsewhere in Asia. At San Francisco he analyzed the nature of the Asiatic challenge: "Across the continent of Asia more than a billion of the world's peoples are churning in one of history's greatest upheavals. All the struggles of man over the centuries—economic, political, spiritual—have come together in Asia and now seem to be reaching a climax." Only by recognizing the aspirations and grievances of the East, he declared, would American people win the struggle for Asia. He criticized the use of hindsight in attacking China policy. "I don't think," he added, "that tearful and interminable post-mortems about China will save any souls for democracy in the rest of Asia, the Near East and in Africa."[17]

Stevenson upheld the Korean War as a major turning point in history—the first historic demonstration of the effective use of collective security. He admitted his pride in the American decision to resist "that ruthless, cynical aggression; and," he continued, "I am equally proud that we have had the fortitude to refuse to risk extension of the war despite extreme communist provocations and reckless Republican criticisms." He pointed repeatedly to what he felt were gains of the free world in holding the line in Korea, but he promised nothing further. Stalemate, he agreed at Brooklyn in October, was abhorrent to Americans. But, he argued, stalemate was better than either surrender or atomic war. To those who wanted greater assurance of future peace and security, he answered candidly: "I promise no easy solution, no relief from burdens and anxieties, for to do this would be not only dishonest; it would be to attack the foundations of our greatness."

Early in the campaign Stevenson voiced his determination to discuss foreign policy in the bipartisan tradition of Vandenberg so that the American people would become educated on matters of world affairs. He urged that the parties face the issues squarely. "Peace is far more important than who wins the election. Whichever party wins, the American people must be sure to win. Let us not place victory in a political campaign ahead of national interests." Thus ran his warning and he added that the nation "could pay a sad price in misunderstanding or miscalculation abroad" by what was said "intemperately, unwisely and hypocritically to beguile the voters in this campaign."[18]

He hoped that the debate would promise no magic solutions but would point up the real problems that confronted the United States and what actually could and should be done about them.

During September Stevenson became disturbed not only at the mounting attack on the past, but particularly that Eisenhower should have joined the attack. He assumed that Eisenhower's real quarrel was with the isolationists of his own party. Soon the Democratic candidate was accusing his Republican rival of promising too much. At Hamtramck, Michigan, early in September he showed some concern for Eisenhower's newly accepted principle of liberation. He believed this a false issue which would needlessly build the hopes and fears of suffering people and the anxiety of all Americans for their liberation. Stevenson admitted a grave American responsibility for such peoples, but he added: "It should never be an issue among Americans, for we are all united in our desire for their liberation from the oppression and in confidence that freedom will again be theirs." Contracting the Iron Curtain, he said, would require more than magic words, slogans, secret agents, parachute drops, or radio propaganda. "Harsh language and 'cold finality' will do us little good unless we are willing to start a third world war which would end by obliterating the very men and women we seek to liberate," he reminded his audience at Albuquerque.

Liberation policy to Stevenson was no substitute for containment, for he could see no alternative to Truman policy except that of initiating a general war. Therefore, he termed it "a cynical and transparent attempt, drenched in crocodile tears, to play upon the anxieties of foreign nationality groups in this country." His solution to the satellite question was a policy of peaceful and relentless pressure, based on collective strength, which eventually would loosen the Soviet grip over these countries.

Stevenson attempted to defend his party against charges of subversion in past policy which "gave away" Poland and China to the Communists. "If there were mistakes, let us discuss them," he said. "But let us never confuse honest mistakes, mistakes of judgment, with the insidious designs of traitors. Those who corrupt the public mind are just as evil as those who steal from the public purse."[19] When Eisenhower by late September adopted the Taft view of why war came to Korea, Stevenson answered in his Louisville speech: "Many Americans of both parties made the same mistake. Better we refrain from competing in denouncing each other in a scramble for votes, admit our common mistakes—and get on with our business."

Eisenhower's promise to go to Korea produced Stevenson's final bitter condemnation of what he termed the partisan use of foreign affairs in the campaign. He concluded that the repeated criticism of Truman policy had gradually forced the Republican party to produce some straight and easily followed road to peace and world leadership. Declared Stevenson in late October: "The General's advisers seem to have assured him that the American people will buy any merchandise so long as you package it gaudily enough." He admitted the hopelessness of competing with Eisenhower's final declaration of Korean policy. "Rather than exploit human hopes and fears," he declared, "rather than promote glib solutions and false assurances, I would gladly lose this Presidential election." And he did.

§ 5

In gaining victory the Republican Party scored more heavily on foreign policy, particularly the Korean War, than on any other issue. By 1952 the American people apparently had lost patience with months of stalemate. Although the Korean War involved fewer men and in many respects was not as bad as the war against Japan, for countless Americans it seemed to lack purpose. "You see," said one young Philadelphia mother, "the last time we knew that the war would be over when we reached Berlin and Tokyo. Now we're fighting way off there in Asia. And I don't know if our real objective is Moscow or not. If it is, then we ought to be fighting a different kind of war. If it isn't, then I don't know what it adds up to."[20] Eisenhower had become increasingly conscious of the popular dislike for the war and had sharpened his attack as the campaign progressed. The climax of his maneuvering came with his promise to go to Korea.

Elmo Roper surveys, conducted for NBC, revealed that Korea began as the key issue of 1952 and became increasingly important until the end of the campaign. Yet opinion on alternative policies remained completely muddled and irrational. The bulk of the American people opposed Truman's policy, but few would accept either clear-cut alternative to the stalemate—a thorough offensive against the Chinese or a complete withdrawal of American troops from the peninsula. It was this same confusion in American opinion that seemed to crystallize the American frustration. It worked to Eisenhower's advantage, for the surveys indicated a three-to-one conviction that the Republican party could terminate the war more quickly than the Democrats. Korea was the Achilles heel in the Democratic record and the General exploited it skillfully.

Eisenhower and his advisers, in short, had shrewdly judged the mood of the nation and had adapted their campaign to that mood. Thomas L. Stokes later recalled those months of 1952:

Our people were plagued with frustrations of all sorts. . . . The Second World War, with all its bloodshed and sacrifice, had been followed by the "cold war" with its constant tensions, and then the Korean War—all identified with the Democrats. The people were aching for a "deliverer," and it was very natural that they should give a thundering welcome to a hero whose name was a household word.[21]

What the American people seemed to demand was a termination of the recurrent crises of a decade.

But victory conveys its burdens, and for the Republican leadership they were acute. In exploiting the hopes and frustrations of the American people they had brought the new isolationism to the highest point of its prestige and influence. The President-elect had accepted its assumptions and had helped to create the illusion, said one critic, that "in the long struggle against Communist aggression there [was] some easy substitute for unending patience and untiring effort."[22] The campaign had magnified the cleavage in American foreign policy opinion between those who accepted the limitations of the Truman-Acheson program and those who adhered to the unlimited expectations of the new isolationism. During his midwestern tour Eisenhower had identified himself with the isolationist wing of his party; when he invaded the East in October, he had praised past American policy in Europe and recommitted himself to the UN and to NATO. Eisenhower, therefore, was claimed by both extremes. In the election he had shown a remarkable capacity to capture the support of both foreign policy groups simultaneously.

Perhaps it is true, as James Reston has observed, that Eisenhower put more spin on the ball in 1952 than a world series pitcher. Writers on American foreign policy have admitted the importance of the Republican tactics in capturing the American electorate. Yet many have regarded the debate of no consequence for American diplomatic history. Such historians as Foster Rhea Dulles have assumed that the Eisenhower election confirmed the basic purpose of postwar American diplomacy. Others have seen continuity in the fact that Dulles wrote the foreign policy platform of 1952.[23] Such writers conclude apparently that whatever Eisenhower and Dulles might have promised during the campaign, they distrusted neither the intellectual foundations nor the purpose and program of the Truman administration.

Yet the impact of '52 on American foreign relations cannot be that easily disposed of. The real question in any campaign is not whether clever campaigning secures votes, but whether it leaves the victor free to develop intellectually sound judgments—whether it permits him to ignore the commitments which he made both on the political stump and to various blocs within his party. It is perhaps true that voters rarely know what promises are included in a party platform, but what matters is whether there is within the victorious party any faction for whom the specific promises, whatever their nature, are essential for building or maintaining their political power. The real issue is whether such party elements will rebel if the party leadership deserts what is promised, no matter how impossible that fulfillment might be. Perhaps the neo-isolationist aspects of the campaign meant little to Eisenhower, but they were urged by Dulles, his eventual choice for Secretary of State. Dulles had formulated the policy of liberation as well as written the foreign policy platform. Either he had accepted the intellectual foundations of the new isolationism or he had become a political opportunist.

Whatever Eisenhower's previous convictions, it was obvious that he could not ignore the foreign policy program of those who fought his nomination at Chicago. Having sought their support during the campaign, he could not turn on them after the election. They were too powerful, and they would not let him. Stevenson observed in November, 1952, "This suggestion that he will doublecross his new-found friends as soon as he gets into office does credit neither to the General's integrity nor to Senator Taft's vigilance." Despite his personal popularity, Eisenhower's power to ignore this group had grown increasingly less. Administration policy would require the support of Congress where the new President would face in the Senate the augmented power, through committee chairmanships, of such neo-isolationists as Taft, Hickenlooper, McCarthy, Bridges, Bricker, Malone, Jenner, and Knowland. The tragedy of the campaign was that Eisenhower, who had been nominated to quell the neo-isolationist tendencies in the Republican party, had actually tightened the grip of such views on the party.

Republican campaigning in 1952 heightened the discrepancy between ends and means with which the neo-isolationists had inflicted American foreign policy as early as 1950. The new isolationists among the party leadership and members of the press interpreted the Republican victory as a mandate for an Asia-first policy that would return Chiang to the mainland and would seize the initiative in the cold war from the Soviet Union. There was also the expectation that Eisenhower would somehow bring the Korean War to a rapid and honorable solution. Yet there was no apparent source of power available which would enable him to reach any of these objectives more readily than Truman. There was danger, moreover, that the promise of peace in Korea would speed the negotiations for a rapid settlement without resolving all the outstanding issues.

Perhaps the greatest intellectual casualty to Far Eastern policy produced by the debates of 1952 was the profound conviction which it created in the American mind that small, limited wars need play no role in United States policy in the Far East. The campaign strengthened the illusion that this nation could really have its way with air and sea power alone. Surveys during the campaign indicated that the majority of the American people were growing less inclined to bear the brunt of Korean-type conflicts. Here the debate on foreign policy had sadly reduced the acceptable alternatives for future American policy in Asia.

Thousands of Americans took seriously the promise of "liberation" in Europe. This was especially true of such key spokesmen of the new isolationism as McCarthy, Knowland, and Jenner. But critics of this concept in both the United States and Europe still regarded the Red Army as the prime reality in the satellite issue. To them containment was no failure, and they doubted that anything short of war would roll back the Iron Curtain. What Europe thought impossible the Republican leadership had promised. And the American public had accepted not only these expectations but the assurance of a reduction in taxes besides.

Eisenhower could not escape the enfilading fire of this debate. As candidate for the presidency in 1952 he rallied, and it appeared with impunity, to the Republican cry for the immediate and inexpensive reduction of Communist power without compromise. As President, however, whatever the avowed stand of his party, he would of necessity assume the responsibility for finding the diplomatic means of living peacefully with Russia and China. Unfortunately, those who opposed him in 1952 approved this presidential role, whereas the powerful bloc of his own party, the neo-isolationist wing, condemned it. Whatever the nature of future crises, any peaceful arrangement would require accommodation and the rejection of the campaign pledge.

Between the intransigence of the new isolationism and the evolution of future Republican policy lay the immense popularity and the unquestioned mandate for peace enjoyed by President-elect Eisenhower. Political forces in 1952 had not eased the task of American leadership, but they had placed in the White House a distinguished citizen. Observers of the American scene everywhere were not without hope that with his prestige he might neutralize the forces within his party and thereby usher in a new era of competence and flexibility in American foreign relations.

5

Eisenhower and the New Isolationism

§ 1

President Dwight D. Eisenhower learned at least one notable lesson from the rough-and-tumble politics of the previous administration—that partisanship can have a destructive effect on the nation's foreign relations. He appeared determined to avoid the political attacks on Executive judgment which had helped to weaken the leadership of President Harry Truman and which subsided only with the 1952 national election. In keeping with this purpose the new President in his first State of the Union message called for a policy developed between the Executive and Congress "in the spirit of true bipartisanship." Such an objective seemed not only laudable but even essential for the achievement of any effective diplomatic policy within the framework of the American constitutional system. It revealed, moreover, that President Eisenhower had some appreciation for what Senator Vandenberg had termed "nonpartisanship" in the building of successful United States foreign policy.

Perhaps he had no alternative. Despite his enormous personal triumph in the 1952 election, Eisenhower was not assured enough Congressional support for any sustained foreign policy without bipartisanship. Undoubtedly he would require far more aid from his political opposition than did Franklin D. Roosevelt, for even in victory the Republican majority was very narrow. Even more significant were the apparent differences of opinion toward basic Asiatic and European policies between the President and the neo-isolationist wing of the Republican party. Nor could Eisenhower overlook the dominance of the Old Guard element in the narrow Republican majority. This group comprised about two-thirds of the party membership in both houses of Congress. Without Democratic votes it seemed doubtful if the new administration could carry out any foreign policy program. Wrote John M. Vorys, Republican Congressman from Ohio:

There are not enough Republicans who are like-minded enough or disciplined enough to jam through foreign policy measures on a party responsibility basis, even under the lead of President Eisenhower. Congress will have to do what the President deeply and sincerely wants its members to do— work out a bipartisan solution on foreign policy measures. If, instead of dropping to the lowest common denominator, Congress rises above partisanship, we may achieve a foreign policy worthy of our great responsibilities and opportunities.[1]

This basic bipartisan approach to foreign policy seemed to be endorsed by the national election. The President's overwhelming victory, following a campaign in which millions of Americans never questioned his internationalism, indicated strong public support behind any realistic policy, either in defense or negotiation. Congressional elections brought the most significant victories to those who had favored collective security, liberal reciprocal trade agreements, the resumption of diplomacy, and a vigorous bipartisanship in policy formulation. Only two

Republican Senators, Irving Ives of New York and John Sherman Cooper of Kentucky, ran conspicuously ahead of Eisenhower, and both were internationalists. Such nationalists as Joseph McCarthy of Wisconsin and William Jenner of Indiana ran far behind him, while others such as James P. Kem of Missouri, Harry P. Cain of Washington, and Zales N. Ecton of Montana were defeated.

Although still a minority within the party, Eisenhower's Republican foreign policy team was strengthened by the election. Governor Dwight Griswold of Nebraska, a devotee of bipartisanship under Truman and administrator of the Greek-Turkish aid program, replaced the late neo-isolationist, Kenneth Wherry. Governor Frederick G. Paine of Maine, an internationalist, succeeded Owen Brewster. Cooper, who returned to the Senate, had served with United States missions to the United Nations. Several key Democratic victories brought new internationalists to the Senate. John Kennedy of Massachusetts succeeded Henry Cabot Lodge, Jr., while Henry M. Jackson and Mike Mansfield replaced the defeated Cain and Ecton respectively. Mansfield had been regarded as one of the most consistent internationalists in the House.

Eisenhower's initial foreign policy appointments gave evidence of his adherence to past policy. They included Henry Cabot Lodge to the United Nations; James B. Conant, former president of Harvard University, to Germany; and Charles E. Bohlen, a Foreign Service officer closely associated with Truman-Acheson policies, to Russia. Furthermore, Eisenhower and Dulles included key Democrats in their early foreign policy conferences.

Democratic leaders during the early months of 1953 sought to assure bipartisan support for Republican foreign policy. Senator Earle C. Clements of Kentucky voiced the constructive ideal that even if there should be a disruption of interparty unity it need bring no cession of bipartisanship. He reminded the Democrats, "We need to present sensible, realistic and constructive alternatives when the party in power fails in its duty to our country." As long as the new administration pursued the formula laid down by Truman and Vandenberg it could anticipate more aid from Southern Democrats, who had seldom opposed the Truman foreign policies, than from many Republicans.

Leaders of the Democratic minority pledged their support, as did both former President Truman and Adlai Stevenson. Richard B. Russell of Georgia, key Democratic spokesman in the Senate, declared: "My disposition is to try to help General Eisenhower in every possible way. Our big objective now is world peace and times are too perilous to indulge in partisanship for the sake of partisanship." Such declarations of purpose gave evidence of innumerable opportunities for cementing bipartisan relationships under the Eisenhower administration which would be reminiscent of the Truman-Vandenberg alliance. Only policy which directly or indirectly flogged previous Democratic administrations or shifted the emphasis of United States action from Europe to Asia through a blockade of the China coast or the bombing of Manchurian bases would meet the determined opposition of the Democratic minority. Eisenhower's spirit of goodwill convinced many observers that he would destroy completely all previous American animosity over foreign policy and reunite the American people again behind one realistic program which would ease world tensions.

§ 2

For Republican leaders the dichotomy within their party on foreign policy matters made the genuine promise of bipartisanship disquieting. Real interparty cooperation could be achieved only through a strong coalition of internationalist Republicans and the great bulk of Congressional Democrats. But any attempt of Eisenhower to employ this combination in the creation of what might be sound and workable policy would alienate completely the Republican Old Guard and widen the internal cleavage within the party. For those who believed the President above party, such action did not exceed their expectations. But they failed to perceive that Eisenhower would soon prove himself a far better Republican on domestic policies than they had anticipated. From the beginning of his administration the President gave evidence of a deep concern for the strength and welfare of his party organization. So apparent was this allegiance that Senator Taft confounded the predictions that he would head the Senate opposition to Eisenhower's leadership and actually became one of the administration's staunchest defenders.[2]

Whatever problems it might create in the formulation of foreign policies, the Republican high command in 1953 could not ignore the continuing task of building political fences. One triumph at the polls does not create a majority party; it merely presents the victorious machine the opportunity to use its power effectively, and through successful governing to annex permanently those voting blocs which made victory possible. Majority coalitions in American history have been built by political craftsmen who have understood the meaning of their success and have translated it into political action that would meet the challenge of the times.

Presidential politics in 1952 had revealed a significant discrepancy between Eisenhower's popularity and that of his party. Few Presidents have been elected so easily. His widely publicized and genuine personal charm, added to an

illustrious military reputation at a time when such a reputation had some relevance to successful leadership, made
his nomination at Chicago almost synonymous with election to the White House. But the November returns
demonstrated also a general reluctance among the American people to accept his party with any comparable enthusiasm. Unless those foreign policy issues of 1952 which had
proved politically successful could be exploited further,
it seemed doubtful that the Republican party could expand
or even maintain its narrow Congressional majority.

Republican leaders could not ignore the role of the
new isolationism in their victory. The stereotypes of Yalta
and Potsdam had been effective in permitting their party to
cut deeply into the normally Democratic vote. Election
returns indicate that Eisenhower's heaviest gains were made
in the most isolationist areas of the United States. As
Samuel Lubell has indicated, Eisenhower ran strongest in
the same areas where William Lemke, Father Coughlin's
candidate in 1936, and Wendell Willkie, the Republican
nominee of 1940, received their largest vote. Eisenhower's
use of the new isolationism in 1952 again tied the old isolationist vote of the nation to the Republican party.[3]

Eisenhower's identification with the Republican attack
on the Truman leadership secured many crucial votes among
minorities whose national origins inclined them to be hostile
to the foreign policies of the preceding Democratic administrations. Yet it was his traditional acceptance of the
Truman-Acheson premises that appealed to the overwhelmingly internationalist suburban white-collar classes. This
powerful element remained in his camp throughout the
campaign, apparently discounting his criticism of past
policies in the conviction that he would maintain the basic
Europe-first orientation of President Truman. If the votes
captured by the neo-isolationist appeal were only a small

percentage of the total cast for the Republican party, they still had to be favored. In the close balance of power which had characterized politics in the United States since 1938, any shift in voting strength of as little as five per cent would creat a new majority coalition.

What made the challenge to the Republican leadership even more acute was its inclination to interpret the victory as a clarion call to effect a conservative revolution in American economic policies. Taft declared 1952 a mandate on the part of the American people "to get a change from the New Deal-Fair Deal philosophy of government." Key members of the administration shared this interpretation. To Sinclair Weeks, the new Secretary of Commerce, the November election "gave a clear mandate to slam on the brakes and move forward in a different direction." In this concept there was nothing strange, for the segments of any victorious machine always tend to interpret victory in terms of their own philosophy. But it was equally clear that many of the Democrats and independents who chose Eisenhower had no interest in traditional Republican economic dogma. Philip L. Graham, publisher of the Washington *Post*, defined the task of the Republican party in terms of domestic policies:

You cannot keep a Tory government in office simply by saying, "It is less wasteful." The challenge to conservatives in America—and that means largely the challenge to American business—that challenge is to show that there can be conservative social programs. Business must demonstrate that all the twenty years of objections and wails and yells over things such as housing, health, and social security programs, were objections to methods, management, and procedure. And if this conservative party is going to be honest, then it is going to come up with a truly sound, well run, conservative social program—one that will affect the people, one that will do something for their betterment.

If, however, the predominant majority of American business begins to regard social responsibility and good works as merely a sort of obsolescent advertising campaign which was needed when those Democrats were in, therefore no longer needed now, then I think the tenure of this administration is going to be extremely brief.[4]

In essence, the Republican party, with its heavy obligations to American business, had to prove to millions of Eisenhower voters that its economic policies, whatever their nature, were operating in the broad interest of the American people. But it appeared doubtful in 1953 if the Republican party could devise any program of social and economic betterment which could be carried through Congress except with a generous portion of Democratic votes. Nor did the times call for action on the domestic front vigorous enough to solidify the Republican gains. Further victory required the maintenance or creation of political appeals that would help tie a liberal vote to a traditionally conservative party.

It becomes evident immediately why Eisenhower's accession to office would produce no abatement in the intense partisanship over foreign policy which had characterized the late Truman years. The very success of such issues in 1952 in aggravating and exploiting the American inclination toward isolationism and nationalism, particularly in the Midwest, meant that the attack on the past would continue. The Republican victory did not bring the Old Guard into power either within the party or in the nation. During the campaign foreign policy comprised the one genuinely partisan contribution to the Republican position. It was the one party issue that transcended the appeal of the man whose nomination that faction had fought at Chicago. The foreign policy question alone gave promise of future Republican victories when Eisenhower's personality would not be involved.

Senator Taft engineered the renewed attack on the Truman policies. He admitted that additional G.O.P. victories would not be won solely by efficiency, honesty, and frugality in government. Writing for *Look* magazine in April, 1953, Taft recommended a political course that would insure additional victories. "The particular job to be done," he warned members of his party,

is to publicize constantly the contrasts between the present administration and the Truman administration. This is the picture which must be kept before the voters. That means that the mistakes at Yalta and other policies that bequeathed us the Korean War must be constantly developed and brought out. . . . In one way or another, there must be presented to the people the failures in the conduct of the Korean War itself—the lack of ammunition, the mishandling of prisoners, armistice negotiations which enabled the Chinese Communists to build up a tremendously strong force and remedy all their deficiencies, and the outrageous dismissal of MacArthur because he thought that the only purpose of war was victory.[5]

Foreign policy to the Taft Republicans had become the pawn in a conservative revolution, with the failures of American policy in the Orient and Europe being attributed not to past subversion alone, but to the very philosophy of New-Dealism and Fair-Dealism itself. Through Congressional investigations they hoped to delve into everything from past treason and corruption to the alleged futility of the Korean War. Fundamentally, however, the Republican campaign strategy was still moored to the concept that President Eisenhower held the affection and trust of the American people, and that whatever was done to perpetuate past national antagonisms, nothing dared deflate the President's stature. Eisenhower's philosophy toward his office made this dual objective totally feasible. His broad tolerance toward Congressional action permitted Republican leaders a wide range in which to establish the assumptions on which American foreign policy would be founded without destroying the illusion that the President was, in fact, charting the nation's course.

Requirements of party cohesion for continued political success necessitated that the Eisenhower administration waive its search for bipartisan cooperation and reject whatever intelligence the Democratic leadership could contribute to American policy. Understandable as such purpose might have been, it was difficult to see how the paralyzing action of continued partisan attacks on the important Truman decisions could prevent the Congressional usurpation of Executive responsibility or the destruction of genuine accommodation with the allies, the countries of free Asia, or the nations of the Communist world.

§ 3

In the evolving pattern of the new isolationism under the Eisenhower leadership Asia continued to receive top billing. This concept stemmed logically from the fixed orthodox belief that the Truman administration had planned the collapse of Chiang Kai-shek and had refused to win the Korean war against the advice of General MacArthur. "So we now reap the harvest," ran the judgment of Frazier Hunt, the noted journalist, "of our stupidity and our moral cowardice, from the northern reaches of the Western Pacific to the warmer waters of the Indian Ocean."

This conviction that the United States could have had its way in the Pacific reached the extreme in vituperation when Senator Jenner asserted that President Truman had sent United States troops into Korea for the specific purpose of having them defeated. The Democratic administration, he charged, had "ordered American youth to engage in a war halfway 'round the earth, in territory the Fair Dealers had carefully stripped beforehand of every American soldier and virtually every American gun," leaving the South Koreans to stand at the Soviet frontier "armed only with policemen's pistols." The administration then deprived American troops of air support and naval blockade, and finally removed their general in the midst of the campaign. When the American forces, not knowing that they were supposed to lose, proceeded to win the war, the Truman administration "gave away the victory our men had won with their blood."

Nor did such neo-isolationists believe that victory need be denied even in 1953. General James Van Fleet continued to inform the American people that they could still gain an easy victory in Korea. "We are . . . thoroughly and completely superior to the Chinese Reds in North Korea," he observed upon his return from the Far East, ". . . all we have to do is to start an all-out effort in Korea and the Reds will come begging to us . . . any time we want to beat the Reds in Korea . . . I guarantee you it can be done." The Communists, he said, were at the end of their resources when the truce came. The armistice was "like a bell saving a beaten and groggy fighter in the last round." The war could have been won, he added, but "the Truman administration got weak-kneed . . . and was wishfully wanting peace without prosecuting the war to win the peace."

Eventually most of the high-ranking American officers in Korea accepted General Van Fleet's contention that success was needlessly denied the United States forces in Korea. General Courtney Whitney charged the Washington leadership with "timidity and abject wheedling" after

the Chinese Communists entered the war. General Edward
M. Almond declared that the Chinese would never have
entered the war if they had not received some assurance
that their bases across the Yalu would not be destroyed.[6]
Both officers agreed that the United States was deprived
of victory by the dual opposition of the enemy in Korea
and the administration in Washington.

Not all American officers accepted such notions of
superiority. General Matthew B. Ridgway replied "casual-
ties unacceptable" when the Pentagon sought his views on
a general Korean offensive in June, 1952. Ridgway was
convinced that the United States would suffer 350,000 to
400,000 dead and wounded if it attempted to reach the
Manchurian border, and that if the war were pursued into
China the figures would become astronomical. "If we had
been successful in a drive to the Yalu," added General
Robert Eichelberger, "we would have faced millions of
Chinese and Russia's best—its Siberian Army. Napoleon
and Hitler fell into a similar trap in Europe and we [were]
lucky to have avoided one in Asia."[7]

Those who accepted the doctrine of American invincibility in the Far East believed that the time had arrived
in the spring of 1953 for the United States to firm up its
Korean policy and break away from the limitations imposed
by the allies. Their denial of power in the Orient made
logical two normally incompatible hopes—that the United
States could secure what it wanted of China merely by demanding it and that it could actually achieve such an illusive
objective by "going it alone." At Cincinnati, Senator Taft
said that this nation "might as well forget the United
Nations so far as the Korean War is concerned." Others
agreed that the time for unilateral action had come. Representative Lawrence H. Smith of Wisconsin declared that
Taft's was "the lone voice that dares to challenge a policy

of drift and equivocation in the state department." David
Lawrence assured his readers in *U. S. News & World Report* that Taft's position was not isolationism, but that the
Senator "just doesn't believe in sitting by and letting
America get buffeted about by allies."[8] War in Korea had
convinced few new isolationists that the West, even at
small effort and cost, need require less than absolute surrender of its adversaries.

Chiang Kai-shek's supporters in the United States declared openly that Eisenhower's election was a mandate
that the administration abrogate the Truman policy toward
China and give all possible assistance to the Nationalists.
A *Life* magazine editorial asserted that the first require-
ment of a sound China policy was the need of binding
"free China's fate and policy to ours with hoops of steel.
Only on that basis will there be anything to defend."
Henry R. Luce, its editor, after a visit to Formosa, declared
that the Nationalists were living completely for the purpose of liberating China from the Communist regime. The
time had come, he believed, to join hands with the Kuomintang in its struggle to free the mainland. Geraldine Fitch,
in her *Formosa Beachhead* (1953), added real expectations
of success to the proposed venture by asserting that the
overwhelming majority of the mainland Chinese were
"working, watching and praying" for Chiang's return.[9]
Any integrated invasion by 600,000 to 800,000 Nationalist
troops, she wrote, would make "the liberation crusade
snowball from South China to Manchuria."

Throughout 1953, members of the Nationalist China
bloc attempted to force the China issue to its ultimate conclusion. They repeated their charges that coexistence with
the Peiping regime was tantamount to total surrender, that
war with Red China was inevitable, and that the Kuomintang was the last hope for American security in the Far

East. "Let us face one simple fact," Jenner warned the Senate. "There can be no American policy for the Pacific if the Communists are allowed to retain the heartland of Asia. . . . All American policy must start from a firm decision to reestablish the legitimate anti-Communist government on the China mainland."[10] Knowland could no longer visualize any long-run alternative to military action against Red China. In his *Collier's* article of January, 1954, he summarized his concept of an adequate China policy:

If we fail to take a strong stand behind Chiang Kai-shek's government and their claim to their rightful homeland, we are in effect handing all of Asia to the Communist gang. We have lost ground to the Communists in Indo-China, and we allowed the Chinese Reds to stop us in Korea. . . . One more defeat at the hands of the Communists in Asia will spell disaster. . . . We must be prepared, then, to go it alone in China if our allies desert us. Such a desertion is likely. . . . We must not fool ourselves into thinking we can avoid taking up arms with the Chinese Reds. If we don't fight them in China and Formosa, we will be fighting them in San Francisco, in Seattle, in Kansas City.[11]

Nor would the United States require more than air-atomic-sea power to achieve total victory over Red China. William C. Bullitt predicted in *Look* magazine that the United States could turn the balance of power against the Communist world "by a concerted attack on the Chinese Communists, employing no American soldiers except those in Korea, but using the American Navy to blockade the China coast and the American air force to bomb appropriate targets, while assigning the great burden of the ground fighting to the Koreans and the Free Chinese. . . ."

Syngman Rhee of South Korea agreed. He informed a joint session of the United States Congress that the Red Chinese could be overwhelmed with American sea and air power supported by South Korea and Republic of China ground forces. The conquest of Red China, he emphasized, would terminate the tensions of Asia by swinging "the balance of power so strongly against the Soviet Union that it would not dare seek war with the United States." McCarthy believed that a sturdy administration could upset the Red regime with no application of power at all. "We can bring the enemy to their knees," he said in late 1953, "without firing a single shot."

These limitless expectations for United States policy toward Red China carried General MacArthur's assumptions of 1951 to their ultimate formula for successful action. Neo-isolationist demands for a strong course rested on the century-old tradition that the West could act tough in Asia with impunity because that continent had limited military power. This concept in 1953 and 1954 continued to reinforce the Asia-first tendencies of American opinion, allowing many citizens who were isolationist toward Europe to demand all-out war against the Chinese. And it permitted all those who advocated war against the Peiping regime to promise an easy victory.

The concept that the United States could have its way in Asia had a corrupting effect on American thought. It continued to deny all revolutionary change in Asia; it reassured the American people that Korea-type wars were unnecessary—that in the air was the source of overwhelming power that would reinstate the weapon superiority which the West had enjoyed in the early days of colonial rule. Such reliance on military strength permitted air power to become a substitute for understanding, compromise, and friends in the Orient. It gave the United States little alternative, however, to the acceptance of the Dulles doctrine of "massive retaliation" in future diplomatic crises in the Far East.

§ 4

Eisenhower could not escape this powerful Asia-first pressure on his foreign policy. Having accepted the neo-isolationist version of the recent diplomatic past, he could hardly as President repudiate politically or ethically what he had failed to repudiate in advance. At the same time his early speeches indicated that he had no intention of uprooting his second major inheritance, the Truman-Acheson foreign policy. Reconciling this conflict between two totally dissimilar foreign policy programs created the most significant and disturbing dichotomy within the Eisenhower administration.

There was much in the President's early foreign policy statements that seemed to promise a continuation of past Europe-orientated policies, with emphasis on maintaining the Grand Alliance. He accepted as the primary task of American leadership that of developing "the strength that [would] deter the forces of aggression and promote the conditions of peace." Under principles of international cooperation and collective security, he declared, "we stand ready to engage with any and all others in joint effort to remove the causes of mutual fear and distrust among nations, so as to make possible drastic reduction of armaments."

Dulles' view of the first ninety days in April, 1953, likewise placed future reliance on the European Defense Community. His purpose, he said, was to strengthen the Western alliance, not to weaken it through a reduction of American commitments. "Nothing that has happened has induced in us a mood of relaxation or any desire to weaken NATO," he assured the nation. Dulles lauded the State Department and believed it worthy of public trust and confidence. "There is a tendency in some quarters," he admitted, to feel that confidence cannot be placed in these career officials because in the past, as was their duty, they served under Democratic Presidents and Democratic Secretaries of State. It is, however, easier than most think for our career Foreign Service men and women to adapt themselves to new Republican leadership. Like career soldiers, Foreign Service officers respect and welcome high-level policy direction such as they are getting under President Eisenhower. They are, with rare exceptions, a splendid and patriotic group of men and women, with a fine tradition.

This early emphasis of both Eisenhower and Dulles on Western unity augured well for bipartisan support. The views of the new administration appeared to harmonize with the opinions of American academicians, key spokesmen of the Democratic party, and the internationalist wing of the Republican party. Any policy changes toward Europe or the Far East semed to be matters only of degree. Whatever new concepts were forthcoming seemed limited to the creation of sterner alternatives to nations who were hampering American purpose. If the Red Chinese and North Koreans insisted on protracting the war in Korea, or the nations of Western Europe insisted on the privileges of nationalism, they could expect to pay a higher price for American cooperation and goodwill.

But such limited purpose would not satisfy those Republican leaders who anticipated the fulfillment of the campaign pledges of 1952. Whatever their private convictions, Eisenhower and Dulles were required by their political commitments to sustain the illusion that this nation could deflate the size and power of the Soviet empire and restore a world of absolute security.

Eisenhower assured the country in his special foreign policy message of February 2, 1953, that the free world would not remain indefinitely "in a posture of paralyzed tension," for it left the initiative of time and place for future conflict to the aggressor. The administration had "begun the definition of a new, positive foreign policy. . . . Our foreign policy," he added, "must be clear, consistent and confident." In his speech before the American Society of Newspaper Editors in April, the President read the list of objectives for the new program. These included an honest peace in Korea and immediate preparation for holding free elections in a united peninsula, the termination of indirect Chinese attacks on Indochina and Malaya, a satisfactory Russian treaty with Austria, and a Soviet agreement to a "broader European community" which would include a united Germany and the "full independence of the Eastern European nations." The President was not long in adopting the apparently limitless goals of the 1952 platform as the official purpose of his administration.

For Asia this new policy of recapturing the initiative became real in the "unleashing" of Chiang Kai-shek. Dulles announced in April that the United States was speeding up its military assistance to Nationalist China, had already stationed an ambassador at Taipei, Formosa, and had instructed the Seventh Fleet to terminate its protection of the Chinese Communists on the mainland. The President added emphatically that the United States had "no obligation to protect a nation fighting us in Korea." To add reality to the concept that the Nationalists had been unleashed and would shortly seize the offensive against the mainland, the administration pressed Chiang hard to put regular troops on the Tachens. Chiang resisted, believing these islands too distant from Formosa. Eventually he conceded and placed his Forty-sixth Division under one of his ablest generals on these distant outposts.

This new posture of firmness conveyed the impression that Eisenhower and Dulles had successfully forged something stronger than the old Truman "containment" policy. George Sokolsky credited the new administration with a program that was "more positive, more nationalistic, more coherent in the philosophic sense than this country has witnessed in two decades." Whatever Europe thought of American policy, it could place new confidence in the "tough-minded, conciliatory but not compromising" policies of the United States. William Henry Chamberlin announced in his book, *Beyond Containment* (1953), that Eisenhower's April speech, which contained not a word of appeasement, "was a move in the right direction."

But the broadest acclaim greeted Eisenhower's promise of a new, more positive policy toward China. Congressional affirmation was acute among those who had opposed Truman's neutralization of the Formosan Straits in 1950. Senator Taft thought the policy "a step in the right direction." Admiral William Leahy termed it a "bright idea" to let the Chinese Nationalists help in settling "problems along the China coast." General MacArthur said it would "correct one of the strangest anomalies known to military history." It would strengthen the American position in the Far East by releasing the Nationalists for raids on the Chinese coast and would give notice to the Reds that their unprecedented sanctuary would now come to an end. "The modification of the Seventh Fleet's orders," he concluded, "should be supported by all loyal Americans irrespective of party."[12]

The "New Look" in military policy spelled out the effort of the administration to find a working arrangement whereby the Republican party could fulfill its campaign pledge of tax reduction and at the same time answer the charge that national leadership was neglecting the country's defense. Under the direction of such noted industrialists as Charles E. Wilson and Roger Kyes of General Motors, who became Secretary and Deputy Secretary of Defense, the administration reduced military expenditures while claiming that greater efficiency was bringing the nation more defense at less cost. Perhaps the United States received more for its defense dollar, but the level of preparation was lower than it was under the previous administration. Since the present administration did not argue that Truman's advisers overrated Soviet power, it might be concluded, as Donald W. Mitchell observed in *Current History* of October, 1954, "that the New Look accepts voluntarily, for the sake of cutting government costs, greater risks than were formerly regarded as acceptable."[13]

As early as February, 1953, the President stated clearly his purpose of tailoring military power to budgetary requirements. "Our problem is to achieve military strength within the limits of endurable strain upon our economy," he said. By May he was speaking of a budget cut of eight billion dollars to achieve the object of creating a situation of "maximum military strength within economic capacities." He recognized the necessity of maintaining the true military power of the nation, but, he added, "the overwhelming majority of the people of the free world appreciate the fact that a healthy economy and a functioning economy . . . are inseparable from true defense."

Neo-isolationists, with their traditional concern for the domestic economy, found the economic foundation of the "New Look" highly attractive. Knowland warned that prolonged defense spending would permit the Kremlin to achieve its objectives without moving a division across one international frontier.[14] The new accent on air-atomic-sea power was equally popular in that it fulfilled the isolationist purpose of Hoover and Taft to reduce United States ground commitments abroad and place major reliance on sea and air power.

This trend toward air-atomic defense fitted the predilections of Secretary of the Treasury George M. Humphrey precisely, for he represented the powerful business
pressure being exerted on the Eisenhower administration to
reduce taxes. Humphrey insisted that the United States
had "no business getting into little wars. If a situation
comes up where our interests justify intervention," he said,
"let's intervene decisively with all we have got or stay
out." The administration's efforts to reduce the military
defense budget were based on political as well as economic
considerations. The ceiling on national expenditures was
being set not by what the American economy could bear,
but by the political strength that the administration chose
to marshal to push through the costs of an adequate
program.

Military writers doubted the wisdom of a military program dictated by economy rather than combat effectiveness. To such analysts as Hanson W. Baldwin it appeared
that Humphrey rather than the Joint Chiefs of Staff
was dictating policy. He wondered whether man power
reductions were essential to a sound American economy,
or whether the United States really was getting more combat power at less expenditure. He charged the administration with "putting a price tag on national security." To
military critics everywhere the concentration on air-
atomic-sea power seemed to leave little preparation for any
eventuality other than a policy of nonresistance or a program of anihilation. Politically the "New Look," with its
asurance that fighting in mud and foxholes had been out-
moded, had unquestioned appeal (Elmer Davis once remarked that in Washington it was generally understood
that only ground troops have mothers). But it was doubtful whether the new accent on reduced expenditures could
really settle the outstanding issues of the cold war unless

American expectations abroad were significantly down-graded.[15]

§ 5

Unfortunately, party requirements demanded that the Eisenhower administration continue to discount the role of external forces in the nation's loss of security, for to do otherwise would have terminated the cold war against the Democratic party. Any precise acceptance of the Truman-Acheson premise of Russian and Chinese power would oblige the President to oppose extreme attacks on the past. Neo-isolationists agreed that there was no threat of dis-loyalty in the new administration, but they feared that the President, in facing the challenge of world pressures, might ignore their assumptions of invincibility and destroy their symbols by defending the bases of past policy.

Attacks on the State Department had to continue, for here allegedly was concentrated the danger to American security. Critics of past policy grew restive at the reten-tion of Truman-Acheson holdovers. That regime was thoroughly discredited, so the argument ran, and all con-nected with it should be removed from office. "Most Americans," wrote Sokolsky, "desire a pro-American State Department and hope that they will get it in due course." Behind this political assault on the department was the struggle to determine the course of Eisenhower policy and to control the Republican party.

Republican irreconcilables in the Senate vigorously opposed the appointments of Charles E. Bohlen to Russia and James B. Conant to Germany, for both had served under the Truman administration. After a bitter Senate fight Bohlen's nomination was confirmed, but the attack did little to increase the ambassador's usefulness to the nation. "He has gone to his post in Moscow under the cloud of a suspended sentence," wrote one Washington reporter. The Bohlen case was a warning to the administration to disassociate itself from the Democratic diplomatic past and to submit no more names of officers who had served under Acheson. Thereafter the administration was more judicious in its nominations, and ignored in subsequent choices such prominent and distinguished career men as George F. Kennan. When a Senate fight loomed, it ran out on the appointment of Mildred McAfee Horton. Nor did it oppose the relentless pursuit of Foreign Service officers who were associated with United States China policy before 1949.[16]

It required only a few weeks for the Eisenhower administration to arrive at a *modus operandi* with Republican leaders in Congress. After Senator McCarthy of Wisconsin had launched his crusade against the Voice of America and the Overseas Books Program and had negotiated his agreement with the Greek ship owners, he announced publicly, after a luncheon with Dulles, that foreign policy was an Executive function. While the administration thereafter defended nothing that occurred prior to January 20, 1953, the Senator and other Congressional investigators began to limit their attacks to events and personalities of the Truman and Roosevelt administrations. When McCarthy, for example, was frustrated during an investigation of the armed forces during the late summer of 1953, he was specific in naming the culprits. The Army, he charged, was doing "what they did under the Truman administration." While there was a better attitude after Eisenhower assumed office, "the political carry-overs are still functioning to cover up, protect, and white-wash."

It was strange, in a sense, that the administration refused to defend the Voice of America, for it had special significance as an agency in the new Dulles policy of liberation. Dulles had written in *War or Peace*, "We have spent little on the war of ideas in which we are deeply engaged and are suffering reverses that cannot be canceled out by any amount of military power. . . ." He informed Congress shortly before he took office that on the effectiveness of an American program to convey truth to the world "may hang the question of war or peace."

What the attack on the Voice accomplished is not clear. Raymond Aron, the distinguished Parisian journalist, wrote in *The New Yorker* that the attack had a purely political objective and that since there had been no charges of Communist activity in the Voice of America staff, the search was not for subversives but for "a cheap political victory against a group of dedicated anti-Communists." So prompt were the State Department's reversals of policy on the Overseas Books Program resulting from pressure exerted by McCarthy that William S. White of *The New York Times* observed in February, 1953: "No greater series of victories by a Congressional body over a senior Executive Department in so short a time is recalled here."[17]

Perhaps the most disquieting account of those early topsy-turvy days of the Eisenhower administration can be found in Martin Merson's *The Private Diary of a Public Servant* (1955). In this brief volume Merson, consultant to Dr. Robert L. Johnson, President Eisenhower's appointee to head the International Information Administration (which included the Voice of America), describes the dismal record of false accusations, ubiquitous resignations under fire, the disintegration of the Voice of America, and the refusal of the White House to oppose McCarthy or defend anyone who challenged him. By July Merson, along with Johnson, had resigned, puzzled by the refusal of Eisenhower to seek out the American people rather than accommodate himself to Congressional pressure, compromise, and expediency.

With Executive Order 10450 the Eisenhower administration sought to fulfill the campaign pledge of ridding the government of security risks. It appointed Scott McLeod, a close friend of McCarthy and former administrative assistant to Senator Styles Bridges, to administer the order. McLeod soon discovered that he could, without difficulty, remove old Acheson associates under the new order, for it enumerated about seventy characteristics for which a government employee could be termed a security risk. These demanded such rigid standards of political conservatism, previous associations, attitudes, and sexual behavior that few statesmen since Washington could have met all the requirements. Henry Steele Commager eventually denounced the system as a fraud, for he doubted if even a minute investigation of an employee's past could foretell with any accuracy his willingness to defend the nation's interests under future duress.[18]

Under the new security system the administration became involved in the "numbers game." As hundreds were released from federal service, the national leadership was never clear on the number of actual subversives found in the State Department. McLeod demurred when questioned: "I don't think that people are concerned with any breakdown. They don't care if they are drunks, perverts, or Communists—they just want us to get rid of them." In February, 1954, McLeod told a Lincoln Day rally in Worland, Wyoming: "In the twenty years from 1933-1953, traitors had free run in high places and low. It is not for me to tell you why—it is up to those who permitted it to tell you why. . . . I wish they would stop squalling 'smear' and stand up like men and offer an explanation if they can. . . ."[19]

Actually in the first seven months under Executive Order 10450 somewhat less than two hundred "security risks" were removed from the State Department, one of whom was a suspected, but unproved, subversive. In June, 1954, Under Secretary Walter B. Smith testified that not one Communist had been found in the State Department under the Eisenhower order. The administration did nothing to correct this discrepancy; if it had uncovered any subversives it did not reveal them. The new security system, although thousands were released under it, did not turn up a single traitor, spy, or subversive whom the government was willing to indict. This barrenness of results gradually led many to wonder whether there ever was any betrayal in the State Department. As one Democratic spokesman said, "As for McCarthy's constant howls about Reds in government—if the President hasn't found more Communists in executive agencies, perhaps it's because there just weren't any there."

Whatever the responsibility of the State Department in the creation of this nation's postwar problems, Hans Morgenthau believes that it was still in January, 1953, a useful instrument of policy. Many of its top- and middle-level officers were men of such experience, ability, and competence that it was doubtful if they could be replaced by a team of equal quality. Yet during the next two years many of these officers had either been dismissed or had resigned voluntarily. The disintegration of the China Service began under President Truman; by 1954 Congressional attacks had almost denuded the government of experts on China and Russia. These years of political assault, plus the refusal of the administration to protect the State Department and Foreign Service from Congressional cannonading, had so drastically reduced morale that it was doubtful if these agencies still had the capacity to serve as the eyes, ears, and brains of the United States in the area of foreign affairs. Foreign Service officers abroad felt deserted in high places. Many became bitter toward Dulles for not defending them. As one officer declared, "If you can't count on your own Secretary of State to stand up for you, what can you count on?"[20]

As a final gesture to those in pursuit of Foreign Service officers connected with China policy, Dulles dropped John Paton Davies from the Service. The Secretary made it clear that Davies' loyalty was not in question, but under 10450 it was "not enough that an employee be of complete and unswerving loyalty. He must be reliable, trustworthy, of good conduct and character." What made Davies vulnerable was the accuracy of his reporting preceding the collapse of Chiang and his refusal to agree that the Nationalists could recapture the mainland. Having accepted the rationale of the Nationalist China bloc on matters of China policy, the Secretary had no choice but to accede to its pressure.

Critics believed that the Davies case would "complete the wreckage of the Service morale." Kennan predicted that it would produce "great sadness and discouragement." Even the administration's staunch supporter, Arthur Krock of *The New York Times*, described the case as "deplorable," and Roscoe Drummond of the New York *Herald-Tribune* predicted that "if the government keeps this up . . . it won't have a Foreign Service worth the cable costs to transmit its judgments." It seemed to many critics doubtful whether anything that the Secretary might do could repair the damage.

The dismissal of highly respected officers for careful analyses in the past produced a rapid decline in the objectivity and quality of diplomatic reporting. James Reston wrote in *The New York Times* of the impact of Dulles' dismissal of Davies: "If his object was to shut off a source of positive information, the Secretary of State can be assured that he has been fairly successful." There was no assurance that the diplomats abroad would ever again tell him the truth. "Mr. Dulles has half-blinded our watchmen overseas," ran a *Harper's* editorial, "at a moment when clear vision was never more needed."

In a special letter to *The New York Times*, published on January 17, 1954, five well-known and distinguished former members of the Foreign Service—Norman Armour, Robert Woods Bliss, Joseph C. Grew, William Phillips, and G. Howland Shaw—warned the nation that the Foreign Service was being destroyed. They declared that, with rare exceptions, "the justification for these attacks has been so flimsy as to have no standing in a Court of Law. . . ." They were disturbed not only at the dismissal of many officers who in the past had reported conscientiously only to have their loyalty and integrity suddenly challenged, but also at the ambiguous and cautious reporting of those who remained. "When any such tendency begins its insidious work," they added, "it is not long before accuracy and initiative have been sacrificed to acceptability and conformity. The ultimate result is a threat to national security. In this connection the history of the Nazi and Fascist Foreign Services before the Second World War is pertinent."

These men wondered whether the Eisenhower security system which attached undue consideration to political and economic views and casual associations, which opened easy avenues to anonymous informers, and which accepted the evaluations of persons inexperienced in affairs abroad, was not "laying the foundations for a Foreign Service competent to serve a totalitarian government rather than the Government of the United States as we have heretofore known it." It would be tragic, they agreed, if the emphasis on security "should lead us to cripple the Foreign Service, our first line of national defense, at the very time when its effectiveness is essential to our filling the place which History has assigned to us."

Whether the security system had produced more security against future subversion was doubtful, but it was certain that the system had done little for the competence, efficiency, and performance of the Foreign Service. Because of personal connections or the inefficiency of the system some of the old hands remained. Of these, Morgenthau wrote recently, "If and when out of the ruins of today a new foreign service will be built, worthy of the traditions and the mission of America, the nation will owe a great debt to these brave, able, and devoted men who defend in obscurity and against great odds the pitiful remnants of a fine tradition."[21]

It was equally apparent by 1954 that the State Department itself had lost much of its former buoyancy and confidence. The dread of McLeod pervaded every corner of the department. Top officials refused to use the phone for fear that the wires were tapped. William Harlan Hale, returning to Washington after a long absence in Europe, recorded his reaction:

I let myself into the State Department and there encountered a few "Acheson holdovers" cowering in their corners. They had aged, and their voices were low. But, oddly enough, some of the new Republican appointees whom I had met seemed to have muffled voices too. There were some things they preferred not to talk about in their offices: it was like Vienna all over again, where we had learned to beware of eavesdroppers. The "New Look" seemed combined with a new hush.[22]

Eisenhower's willingness to accept the neo-isolationist illusion of domestic subversion posed a curious dilemma.

In his administration's gesture at "unleashing" Chiang Kai-shek, its unwillingness to define policy for Asia in terms of intense nationalism, its dogged pursuit of Owen Lattimore and its dismissal of John Paton Davies, its refusal to defend the State Department, and its vigorous employment of Executive Order 10450, it either believed that a few Americans were solely responsible for the collapse of the Kuomintang or it was willing to pay an exorbitantly high price for party unity. It was not clear how the administration could quiet the continuous neo-isolationist insinuations of past treason and protect American policy from the effect of such attack on both the nation's understanding and its diplomacy unless it were willing to defend vigorously the premises of its basic Europe-first emphasis. For although the President did little to contest the new isolationist notions regarding American will abroad, he still refused to formulate actual policy on these assumptions.

§ 6

President Eisenhower could depend on the liberal Republicans in Congress to support him on both foreign and domestic policies. To meet the challenge of party politics and important economic questions he sought a larger Congressional coalition which corresponded roughly to the united Republican party. To build this coalition the White House in 1953 accommodated itself to Republican Congressional leadership and refused to defy the actions and dogma of the new isolationists. Eisenhower required also a foreign policy coalition which included a large element of Democratic support. Unfortunately, any purposeful move to solidify the latter group would have undermined the effort to build G.O.P. unity. In practice, therefore, the President discarded the machinery of bipartisanship and ignored his foreign policy coalition. This did not injure his program, for in each crisis he received Democratic support anyway. It was the neo-isolationists whose favor he curried who remained rebellious at his leadership in foreign affairs.

Their persistent determination to seize and maintain the initiative in foreign policy formulation and to subordinate the President eventually took the form of the Bricker Amendment. This document was designed to give Congress primacy over treaties and executive agreements. It was basically an effort of neo-isolationist Republicans to gain firmer control over party policy and to assure an isolationist program for the United States. Eisenhower Republicans with the support of Democratic votes were able to defeat the measure in the Senate. But the close vote was a warning to the Executive not to ignore the views of the principal Republican leaders in Congress in the creation of future policy.

To Dulles fell the task of appeasing the Republican right wing. The specific problem of the administration was to prevent Knowland, Bridges, and Jenner from pushing the United States into a war against Red China and McCarthy from abusing the State Department. To quiet these neo-isolationists Dulles breathed fire in defining American purpose abroad while he offered only negative policies. This maneuver seemed to work, for at heart the neo-isolationists, bent on tax reduction, really wanted no more trouble than did the administration.

Whereas Dulles' hard, intransigent line looked to the Old Guard of his party, Eisenhower's persistent attitude of conciliation, his emphasis on peace, negotiation, and Western unity looked to the world and to the American people in general. This cleavage was so obvious in the Eisenhower and Dulles speeches before the American

Society of Newspaper Editors in April, 1953, that it produced a sharp reaction in Europe. One Paris editorialist declared that the President's "conciliatory words and generosity of tone" had been followed by "a harangue in which intransigence competed with mock innocence." The London *Times* found Dulles' remarks "strangely hard to reconcile with the spirit of the President's speech."

This concerted effort to bridge the foreign policy gap within the Republican party prevented Eisenhower and Dulles from putting external affairs on a bipartisan basis. Strong bipartisan policies require the vigorous definition of goals and sources of power to achieve them in terms on which leaders of both parties can agree. But the hard line of liberation and the continuous attack on the past created premises of power with which the bulk of the Democratic party had little sympathy. Whereas Democrats, in general, continued to be intellectually Europe-first men, the President did little to break the powerful Asia-first orientation of his own party. If vocal opposition to Republican foreign policy was almost nonexistent among Democratic spokesmen, bipartisanship, as Senator Vandenberg understood it, was absent from the Washington scene.

Whatever hope President Eisenhower had in January, 1953, of creating a truly bipartisan foreign policy, that purpose lay buried by 1954 under the blanket charges of treason. He had appointed no Democrats to important policy-making positions in the State Department. Those with long experience in foreign affairs were no longer being consulted. Their attendance at conferences would have made little contribution to American foreign policy anyway, for neo-isolationism had made too many inroads into the administration's diplomatic goals. Perhaps the only real contribution which Democratic leaders could make to Eisenhower policy was to withhold their criticism.

Although Eisenhower made no particular effort to cultivate it, he was able to rely on Democratic support for most of his foreign policy program. Democratic leaders pointed out that their build-up of Chinese Nationalist forces on Formosa during the two previous years had anticipated a move commensurate with the President's withdrawal of the Seventh Fleet. Furthermore, many of them believed that the time had arrived to demand more purposeful defense activity from Western Europe as a condition to further aid. This Democratic cooperation, based solely on conviction, accounted for the smoothness of the administration's relations with Congress. The President enjoyed the support of two Congressional coalitions simultaneously, one on domestic and one on foreign affairs. The core of Eisenhower's political success lay in the fact that the Democrats defended his foreign policies in Congress without demanding in return that he defend them from Republican neo-isolationist attacks.

United States foreign policy evolved into a pattern far better than the administration's intellectual commitments to the new isolationism would suggest, for it was the President's unwillingness to pursue the unlimited objectives of the new isolationism in practice that maintained the support of Democrats, liberal Republicans, and independents. Yet his unwillingness to destroy party symbols limited his triumphs, extensive as they were, to areas of action which would not challenge the stereotypes of Tehran, Yalta, and Potsdam. The administration resisted those who would build fortress America on air and sea power alone and terminate aid to the allies. It sought a truce in Korea rather than follow party demands for a renewal of war and a thorough conquest of the Chinese forces. It fought valiantly to maintain the European Defense Community intact. These comprised in a sense the greatest foreign policy achievements of the new administration. There were occasions when the President eschewed some tests which he could have carried with Democratic votes rather than antagonize the Republican right wing.

Republican unity demanded a high price of the administration. No matter how successful its foreign relations might be, it would remain vulnerable to attack, for it would not fulfill its promises of 1952. Unless the administration challenged the premises of disloyalty and subversion upon which the oversimplified assumptions of invincibility were founded, there was no way that it could free itself from its internal contradictions of claiming it could achieve what continuing experiences demonstrated it could not achieve. The full irony of the new isolationism had become clear with Eisenhower's victory of 1952. No change in American leadership would alter Russian or Chinese power and purpose; nor would it reduce the force of nationalistic upheaval in Asia and Africa. Whatever external challenges the United States had faced in the post-war years would continue to exist, but men in power were forced to act as if a new, dynamic foreign policy was actually available which could achieve the goal of security at reduced cost. It was not clear, however, how the Eisenhower administration's premises of invincibility could create a firm foundation upon which to build an effective program which could bring both ends and means, both commitments and power, into balance.

6

In Lieu of Diplomacy

§ 1

Dwight D. Eisenhower's promise of a new, dynamic foreign policy that would deflate the Russian and Red Chinese empires at reduced cost placed an enormous burden on American diplomacy. Enough crusading zeal had accompanied the creation of the Truman cold war policies to rule out all hope of immediate accommodation with the Soviet bloc. But the Republican platform of 1952, having attributed the enslavement of hundreds of millions of Europeans and Chinese to the handiwork of Democratic officials, made the destruction of the Communist hegemony in Asia and Eastern Europe the moral commitment of the Republican party. Thereafter its leaders were forced into the ironical position of having to predicate their future demands on the world on assumptions of American invincibility. After they had captured the isolationist vote through the condemnation of past weakness, they could find no escape from their promises. For to alter their course would either destroy their powerful symbols of past iniquity or expose the fallacy of their position regarding the nation's power to recreate a prewar world of absolute security. Unfortunately, the continued insistence that such illusive goals were actually attainable effectively eliminated all diplomacy, for any success in foreign affairs required nothing short of unconditional surrender from the enemy.

Neo-isolationist purpose reduced the area of negotiation with Russia almost to the vanishing point. Yet neither Eisenhower nor Dulles would defy the promises of '52 by compromising their high expectations of rolling back the Iron Curtain. Dulles affirmed the administration's goal of liberation before the American Society of Newspaper Editors in April, 1953. "It is of utmost importance," he said, "that we should make clear to the captive peoples that we do not accept their captivity as a permanent fact of history. If they thought otherwise and became hopeless, we would unwittingly have become partners to the forging of a hostile power so vast that it could encompass our destruction." The Secretary promised the American people at the outset that there would be no diplomacy on the basis of the *status quo* in Europe. To prove his conviction he dropped ex-Ambassador George F. Kennan, who knew as much about the culture and characteristics of the Soviet Union as many men in the Kremlin, from the diplomatic service because of his previous identification with the Truman policy of "containment."[1]

President Eisenhower, in his first State of the Union message of February 2, 1953, criticized the American agreements which allegedly had brought Russian dominance to millions of Europeans. He would ask Congress, he said, to pass a resolution making it clear that the government of the United States recognized no past accords which condoned such enslavement. This proposed resolution, however, by previous agreement with influential Democrats, did not approach repudiation of Yalta. When it condemned Russia rather than the Roosevelt leadership, it proved totally unacceptable to Senate Republicans. Taft

of Ohio demanded no less than the repudiation of Yalta;
Senator Arthur Watkins of Utah reminded his Republican
colleagues of the campaign pledges. Dulles refused to defend
the resolution in its original form and the entire project col-
lapsed. His Democratic supporters discovered early that
the Secretary was unprepared to defend them in their
quarrels with the isolationists of Congress.

Nor did the Republican high command in Congress,
led by Senator Knowland, cease its exertions to limit
all diplomacy with the Soviet Union until that nation
agreed to release her control over other peoples of Europe.
Tehran, Yalta, and Potsdam—all symbols of failure—
should militate, they agreed, against any further conferences unless the Kremlin made all possible guarantees for
successful negotiations in advance. Senator Bourke Hickenlooper of Iowa warned against "round robin" discussions
with the Soviets. Former President Herbert Hoover
charged that American "acquiescence" to Russian annexa-
tionist policy had "extinguished the liberties of tens of millions of people" in Eastern Europe and should not be
recognized by the Republican administration. Taft rebuked the British and French in May, 1953, for their willingness to abandon the Poles, Czechs, Hungarians, and
Rumanians to the mercies of the Soviets; and Senator Mc-
Carthy warned the administration late that year against
adopting the Truman-Acheson policy of "perfumed notes"
and "whining, whimpering appeasement."

President Eisenhower resisted the Bermuda conference
of December, 1953, and attended it finally as a tough
bargainer. Shortly before the meeting Dulles assured a
House committee that the United States would welcome
the opportunity to settle specific disputes with the Soviet
Union, but he added, "We do not look on the conference
table as a place where we surrender our principles, but

rather as a place for making principles prevail."[2] If Winston Churchill and Premier Joseph Laniel hoped to extract a realistic policy toward Russia from the United States, they were disappointed. Instead, the Bermuda declaration repeated the American rollback policy toward Russia. In its reassurance to the enslaved peoples behind the Iron Curtain it declared: "We cannot accept as justified or permanent the present division of Europe. Our hope is that in due course peaceful means will be found to enable the countries of Eastern Europe again to play their part as free nations in a free Europe."

Whatever the possibilities for successful negotiations with the Russians at the Berlin Conference of January and February, 1954, Dulles' deliberations were doomed by Congressional pressure before he arrived. The Secretary's intransigence permitted the Soviets to make one proposal after another, forcing the American delegation to argue down every move. And because of domestic commitments, the American delegation could advance no ideas of its own. Whether the Russian proposals were sincere, idiotic, or phony made no difference. The Soviets appeared as the genuine seekers of peace, whereas the Americans seemed to be responsible for blocking it. At Berlin the United States might have made some moderate proposals for easing tensions, but the neo-isolationist tradition of American diplomacy ruled out any such possibility. Finally Dulles braved the wrath of Congressional leaders when he agreed to a meeting with Communist China at Geneva late in April, 1954, to seek solutions to the Korean and Indochinese questions.

Eventually American diplomacy, characterized by Dulles' new, hard line, could not even save the European Defense Community. In February, 1953, Dulles visited six European Defense Community countries and Great Britain to warn them that a policy of drift and disunity would dry up the sources of United States military and economic aid. He urged the nations of Europe to perfect the organization of EDC. Having revived the project, he predicted that its completion would shortly be realized. It had become, he informed the nation, "the livest single topic before the six parliaments of continental Europe."

Throughout 1953 and the early months of 1954 Dulles continued to apply the "shock treatment" to France, forcing the issue of EDC ratification on both the French Assembly and the French people. At length he warned that the United States would undertake an "agonizing reappraisal" of its policies if the French did not approve the plan quickly. Europe recognized in these demands a veiled threat that this nation would either return to this hemisphere and rely on air-borne striking power or it would proceed to rearm West Germany without French approval. To European observers such strong alternatives appeared unreasonably severe.

In August, 1954, the French Assembly finally delivered its *coup de grâce* to EDC—a resounding defeat for Dulles' policy of acting tough. It left the West scrambling for the means to tie Germany to an integrated western Europe and to utilize German power in Western defense. Into this vacuum moved the British, deserting their traditional isolation from the continent. Britain feared that any United States move to rearm Germany by by-passing France would expose that nation even more to bitterness and internal dissension. Britain, moreover, shared France's dread of German power and viewed with disapproval a combination of uncontrolled German and United States forces in western Europe that might increase pressure on the Soviet Union. British leaders never accepted Dulles' purpose of rolling back the Iron Curtain; they never shared the moral scruples of the United States regarding the Russian position for they never believed it the creation of Yalta. Nor had they any interest in an aggressive policy that would challenge the *status quo* of Europe.

In the crisis Sir Anthony Eden committed four British divisions to the continent "as long as a majority of the Brussels partners want them there." He saved NATO by placing curbs on Germany satisfactory to the French. Suddenly western Europe enjoyed more unity than had existed earlier. President Eisenhower lauded the new accord as perhaps "one of the greatest diplomatic achievements of our time." At the nine-power conference in London in September, 1954, American policy finally revealed a more compromising tone. Dulles remained calm at French demands for arms control and did not threaten to pull the United States out of the meeting. During the following month the foreign ministers met at Paris to approve the new agreements with Germany. Chancellor Konrad Adenauer of West Germany made the necessary concessions to France on the Saar. Germany received independence and membership in NATO, thus becoming tightly linked to Western defense. British initiative and American cooperation had saved the Western coalition. Yet one diplomat at London still revealed his distrust of American purpose. "This is fine," he admitted, "we will accomplish what we came here for; but please, let us not try to do more, let us not embark on any American 'papers' to turn the Russians out of Poland."[3]

§ 2

United States purpose in Asia, as defined by Dulles in March, 1953, was that of "disengagement." The administration agreed that another ground war in Asia would again pin down the United States and give the Soviets a free hand elsewhere. American security in the Far East required a new balance of power that would allow this nation, like Russia, to play the role of interested bystander. Yet the United States could build this requisite balance only on the support of the neutralist bloc of southeast Asia, for there was no other power on the continent, moral or military, that could contain the aggressiveness of Red China. The specific burden of American diplomacy in the Orient was that of achieving the approval of Asiatic intellectuals before their differences with United States policy would become irreconcilable. This significant group comprised the one great hope of future peaceful and stable American relations with the Far East. Should the alienation become complete, armies, money, and pacts would be of no avail.

In the Korean truce of July, 1953, the administration achieved its first step in its policy of disengagement. Both Eisenhower and Dulles gave the illusion in 1953 that they were willing to use stronger methods to bring an end to the war. When Eisenhower returned from Korea, he admitted publicly in New York that "we face an enemy whom we cannot hope to impress by words, however eloquent. But only by deeds—executed under circumstances of our own choosing." As the negotiations continued through the early months of 1953 Dulles informed the Chinese that unless they agreed to some truce the United States would strike at their Manchurian bases. Nor would the administration accede to the Chinese insistence on "compulsory repatriation" for all prisoners. Eventually a compromise was reached in which each prisoner would be granted his own choice. These became the conditions of the armistice.

Agreement in Korea came hard and promised only temporary relief. What complicated the issue for the administration was its commitment to a united peninsula under Syngman Rhee. Such goals seemed to ignore the reality of Chinese influence and the limited objectives of both the United Nations and the allies during the Korean War. The United States, furthermore, had backed Rhee's demand that India, a neutral nation, be regarded as a member of the Communist bloc. This was not only a grossly untrue analysis of the Indian position, but it also denied to the United States the good services and moral leadership of that important nation. Free Asia was committed neither to Rhee nor to a united Korea. The goal of Korean unification had little support outside the United States and was tantamount to demanding that the Communists surrender at the conference table what they had not been made to surrender on the battlefield.

Korean negotiations also placed the United States in the embarrassing position of dealing with a regime whose existence officially it could not recognize and one to whose downfall it was politically and morally committed. It is never simple to make satisfactory arrangements with a government that cannot be recognized, and Dulles could hardly make an agreement without admitting that the government of continental China did actually exist. Yet the Secretary remained firm. Even an armistice, he said, "would not automatically lift our embargo on strategic goods to Red China or lead to the acceptance of Communist China in the UN."

Eisenhower and Dulles rightly hailed the Korean truce as a triumph for both the administration and the United Nations. Amid the universal relief the administration appeared to overlook certain aspects of the new status of Asia as it planned future policy: This nation had not defeated the Chinese army, it had not united Korea; it had not evolved policy acceptable to the spokesmen of free Asia; it had not settled the Chinese civil war; and it had agreed to truce terms so loosely drawn that they could be intentionally misinterpreted. Hans J. Briner, the Swiss member of the Neutral Nations Supervisory Commission selected to carry out the armistice terms, concluded after his frustrating experiences in Korea that the implied promise of a quick settlement in 1952 had so weakened the United Nations bargaining position that the formula it had secured was actually unworkable.[4]

Whether the United States could extract itself completely from the problems of the Orient which still remained, without recognizing certain claims of Red China, was not clear. Joseph C. Harsch, Washington correspondent of the *Christian Science Monitor*, posed this question in September, 1953:

If Secretary Dulles is firmly set on a policy of "disengagement" from the Far East and if Ambassador Lodge really expects to get American troops out of Korea, then both of them must contemplate the possibility of some sort of progression from the Korean peace conference which would lead to a seat for Communist China in the UN.[5]

Republican stalwarts had already committed the administration to their policy of indefinite nonrecognition of Red China. They had first extracted this promise from Secretary of State Acheson during the MacArthur hearings. Then in June, 1953, they closed in on the Eisenhower administration by attaching a rider to an appropriation bill which declared that the United States would cut off all financial support to the UN if it should seat a Red Chinese delegation. Senator Knowland soon monopolized the headlines when he announced that he would resign his position as majority leader of the Senate and devote his full efforts to seek the withdrawal of United States membership if the UN admitted the Peiping regime. Eventually the Senate neo-isolationists relaxed their pressure on the

President, but only after he had assured them personally that he would oppose vigorously any effort to bring the Peiping government into the world organization. Irreconcilables in Congress still appeared committed to the restoration of Chiang Kai-shek, although it was never certain how they intended to accomplish this purpose. But their approach to the China question was not even challenged in high places.

President Eisenhower improved his liaison with the China bloc by appointing Walter Robertson to the position of Assistant Secretary of State for Far Eastern Affairs. Robertson in China after the war had opposed a coalition government for that nation. Upon his return to the United States he allied himself with the viewpoint of Representative Walter Judd, of Senator Knowland, and of General Albert Wedemeyer, who had shifted by 1953 far from the views of his exhaustive 1947 report on the incompetence of Nationalist China. "If we had paid attention to the reports of Walter Robertson," Knowland once said of him, "we wouldn't be in the mess we are today." In his appointment of Admiral Arthur W. Radford as Chairman of the Joint Chiefs of Staff, the President also placed in high advisory position a powerful member of the Nationalist China bloc. Radford had made no secret of his belief that the Red China regime must be destroyed even if it required a fifty-year war to accomplish it. With Secretary Dulles these men comprised a strong voice in the top echelons of the Eisenhower administration demanding relentless opposition to Red China.

Nowhere was it evident in 1953 that the new administration was ready to come to grips with the most significant alteration of power at mid-century—the consolidation of Communist authority over the mainland of China. The President readily admitted to newsmen that the United

States could not eliminate the Red regime and therefore had to seek the means of living with it peacefully. But in his diplomacy he preferred to keep the question in limbo through continued indecision and temporizing. The President remained officially committed to Chiang Kai-shek.

Alfred Jenkins, State Department officer in charge of Chinese political affairs, defined American policy succinctly in 1954 when he recounted the many misdeeds of the Peiping regime and suggested that United States recognition would deliver a blow to those resisting communism elsewhere in Asia (the most common argument used by those who defend nonrecognition). Then he contrasted the quality of the Communist government with that on Formosa, which, he added, "is far more representative of the will of the Chinese people than is the Peiping regime."[6] Consequently the United States had no intention of tolerating a Red Chinese representation in the United Nations.

This official policy received a vigorous endorsement in *Foreign Affairs*, October, 1955, from Stanley Hornbeck, former Chief of the Far Eastern Division of the State Department. He maintained that recognition confers on the government recognized a body of rights and duties which he doubted the Red Chinese government could properly discharge. American policy, he recalled, had always followed the principle that recognition be deferred until governments gave evidence of governing in conformity with the will of their people. "The American policy," Hornbeck asserted, "is rooted in a belief in the reality of a corpus of moral and divinely ordained law and in practical application of principles evolved and expounded in the corpus of Christian doctrine."[7]

Both Jenkins and Hornbeck objected to recognition on the dual grounds that material advantages alone were no

acceptable criteria for recognition, and that Peiping probably would honor no agreements anyway. As Jenkins said
of the government of Mao Tse-tung, "we recognize with
concern an increase in the incidence of cancer in recent
years, but we refuse to recognize cancer as the inevitable
wave of the future."

United States China policy illustrated the powerful
unilateral tradition of American isolationism that this nation
has the moral and legal right to judge for itself the quality
of an opposing regime. Whatever other countries might
believe, this nation dared cling, because of its power and
virtue, to diplomatic policies with which the bulk of the
world might have little or no sympathy. It suggested with
equal clarity to what extent purely domestic political forces
could conduct this nation's diplomacy. Actually the United
States has recognized countless new governments which
had not demonstrated in advance their ability or willingness to fulfill their domestic and international obligations.
American policy at best has been somewhat less logical
than those who upheld indefinite nonrecognition might
have admitted. But perhaps it was true, as Mr. Jenkins
suggested, that if the cancer were properly ignored it
would eventually disappear, and even without a quarantine.
Perhaps it was equally true, as Eric Hoffer wrote in
Harper's, that "an uncompromising attitude is more an
indication of inner uncertainty than of deep conviction.
The implacable stand is directed more against doubt within than the assailant without."[8]

That the United States was committed to two incom-
patibles in the Orient—an eventually united Korea and the
nonrecognition of Red China—presented no problem to
those who denied the existence of competing power in the
Far East. But these purposes left little margin for com-

promise and thus destroyed United States initiative in the solving of Far Eastern problems. China, like Russia, placed an enormous political burden on the Eisenhower administration, for any movement toward genuine accommodation in Asia would challenge the powerful isolationist symbols. During the first twenty months in office the President announced no program for east Asia which stated conditions for permanent peace except the destruction of the Red Chinese regime.

§ 3

Indochina loomed as the first important crisis area to challenge the Asiatic policies of the Eisenhower administration. There was nothing strange or unique in the Indochinese situation of 1953. For seven years Saigon, its beautiful, French-architectured capital, had been the nerve center of a ruthless civil war. The nationalist movement of the region, vastly strengthened by the Japanese successes in southeast Asia during World War II, had been captured by the Communist leadership of Ho Chi Minh. With the collapse of the Japanese empire in 1945, Ho expected to fill the political vacuum with the creation of an independent republic. But the French had other plans. In 1946, with British help, French forces recaptured control of Saigon and soon came face to face with Ho and his Viet Minh forces to the north.

France was in no mood to see her declining prestige in the Orient vanish with the loss of Indochina, and the French constitution of 1946 anticipated neither independence nor dominion status for her great colony. As French diplomacy with Ho gradually disintegrated into civil war, the United States sided with the French and by 1950 had recognized the French puppet regime of Bao Dai. From the beginning of the civil war American observers predicted eventual French defeat, for they saw that Indochina's powerful nationalistic upheaval was working for Ho. But for American neo-isolationists after 1950, having denied the revolutionary content in the Chinese civil war, the struggle for Indochina remained a matter of pure Communist aggression emanating from Peiping and Moscow which would be resolved with military power alone.

Repeatedly, following the Korean armistice Dulles had warned the Chinese of "grave consequences" if they transferred their forces from Korea to Indochina where, despite continued and extensive American military aid, the French forces were still in retreat. Nowhere on the horizon was there any coalition of power sufficiently in sympathy with French purpose to resist the thrusts of Ho Chi Minh and his allies. The free nations of Asia had no interest in the war (except to see the French driven out). Even the French, after seven years of futility, were ready to compromise with the Viet Minh forces. Nor could the United Nations step into the breach, for the American threat of action had been unilateral and no other power had enough concern to invoke the good services of the world organization.

Yet the growing threat of Communist victory in Indochina found the administration in a noncompromising mood. During his tour of Indochina in late 1953 Vice President Richard Nixon warned the French:

It is impossible to lay down arms until victory is completely won. . . . If your country [Indochina] is to be independent and free, it is first necessary to defeat the representatives of Communist imperialism on your soil. . . . Those who advocate [removal of the French troops from Indochina] must know that if such a course is adopted it will mean not independence but complete domination by a foreign power.

So patent was the American drive to stop at nothing in blocking Communist success in Indochina that Eden at Bermuda felt compelled to caution the American leaders not to "go it alone" and thus destroy the entire working alliance of the West.

Indochina confronted the Eisenhower leadership with the gravest foreign problem that it had faced. Dulles had to reassure those new isolationists who feared the Communist dominance of all southeast Asia that the United States would remain firm. At the same time he had to soothe the old Eisenhower Republicans, the Democrats, the British, and the free Asians that his policies would not involve the world in another war. Daily the earlier French assurances of ultimate victory were being disproved. In the crisis Dulles required a coalition of powers if he would hold the line, but the nations of Europe and Asia had no sympathy for official American objectives in Indochina.

Having repeatedly agreed with the new isolationists that the French province was the key to all southeast Asia, the Secretary had no choice but to revise downward the American estimation of its strategic importance or to commit the United States to a policy of defending the region alone. His response to the challenge was clear. If the Red pressure continued, he declared in his noted speech before the Council on Foreign Relations in New York in January, 1954, the United States would draw deeply enough on its air-atomic resources to counterbalance the shortage of allies.

Dulles, to fill the vacuum in Western policy, placed new emphasis on the "deterrent of massive retaliatory power" to supplement the reliance "on local defensive power." This nation now would "depend primarily upon a great capacity to retaliate, instantly, by means and places of our own choosing." This implied the bombing of areas beyond the range of immediate aggression; these places were assumed to be the cities of China and Russia. Critics in the United States, Europe, and Asia predicted that this policy would narrow the freedom of choice to either complete inaction or the mushroom cloud. Dulles explained his original statement more fully in *Foreign Affairs* of April, 1954:

The essential thing is that a potential aggressor should know in advance that he can and will be made to suffer for his aggression more than he can possibly gain by it. This calls for a system in which local defensive strength is reinforced by more mobile deterrent power. The method of doing so will vary according to the character of the various regions. . . . Local defense is important. But in such areas the main reliance must be on the power of the free community to retaliate with great force by mobile means at places of its own choice.

Dulles assured Congress that the capacity to retaliate instantly did not impose the necessity of unleashing atomic power in every instance of attack, and he concluded that "it is not our intention to turn every local war into a general war." Senator Knowland, rising to Dulles' defense, assured the nation further that the new policy did not mean the use of atomic weapons alone. It could embrace also, he said, "a naval blockade, conventional air harassment of Communist communications lines or greater supplies of arms and ammunition to non-communist governments and to people behind the iron curtain who are engaged in the struggle against communism." Whatever form the new American policy might take, it assured the American people that they would become involved in no further local wars in Asia.

In massive retaliation was the Eisenhower administration's fulfillment of its promise of a more dynamic foreign policy. "The doctrine is a departure from the policy of 'containment' which we have heretofore followed in recent years," wrote Knowland in March, 1954. "It is clear, therefore, that this Administration intends to change our defense emphasis to a point where we are no longer dependent on merely reacting to Soviet initiative within limits planned and desired by the Kremlin."[9] This new threat of massive destruction would restore the "strategic initiative" to the United States and guarantee unlimited victory in any future contest in Asia without the commitment of American ground forces.

Dulles scored a second political *coup* when he assured the American people of "more security at less cost." His speech announcing the new policy contained repeated references to the prohibitive costs of American defense. Massive retaliation, as Dulles had explained it as early as 1952, was a policy designed primarily to guarantee the American nation the fulfillment of its will under conditions of reduced expenditures. Said Senator Henry M. Jackson of Washington regarding Dulles' announcement, "I believe it has become quite apparent that cutting the budget was uppermost in mind when the policy was formulated."

Massive retaliation conformed perfectly to the neo-isolationist dogma that all Communist gains in Asia had resulted from pure military aggression emanating from Russia and China. Such aggression had allegedly driven Chiang onto Formosa; now it was threatening to overrun Indochina. Nixon had described the struggle within Indochina as a simple matter of Communist imperialism on French soil. Dulles himself limited the threat to "the mighty land power of the Communist world." It was this great landed force that demanded "the further deterrent of massive retaliatory power," for otherwise a potential aggressor, glutted with man power, "might be tempted to attack in confidence that resistance would be confined to manpower." Knowland voiced the theme more succinctly. "Communism is a global and not a mere area menace," he said, which advanced on "the conspiracy to destroy freedom which exists in the world." To Knowland the answer to the Communist threat in Indochina lay in a military alliance of the Philippines, Thailand, Cambodia, Laos, Viet Nam, and the Republics of China and Korea. None of these national spokesmen could detect the underlying internal revolution of Indochina that since 1946 had been relentlessly driving the French from the scene.

Massive retaliation satisfied those Americans who were determined to hold the line in the Far East while they avoided jungle wars and reduced military expenditures in the United States. Basically it offered an inexpensive method whereby the nation could have its way all over the world. As many predicted from the outset, the new policy disturbed the European allies and the free nations of Asia more than it did the Red Chinese who called the bluff and proceeded in their support of the Indochinese insurgents.

§ 4

From the besieged Indochinese fortress of Dienbienphu in March and April, 1954, came the crucial test for Dulles' new Asiatic policies. General Paul Ely, French Chief of Staff in Indochina, informed American leaders that the time for allied intervention had arrived. Dulles used his address before the Overseas Writers in New York on March 29, 1954, to call for the internationalization of the Indochinese war. He warned that the "imposition on Southeast Asia of the political system of Communist Russia and its Chinese Communist ally, by whatever means, would be a grave threat to the whole free community. The United States feels that the possibility should not be passively accepted, but should be met by united action. This might involve serious risks. But these risks are far less than those that will face us a few years from now, if we dare not be resolute today."

Numerous American political and military leaders, especially those who recognized in this new crisis the opportunity (denied them in Korea) to destroy the Red Chinese regime, demanded that the United States save the French province. Nixon informed newsmen in Washington that the fall of Dienbienphu would be catastrophic. To Knowland the free world had reached the "jumping off place," and if it did not react properly it would witness the loss of all southeast Asia. Dulles even warned that a situation might arise in which the United States might be forced to act alone. President Eisenhower affirmed Dulles' stand that this nation block Communist expansion by whatever means were available. He warned that if one more nation goes down, the others, like a row of dominoes, would follow.

During the crisis month of April the public statements of national leaders revealed far less consistency. On April 7 the President was quoted at a press conference as saying that "we simply cannot afford to lose Indochina." Nixon on April 16 told the American Society of Newspaper Editors: "If, to avoid further Communist expansion in Asia and Indochina we must take the risk now by putting our boys in, I think the Executive has to take the politically unpopular decision and do it." So violent was the reaction to Nixon's speech among Republican editors that the administration demurred. Four days after the Vice President's speech Dulles admitted that the administration believed it unlikely that American troops would be employed in Indochina, and on April 28 he declared more emphatically that the United States would avoid sending troops to fight in Indochina or anywhere else if it could.

Meanwhile Dulles and Radford (who admitted that he was not speaking for the Joint Chiefs) had moved to obtain Congressional support for an air strike to relieve the embattled fortress of Dienbienphu. Then to secure British approval for his policy of "united action," Dulles conferred with Churchill and Eden in London. The eve of the Geneva conference in April still found the French seeking military aid from Radford and Dulles in Paris. But at the eleventh hour the British cabinet rejected the plan for united action while the British chiefs of staff predicted that within forty-eight hours after the initial air attack the demand for ground forces would become irresistible. The British feared that allied intervention would provoke a direct countermove by the Chinese Reds and greatly enlarge the Asian war. Facing consistent opposition in both Britain and the United States, Dulles' plan for military involvement ground to an abrupt halt. With the fall of Dienbienphu in May, the struggle for Indochina was transferred to the conference table at Geneva.[10]

Throughout the siege of the fortress the reality that Indochina lay at the extremity, not the center, of America's vital interests became increasingly the basic determinant in United States action. Many Congressmen and members of the press argued that the United States dared not become bogged down alone in another war on the Asiatic continent. To the end some of the Congressional neo-isolationists were willing to "go it alone" but not the administration. As April wore on, the President became more responsive to the views of Generals Matthew B. Ridgway and Nathan F. Twining of the Joint Chiefs of Staff, key members of Congress, and leading editors, all of whom were opposed to American intervention. Radford, Knowland, and Dulles did not have their way.

Yet the new isolationism was still influential enough to set the booby trap for Dulles at Geneva, for the Secretary attended the conference limited by the political attitudes of Republican leaders at home. Without either allies or Congressional backing, he had the choice of bluffing or compromising. Unable to exert pressure on the Chinese, he had recourse only to negotiation. United States leadership at that moment required that the Secretary have the necessary freedom to discuss, negotiate, and bargain. Instead, his diplomatic powers were completely circumscribed. He had been warned by powerful Congressional neo-isolationists (whom the administration would not defy) against an Asian "Munich" or a "sell-out." That ruled out even a glance at the Chinese delegation, and Dulles could assure Republican leaders upon his return that he had acceded to their demands. At Geneva he could do nothing but call for free elections and a unified Korea and then disengage himself from the conference as quickly as possible.

United States intransigence toward China had made it possible for Peiping and Moscow to offer terms acceptable to all Europe and Asia without running the risk of facing their acceptance by the United States. Neo-isolationist demands for action, countered by a strong reaction at home, had forced the President to lean over backwards in assuring the world that the United States would not fight. Politicians at home made it clear that the Chinese and Russian bluff would not be called. With this nation on the sidelines, the French were forced to negotiate alone. The American failure of leadership seemed to prove the Russian and Chinese contentions that if the free nations would ignore the United States, the great tensions of the world could be resolved.

Many writers have been critical of this undermining of United States diplomacy by the irreconcilables in Washington. "They have raised the false hopes which have then had to be denied," Lippmann has charged. "They have made a united front impossible by their extremism, their contempt for negotiation, their advocacy of a big war. They have frightened off, indeed they have lined up against us, all the important nations that were needed if there was to be a united front." Such diplomatic setbacks would be repeated, he believed, as long as the State Department remained a "paralyzed instrument of policy" and a "bureaucracy intimidated by demagogues."

After May, 1954, Eisenhower and Dulles modified their domino theory by declaring their intention to strengthen the other nations of southeast Asia so that if Indochina should fall the others would stand. With this intention Dulles struck back from his failure to uphold American prestige at Geneva with the Manila Pact of September, 1954, which established the Southeast Asia Treaty Organization. The new alliance, which included the United States, Britain, France, Australia, New Zealand, Pakistan, Thailand, and the Philippines, was designed to insure southeast Asia against further encroachment of Communist power. The eight signatories promised to act jointly against "any fact or situation which might endanger the peace of the area" south of Formosa. As a military arrangement, however, it demonstrated the weakness rather than the strength of American policy, for the only nations that could have made it a success in building the needed balance of power in the Orient refused to join it.

Collective defense in southeast Asia without the allegiance of India, Burma, Ceylon, and Indonesia, observed Drew Middleton, was as absurd as a NATO without France and Italy. The Asian bloc represented by the Nehru school charged SEATO with violating the neutralist third force tactics of free Asia. This middle way, Asian spokesmen believed, would serve as a brake on the two power groups and would best protect Asia against involvement in another general war. To them communism was not an external military threat, but rather the product of economic misery and political misrule that could be dealt with by eliminating the conditions. They regarded Communist success in China as the product of this underlying nationalistic upsurge, and they believed that United States pressure in Asia, as represented by SEATO, would perpetuate Chinese aggressiveness and prevent Peiping's detachment from Moscow.

§ 5

Statesmen and writers throughout the non-Communist world evinced little sympathy for American Far Eastern policy as it evolved in 1954. To the British, India—not China—was the key to a stable Orient; Indian welfare was the vital Western cause in Asia. They recognized Indian neutralism for what it was—the reaction of a young nation to foreign policies that demanded military alliances, that appeared to be substituting power for diplomacy, and that seemed to ignore the non-Communist goals of Asian nationalism. They recalled the neutrality policy of the United States in the 1790's and wondered why this nation would criticize Nehru for attempting to avoid entangling alliances in 1954. The British had little interest in SEATO. They did not regard military alliances as the foundation for successful policy in the Far East; and since SEATO excluded India, they viewed it as a barrier to full British and Indian cooperation.

Britain shared the Indian fear that the United States was indulging in policies which could provoke war and annihilate the political, social, and economic gains of all free Asia. The *Manchester Guardian* in mid-1954 revealed the British alarm at Senator Knowland's inflexible stand toward Red China:

Mr. Knowland does not want peaceful co-existence. He wants to root the Communists out of China and give it back to Chiang Kai-shek. He cannot yet carry the American people along with him in his crusade, but he is pushing them in that direction. . . . With the kind of ideas which Mr. Knowland represents there can be no possibility of compromise from the British or European side. He is against "entangling" alliances, against listening to Mr. Nehru, against any negotiation with Communists, against peaceful co-existence, against atomic partnership with Britain. He is a supporter of the idea that the United States must hasten the "disintegration" of Communist China by "maintaining pressure" on it, and he favors taking risks in the process. He supports, in brief, a belligerent policy short of actual aggression.[11]

British and Indian leaders were as critical of American China policy in 1954 as they had been in 1950. Their judgment did not condone what the Chinese leaders had done at home or abroad. Nor did the acceptance of their views infer that Red China be recognized by the United States immediately. But a study of their convictions suggested why most of the world's opinion was opposed to the American posture of intransigence and why the price of nonrecognition was diplomatic isolation in the Far East. Bertrand Russell summarized the British view:

Governments are not recognized because they are thought to be good; they are recognized because they hold *de facto* power. To refuse to recognize the *de facto* Government of China and give it its due place in the United Nations involves an entirely useless prolongation of ill feeling. It would only make sense (of a sort) if it were a prelude to a war against China for the restoration of Chiang Kai-shek. But since such a war would inevitably be a world war, no sane man can regard it as an aim of practical policy. The recognition of the existing Government of China is an essential step in diminishing tension of the Cold War, and no legitimate purpose of statesmanship is served by postponing it.[12]

Harold Macmillan, former British Foreign Secretary, has been equally critical of United States policy. "Recognition of a government," he observed, "never used to be a sort of diploma or certificate of approval. I think rather a false diplomatic doctrine has grown up about all this in recent years. We do it, to be frank, to benefit ourselves— not to please them. This was the older doctrine and I think the right one." Clement Attlee, one-time British Prime Minister, has termed it ironic that the United States insisted on viewing the China of Chiang Kai-shek as a great power and placing it on the Security Council, but now that mainland China has evolved into a nation of considerable power denying it a seat.[13]

Nehru, who above all others is viewed as the spokesman of free Asia, asked, "Why should the United States *not* recognize China?" Apart from liking or disliking the Chinese regime, he believed it difficult to ignore its existence or its place in Asiatic affairs. Similarly, C. Northcote Parkinson of the University of Malaya recently made a plea for recognition. "Diplomatic courtesies," he said, "imply no approval of the way a land is ruled. If they did, Great Britain need never have recognized the independence of the American colonies. In recognizing their independence, the British were not viewing the matter with enthusiasm. They were merely recognizing a fact." Asia, like Europe, had deserted Chiang.

Critics of United States policy on China believed that it was contributing to the diplomatic advantage of both Moscow and Peiping. So completely did nonrecognition tie China's voice to that of Russia that observers wondered why the Soviets brought up the issue each year. One Yugoslav diplomat supplied an answer: "Obviously because she thinks the effect in China will be to increase anti-Western sentiment. And why does she always seem to bring it up at a time when it is most likely to call for a particularly sharp turndown from the United States? Obviously to create trouble between the Western allies and to convince the world that America is anti-Asian."[14] Thus for Peiping there were advantages also, for the Red leaders understood well that United States policy of refusing to recognize a colored nation was a constant affront to the anticolonialism of Asia.

British experts on Russia and China agreed with those of the United States that a flexible policy could cut China loose from her Russian moorings. The fact that Mao Tse-tung owed little or nothing to the Russians for his success, that China was large and independent in tradition, with a strong sense of nationalism, that its long common boundary with Russia was a source of irritation, that China was overpopulated and Siberia was not, and that in the long run China required more technology than Russia could supply, indicated that the alliance between Peiping and Moscow was neither stable nor permanent. The words of the Russian Foreign Minister, Sazonov, uttered in 1912, still have meaning today: "Germany is interested in China as a market and she fears China's disintegration. . . . Russia, on the contrary, as a nation bordering China, and with a long, unfortified frontier, cannot wish for the strengthening of her neighbor: she could therefore view with equanimity the collapse of modern China."[15]

United States success in blocking continental China in the United Nations had by 1954 made few converts to the wisdom and justice of the American cause. The quality of any policy must be measured in cost, and the cost to the nation of its China policy was exceedingly high.

Like American policy in China, Dulles' new program of massive retaliation met with wide and vigorous criticism in the United States, Europe, and Asia. Somehow its very simplicity raised serious doubts, for it guaranteed too much. It promised to hold the line against the Russo-Chinese alliance in the vast continent of Asia, with primarily one type of weapon, yet without effective allies, while reducing both the available man power and the military budget. Students of American foreign policy challenged Dulles' statement that the United States could afford no more Korea-type wars. For many there was no other type that the nation could afford. Morgenthau averred that "a Korean war, even one fought in perpetuity, is cheaper in every respect than an atomic war."[16]

Lester B. Pearson, Canada's Secretary of State for External Affairs, in his *Democracy in World Politics* (1955), accepted massive retaliation as one component in democratic strategy, but he opposed the use of more force than necessary to stop an aggression. He argued for limited wars ending in negotiated settlement. "If hostilities ever again break out," he warned, "surely every effort must be made, not only to prove that aggression does not pay by repelling and defeating the aggression, but also to localize the hostilities, to bring them to an end as soon as the limited objective is accomplished; and then to work at once for a peace which will be just but not savage, the kind of peace that will not have planted in it the seeds of future war."

Critics predicted that Dulles' policy of massive retaliation would prove a failure in action as well as in concept. They saw that under conditions of revolutionary change sweeping the Orient, whether successfully exploited by

Communist spokesmen or not, the real challenge to the *status quo* was a state of mind—an ardent quest for a better existence—arising wholly out of indigenous conditions. It was this state of mind in Indochina that gave power to the straggling forces of Ho Chi Minh, and it was not clear how the dropping of bombs on such Asiatic targets could ease the demand for change which was exerting itself, not through overt military aggression, but through an internal upheaval anchored to emotion and spirit.

Bombing of human targets in Asia (since purely military and industrial installations would be hard to find) appeared certain to alienate hundreds of millions of Asians. It was doubtful if the coolies of Shanghai would understand that they were being vaporized for the brutal and sadistic treatment meted out to United States prisoners in some distant Chinese camp. Chester Bowles once queried, "Would not the atomic destruction of defenseless Chinese cities—while Russian cities remained untouched—turn all Asia into our bitter and unrelenting enemies?"[17] Nor was it certain that massive retaliation could guarantee a cheap and easy victory. It assumed zero enemy capability from an enemy with access to atomic bombs, and it ignored the oft-stated fact that "preventive war is war."

Dulles' policy of instant retaliation seemed to break the primary rules of coalition diplomacy. These principles require that policy either strengthen and cement the coalition more closely together or weaken the opposing coalition and loosen its bonds.[18] Any program that accomplishes either purpose is successful; any course that fails in both is clearly harmful. In his speech announcing the new policy Dulles stressed the need for joint action. "We need allies and collective security," he said. "Our purpose is to make these relations more effective, less costly." But if he believed that the free nations would respond favorably to his use of power as a substitute for diplomacy, he overlooked their fear of atomic warfare and their lack of sympathy for the goals and the inflexibility of American purpose.

Diplomatically the weakness of massive retaliation was clear. Any threatened employment of atomic bombs in any crisis created even partially by United States intransigence toward Red China would cretainly not strengthen the Western alliance. On the other hand, such a threat would strengthen the ties of Asiatic aggressors to the Soviet Union as the sole source of atomic power to counter that of the United States. Massive retaliation, like United States policy toward China, was the creation of the powerful isolationist tradition which emphasized unilateralism and the concept of omnipotence. Europeans and Asians indicated in their reaction to both major United States policies in the Far East how completely the trends of American foreign relations defied the will of the non-Communist world.

§ 6

Having cast its lot with Chiang Kai-shek, the United States was assured from 1950 onward that eventually it would be trapped in a renewal of the Chinese civil war. Only a heavy fire by Chinese Red artillery and air bombardment on Nationalist-held offshore islands in September, 1954, especially in the vicinity of Quemoy and the Tachens, was required to involve the United States in another Far Eastern crisis. What made these attacks particularly disconcerting were assertions by Chinese leaders that they were a prelude to the conquest of Formosa. After a lull Chou En-lai announced on January 24, 1955: "The government of the People's Republic of China has repeatedly and in solemn terms declared to the world that the Chinese people are determined to liberate their own territory of Taiwan [Formosa]. . . . Taiwan is an inalienable part of China's territory."

The threatened assault on the Nationalist stronghold created a situation of far greater tenseness than did the Indochina crisis. First, the island of Formosa was the keystone in the American defense perimeter from the Japanese islands to the Philippines. Second, the United States had stronger and more direct commitments to the Nationalist regime than it did to the French in Indochina. On December 1, 1954, Dulles had anounced a new security pact with the Republic of China which made it clear that the United States would defend Formosa and the Pescadores and other Nationalist-held islands by special agreement. Chiang agreed not to attack the mainland without previous consultation with the United States. With the Communist threat on Formosa in January, 1955, Dulles again assured Chiang and the world that the Nationalists on Formosa would not "stand alone" against any invasion from the continent.

Nor was this American purpose unacceptable to the non-Communist world (except among Asiatic leaders who had no interest in Chiang or in American defense plans). Strategically the Dulles declaration seemed feasible because it was based on this nation's power to control the sea and the air in the Formosan Straits. Legally the United States had a defensible claim based on the fact that Formosa had been returned by the Japanese in 1945 to the victors in the Pacific war and not necessarily to China. At worst Formosa's legal status was uncertain. With Formosa protected from the mainland by a hundred miles of water, the United States commitment did not appear to Europeans as particularly dangerous.

What quickly subjected the Eisenhower administration to open criticism all over the free world was the doubtful posture which it assumed on the question of the offshore islands. With the President's decision to order a retreat from the Tachens went the tacit promise to Nationalist Foreign Minister, George Yeh, that the United States would defend Quemoy and Matsu, the offshore islands along the China coast facing Formosa.

Yet official American policy remained vague. Dulles announced that the United States would fight for the offshore islands if their seizure appeared a step toward an attack on Formosa itself. But the future course of Chinese policy could hardly be determined with any certainty by an attack on Quemoy and Matsu. Perhaps Dulles had two purposes in mind, both designed to prevent trouble. On the one hand, by taking no firm stand he seemed to be telling the world that the offshore islands were really negotiable and that they would be released in exchange for a cease-fire. On the other hand, the American posture of doubt might deter the Reds from attacking and thus prevent war and save the islands for Chiang. Dulles even intimated that the United States might use some form of "massive retaliation," including the tactical use of atomic bombs, to defend the offshore islands.

Nor did the administration's request to Congress in January, 1955, for a resolution to grant the President permission to employ United States armed forces in the defense of Formosa and the Pescadores clarify the official American position. The President agreed to use United States forces only in situations which were recognizable as part of a general assault on the main position. His purpose, he said, was to demonstrate United States unity and determination to maintain its commitment to the defense

of Formosa. Congress neglected to demand a precise definition of what that commitment might be in a crisis.

Such indecision assumed a calculated risk. Dulles himself admitted to newsmen that the Reds were amassing
enormous forces of air and man power along the coast
opposite the offshore islands. He predicted that an attack
could come at any moment. Yet any Chinese assault would
have left the United States two alternatives, neither of
which would have been wholly in the nation's interest. If
American forces rushed to the aid of Chiang's exposed
position, the United States would be involved in another
open conflict with China; if it, as Dulles had warned, used
atomic weapons, the world might shortly be involved in
another general war. If the United States backed down
and deserted Chiang, as it did in the Tachens, it would
suffer another tremendous, if unnecessary, loss of prestige.
The secret of successful diplomacy has always entailed the
avoidance of the hard decision between war and diplomatic
defeat. Yet any all-out Chinese attack on Quemoy or
Matsu would have placed the United States in exactly that
dilemma.

This crisis in the Formosan Straits demonstrated again the
irony of the new isolationist policy toward China. It was not
the strength, but the weakness, of the Nationalist regime that
forced the administration to risk war over the defense of
two tiny islands hugging the China coast. These offshore
islands were not even remotely required for the defense
of Formosa. C. L. Sulzberger of *The New York Times*
reported from Tokyo after a visit to Formosa: "Chiang
Kai-shek would like to see a battle for the strategically unimportant offshore islands developed into a world war so
he could gamble on returning to the mainland. But as
far as we are concerned they have no military value."

To Chiang the offshore islands, as stepping stones to the continent, were symbols that the Nationalists would again one day return to power over all China. With a fourth of his best troops on Quemoy and Matsu, placed there largely at the encouragement of American officials, Chiang continued to assert his right to hold the islands as essential for his ultimate victory in the Chinese civil war. Without such anticipation of success his regime was in danger of disintegration. Tingfu F. Tsiang, Chinese representative to the UN, defended the Kuomintang position in June, 1955: "We cannot do that [give up the offshore islands] because withdrawal from Matsu and Quemoy weakens our material strength and undermines our moral position." Any effort to force compromise on the Nationalists, he said, would "liquidate the Republic of China."[19]

The administration admitted in its arrangements with Chiang in December, 1954, that he would not return. Yet it feared that United States policy anchored to that conviction would inflict such damage to Nationalist morale that it would produce a wholesale desertion of Kuomintang forces and their return to the mainland. Said Lippmann of American policy, "If, as a matter of fact, the internal strength of Nationalist China rests on the fantasy that Chiang Kai-shek will some day return to China, we are headed for trouble."

President Eisenhower's decision to remain in the thick of the Chinese civil war soon isolated American policy from the bulk of non-Communist opinion. Churchill was careful not to place any pressure on the President to define his position, for he understood the enormity of the political compulsion under which the President was laboring. But Eden in the House of Commons was somewhat more outspoken, and the London *Times* and *Manchester Guardian* both lectured the United States and Chiang openly on the folly of trying to hold the offshore islands. Said the *Times:* "What is most regrettable is that Dulles should still oppose so strongly any Chinese Nationalist withdrawals from the offshore islands opposite Formosa. Mr. Dulles is chiefly concerned with the defense of Formosa, and many are with him there. But even on the score of defense, it is surely better to put 100 miles of sea between the two sides than leave provocative and exposed outposts on [Red] China's doorstep." Foreign Secretary Pearson of Canada warned the administration that his nation would not join the United States in any military involvement in the Formosan Straits.

For Nehru and the leaders of free Asia the Chinese civil war had been settled long before. In their judgment even Formosa belonged to Red China. At New Delhi, wrote A. M. Rosenthal, Indian leaders blamed the United States rather than Communist China for the tension in the Straits.[20] Critics everywhere hoped that the United States would avail itself of the 100 miles of blue water to gain time— time in which the UN might acquire some jurisdiction over Formosa and extend to the island people the opportunity to determine their own destiny. It was apparent that no final settlement could come to the region until the Chinese civil war ended in some acceptable arrangement. One St. Louis *Post-Dispatch* editorial summarized the criticism of United States Formosan policy:

As they consider this new crisis, the leaders of the Eisenhower administration should remind themselves that an Asiatic war entered via Quemoy island would be no more in the American interest than an Asiatic war entered via Indochina.

They should remind themselves that defending Formosa is one thing, and permitting Chiang Kai-shek to involve us militarily in an attack on the Chinese coast or coastal islands is quite another.

They should remind themselves that Europe remains the most vital world theater, that the United States cannot afford to undertake unilateral adventures in Asia, and that this country should not act without the fullest support of our European allies.

They should remind themselves above all that they are not supermen, but fallible human beings who, having almost blundered into war last spring, need to approach Far Eastern problems with a special caution today.

It would seem that the loss of respect and goodwill among the uncommitted nations of Asia and the allies of Europe would be a high price to pay for a policy that offered little hope of success. American China policy, born of politics, had reached the dead-end predicted for it five years earlier by American writers, for it had from the beginning ignored the realities of power and revolution in Asia and the demands for peace in the hydrogen age.

Only the President could disengage the nation from the danger of conflict in the Formosan Straits. Yet he could avoid antagonizing the friends of Chiang in Congress only by keeping the line which he would defend purposely smudged. Administration leaders seemed to prefer running the risk of war to revamping their China policy. Even a limited war would, of necessity, terminate in some kind of peace, and how could the United States make peace even then without some revamping of its China policy? If eventual peace with China required some redefinition of this nation's objectives, noted *Business Week*, then why should not that adjustment precede rather than follow another war? United States policy appeared logical only if it contemplated total war in which it could pursue the unconditional surrender of China.

Max Ascoli has suggested that one reason why the President called for a Congressional resolution early in

1955 was to place some responsibility on the Democrats in Congress and on the United Nations to extract him from his political commitments. It was precisely a combination of Congressional support and external diplomacy that extracted President James K. Polk from his political defile on the Oregon boundary question in 1846. It was disturbing but clear that the administration, with its domestic obligations, could not assume the initiative in any diplomacy with Red China.

However one analyzed the Asiatic challenge to American security in 1955, one stumbled hard against an unavoidable fact—the power and purpose of Red China. It was the American posture toward the Peiping regime that had placed the triple burden—military, diplomatic, and intellectual—on Dulles' final answer of massive retaliation. The military task of confining that nation's aggressiveness was serious enough. It ran counter, moreover, to Dulles' avowed purpose of eventual United States "disengagement" from the Far East, for it was useless to talk of disengagement when American air power alone could effectively confront the manpower of Communist China. Diplomatically the problem ran deeper. The fact that the United States stood almost alone in its purpose in the Korean, Indochinese, and Formosan crises suggested that any policy which stemmed from a set of specific attitudes which this nation held toward Red China would be merely tolerated in Europe and actually resented in Asia.

Intellectually, American Far Eastern policy produced its most troublesome dilemma, for American intransigence toward Red China which had called forth the doctrine of massive retaliation was based on the assumption that the Peiping regime gained power largely through American stupidity or treason, and therefore merited neither respect nor acceptance. Whatever the justification for this position, it rendered illogical the very recognition of the vast revolutionary fervor sweeping the Orient as the factor determining the outlook and purposes of all Asiatic nations. Dulles' policy of massive retaliation carried not only a military responsibility, but a diplomatic and an intellectual one as well. This suggested from the beginning why the policy's long-term success was questionable. Military policy alone could hardly create the needed balance of power in Asia.

Perhaps what was required was the ability of the United States to bring its objectives into harmony with what the European allies were willing to defend and what the free nations of Asia would recognize as being in their national interests. For the United States this meant the avowed purpose of keeping small wars small and of winning the support of the indigenous peoples of Asia. This, in turn, required essentially an understanding of what Asia wanted. But at heart the problem was Red China; and perhaps the final answer, if one existed at all, rested in arriving at some *modus vivendi* with that regime. Until the free nations of the Orient had the power and economies to resist Communist pressure, and until those nations could be drawn together diplomatically to oppose Chinese aggressiveness, the United States commitment to military force had no apparent alternative. The dearth of indigenous support in Asia left the United States with its policy of massive retaliation. Such policy at best extended time to the Eisenhower administration for making some hard decisions —time for redefining its relationships with both China and the nations of free Asia.

7

The Dilemma of Politics

§ 1

John Foster Dulles, like his predecessor, Dean Acheson, entered the office of Secretary of State with an established reputation in the area of foreign affairs. Like Acheson, he had defined his concept of the nation's mission in concrete terms and had formulated the principles of policy which would achieve it. For three years American foreign policy has borne the indelible stamp of his knowledge, philosophy, and personality. His contribution to Republican policy began as early as 1952 with his concept of "liberating" the satellites; he introduced that doctrine into the platform and eventually sold it to the Republican leadership as national policy. Thereafter his diplomatic experience has been characterized by a series of slogans of his own creation. In the President's message of January, 1953, he "unleashed" Chiang Kai-shek to invade the China mainland. In 1954 he announced that he would make an "agonizing reappraisal" of American policy if France did not join EDC. At the same time he announced formally his policy of "instant retaliation" and "united action" to warn the Chinese Reds not to move into Indochina.

By late 1954 Mr. Dulles had been forced to backtrack on each of these purposes and to spend considerable time in explaining what he meant by his pronouncements. He had made it clear that he meant "peaceful liberation" in Europe, although he never explained just how he was going to accomplish this objective. He had leashed Chiang Kai-shek again. He had swallowed France's rejection of EDC without any "agonizing reappraisal," had failed to achieve "united action" in Indochina, and had made it clear that there would be no "massive retaliation" except in response to some momentous Communist move that actually threatened the security of the United States. Dulles' record has been consistent: in each crisis since 1953 he has promised more than he or the nation could achieve and has rejected the normal devices of diplomacy which take cognizance in advance of the wills and purposes of other nations. For that reason Dulles' policies can be understood only in terms of the neo-isolationist assumptions of American omnipotence.

This illusion of invincibility in the Secretary's statements has exposed him to new isolationist accusations that he has made the United States appear as a "paper tiger," for this element recognizes no power on earth sufficiently great to force the Eisenhower administration to back down from its declared objectives. But Dulles' chief critics have been those writers in Britain and America who have expected far less of United States power. They have been disturbed not at his failure of purpose, but at the fanfare, irresolution of policy, saber-rattling, and the isolationist tendency of unilateralism in his actions. If these qualities must characterize American policy, they would prefer that the United States appear as a "paper tiger" than that it engage in a war in Europe or Asia.

These critics have doubted that this nation's recent external affairs have revealed the patience, magnanimity, and urbanity demanded of a great nation by a world endangered by atomic destruction. No great country such as the United States, arriving at the threshold of world leadership, can expect love. If its policies are calm, poised, reasonable, and consistent, however, it can evoke respect. But foreign policy to be reasonable must take stock of the nation's assets and liabilities so that it not promise its own people more than it can achieve; it must not demand of its allies more than they might willingly contribute, and of its opponents more than the balance of power might force them to concede.

Any adherence to such limited goals for American policy in 1954 was rendered illogical by the continued partisan attack on the past. Senator McCarthy's strategy of exposing the Democratic record culminated in February, 1954, with his charges of "twenty years of treason." The Eisenhower administration itself had entered the crusade against the Truman leadership when Attorney General Herbert Brownell reopened the Owen Lattimore case in the early spring of 1953 and the Harry Dexter White case in the following November. The impact of these attacks on past traditions of American foreign policy was disturbing, for it was difficult to see how the administration could condone this procedure without being forced to accept the assumptions of American invincibility on which the attacks were based. The real danger was not that the American obsession with internal security would stifle freedom of thought and expression in the United States, but that it would force its foreign policy into rigid and inflexible patterns based on emotion rather than on a realistic measure of the nation's power. What was essentially at stake was the integrity of the State Department and the intellectual foundations of American foreign policy.

Seldom had such violent disagreements over past policy and such predictions of dire consequences challenged the motives of fellow Americans on so vast a scale as during the first eighteen months of the Eisenhower administration. Continued debate over previous China policy produced a schism among Americans that Paul G. Hoffman termed "deep, ugly, and shockingly wasteful." It seemed to dissipate the energies and obscure the goals of the nation. The ubiquitous charges of subversion seemed to convince millions of Americans that by the destruction of the efficiency and reputations of leading citizens they could solve all national and international problems. Lippmann warned that this effort to build political fences through the deliberate falsification of history would create irreconcilable cleavages in American society. "When men accuse their fellow citizens of treason," he said, "they can never live at peace with them again. The accused can never forgive the accuser. . . . There is a line beyond which political passions must not go, or they will break the bonds of affection which hold the nation together in time of trouble."

§ 2

Perhaps the most disquieting implication of the continued partisanship under President Eisenhower was the failure of will. Divisions at home seemed to prevent the United States from getting a grip on itself and formulating policy that appeared realistic enough to promise peace rather than prolonged tension. Richard H. Rovere, writing in *The New Yorker*, reported that the administration had fallen "into a condition for which the only proper clinical term is paralysis." Having done little to discourage the partisan debate, the administration had helped to perpetuate those isolationist emotions which plagued its leadership and kept the nation divided. Isolationism was at best a weak reed on which to build the foreign policy of a great nation at mid-century.

As late as 1954 there was little evidence of Executive judgment in the policy statements emanating from Washington. There was no recognizably coherent program which defined United States objectives abroad in terms of the limitations of power. There was no challenge in high places to the concept of Congressional neo-isolationists that whatever caused the weakening of American security after 1945 the nation could still have a world of its own choosing. When any national administration responds to partisan pressure and in a sense allows it to dictate policy, invariably American diplomacy begins to lose its effectiveness. "Having accepted as their own the standards of the opposition," Hans Morgenthau has observed,

the fearful politicians, counting and miscounting votes, find no escape from the vicious circle. Prisoners of their critics, they obligingly commit every blunder that the opposition suggests— but is itself spared from making. Thus, by the very logic of its course, the Administration is never able to satisfy its critics or do for the country what needs to be done. And while the Administration involves itself ever more deeply in contradiction and confusions of its own making, the interests and the very safety of the country are imperiled.[1]

What was unique in this Executive dilemma was that the partisan opposition to his leadership stemmed from members of the President's own party. Nor did the friends of the administration in Congress make any effort to defend the President's constitutional prerogatives in the conduct of foreign affairs. As late as 1954 Senator McCarthy appeared to hold the United States Senate paralyzed in terror, so that not even the Democrats would question the course and premises of American foreign policy.

There was no agency outside the Executive that could defend United States foreign relations from the onslaught of the new isolationism. It was certainly not clear how that

"'scuffle of local interests," as Herbert Agar once described
Congress, could fill the vacuum in leadership. Nor was it
apparent how an Executive that was weak at home could
be effective abroad. The challenges to American policy
all over the globe demanded the strengthening, not the
weakening, of the Presidency. As Samuel Lubell noted in
The Future of American Politics: "Only through Presidential leadership can national unity be achieved, a coherent foreign policy formulated and the resources of the
nation mobilized to meet the needs of the cold war."[2]
Without unifying leadership, George F. Kennan observed,
the United States was no longer in 1954 in a condition to
unite with the Atlantic democracies. "Sometimes," he
added, "I think it is scarcely in a condition to unite with
itself."

Unwilling to antagonize the new isolationists, the President could find no way out of his political dilemma, for
while he attempted to live peacefully with his party he still
faced the obligation to lead the free world. To have relieved his leadership of domestic pressure would have
required a purposeful destruction of the new isolationist
version of Chiang's initial loss of power in 1949. It would
have necessitated an agreement with Britain and free Asia
that the Chinese civil war was over, that Yalta did not
deliver the satellites to the Soviet Union—that the nation
was not omnipotent. But President Eisenhower was unable to accept the challenge of marshaling public opinion
behind the acceptance of a more conciliatory attitude toward the world. His own declarations of policy and the
forces within his party tied his hands both diplomatically
and politically. Increasingly he was trapped between the
ultimate necessity of negotiating some cold war settlements with Russia and China and the immediate necessity
of supporting the "ultras" of his party. In identifying him-

self during the campaign of 1952 with the neo-isolationist
position of his party, he ignored the warnings that he was
politically accepting certain objectives abroad that were
incompatible with the diplomatic settlement of any significant issues in the cold war.

American foreign policy, with objectives anchored to
the quest for party unity, reflected graver concern for the
opinions of Senator Knowland and Chiang Kai-shek than it
did for those of such Republican leaders as Paul G. Hoffman or Harold Stassen, of British and French spokesmen,
to say nothing of the leaders of India, Burma, Indonesia,
and Ceylon. Democratic leaders experienced in foreign
affairs criticized this trend in Eisenhower policy. Averell
Harriman asked that the administration "decide whether it
will unite the Republican party or unite the free world,"
for he doubted in 1954 if it could do both. Adlai Stevenson observed in retrospect in his *Look* magazine article of
September 20, 1955: "The anxiety at home and lost confidence abroad that resulted from trying to please both
wings of the Republican party by policies of bluff and
backdown and by pronouncements alternately hot and
cold, tough and timid, are, I think, President Eisenhower's
most serious failures."[3]

Alastair Buchan, Washington correspondent of the London *Observer*, leveled the same charge at Eisenhower
policy. He analyzed correctly in 1954 why the triple
threat of massive retaliation, the hydrogen bomb, and
united action did not add up to the immediate danger that
terrified the British. Mr. Dulles, he wrote, had one foreign
policy for the world and another for the United States
Congress. What made American policy seem belligerent
and confused was Dulles' insistence on speaking to two
different groups simultaneously. American policy would
respond to its challenges, he thought, when the Secretary

would accord the same attitudes toward the world that he did toward the Senate.[4]

Dulles' repeated failure to carry out his vigorously enunciated purposes illustrated the powerful dichotomy within the Eisenhower administration on matters of foreign affairs. That the national leadership readily compromised in each crisis with its avowed objectives suggests either that its initial goals were based on a flagrant misreading of the national interest, or that they were created merely to satisfy the new isolationists in Congress. Either the administration might have engaged in less bluff, or, if it believed that it had gauged the national interest correctly, it might have increased the nation's striking power with the object of fulfilling its declared purpose. Unified policy reflecting a united nation, it seemed, could be created only when the American people could again agree on the nature of the forces that made the American position precarious. Eventually they would have to agree on whether the danger had been created by trends at home or abroad. As long as the national leadership contributed little to the settlement of this question, the lack of unity over American purpose would continue.

After two years in office the Eisenhower administration still issued policy statements that reflected the neo-isolationist faith in American invincibility, but in action its policies were far more realistic than its words would indicate. Before the end of 1954 it had placed less emphasis on "liberation" and more on "containment." It had deserted the campaign platform of 1952 although it still voiced the limitless expectations of liberation. Its program in Asia, not as voiced by Dulles, but as executed by the President, tended toward disengagement rather than involvement. Eisenhower had asked for the evacuation of the Tachens and insisted that Dulles' treaty with Chiang contain no

pledge on the offshore islands. There was less emphasis
on the possibilities of all-out war, on atomic retaliation, and
on unilateralism in world relations. The administration
spoke less of a balanced budget. In performance its policies
looked increasingly like those of Acheson.

Despite the pressure of the new isolationism, the evolving
Eisenhower program had accomplished much, but still in
those areas only where it would not challenge the symbols
of past iniquity. James Reston wrote in *The New York
Times* of January 16, 1955, with considerable truth:

> Divided within itself, harassed by the collapse of French prom-
> ises in Europe and policy in Indochina, confounded by its own
> twenty-year foreign policy record and campaign promises, it
> has, nevertheless, maintained and extended the alliance [with
> the addition of West Germany], greatly improved the situa-
> tion from Trieste to Tehran, achieved its main objective of
> preventing the big war, and diverted the Communist energies
> from open aggression to a vast war of subversion all over the
> world.[5]

§ 3

Political forces in the United States created a significant
dichotomy between the opinions of national leaders and
professionals on matters of diplomacy in the cold war. The
recurring cycle in Eisenhower policy from bold declarations to limited action found no intellectual adjustment
whatever in the claims to invincibility on which its original
"new, dynamic" policies had been predicated. While the
administration sought to assure Europe that it would engage in no venture to liberate the captive people of Europe,
unleash Chiang Kai-shek, or risk involvement in any unnecessary war, it did not grade down the conditions under
which the United States would agree to negotiate away the
issues of conflict with the Soviet world. In refusing to
destroy the myth of past treason or attribute publicly the

problems of American security to external rather than internal forces, the administration still found it feasible, whatever the limitations of its achievements, to cling to limitless expectations and refuse negotiations until they were met.

Certainly the nation lacked nothing in intelligence, power, and good intentions, but critics of its diplomacy believed that it was failing as a world leader because for too long it had been unable to engage in discussions either in Europe or Asia which were based on anything but conditions which the nations of the world, free and slave, regarded unrealistic. Nowhere in its underlying diplomatic objectives could one detect attainable goals upon which tensions of the cold war could be accommodated.

Howard K. Smith, foreign affairs analyst of CBS, suggested that the Republican Party had become the victim of the symbols that it had so laboriously created to discredit its opponents. "There is a myth," he said,

that half a dozen men in the State Department caused the Chinese Communist revolution—diplomats therefore are not to be trusted. There is the myth that areas of Europe were given to the Reds at the Yalta conference—therefore negotiation at a conference equals appeasement, and should not be permitted. . . . These myths are made the stuff of U. S. policy by intimidating, purging, and dishonoring officials who might utter an independent or questioning thought. Thus Mr. Dulles, who is probably as capable a Secretary of State as we have had, is not permitted . . . to negotiate. Nor is he trusted to create any other policy but one of words and bluff.[6]

Writers in Britain and the United States who accepted the power and prestige of the Soviet Union as the creation largely of massive historical trends going back at least a century did not anticipate policies that would predict how and when the Soviet empire would be toppled from its pedestal. To those who accepted firm allied unity as the best hope to exert pressure on the Soviet world, to heighten its internal dilemmas, to force its leadership to reverse its expectations, American intransigence and the demand for perfectibility among friend and foe alike appeared a threat to the Western coalition. Peter Viereck observed that the hard line of the new isolationism had found its mirrored image in the soft line of British socialism. Whereas the American right, led by McCarthy, attacked the British left for its willingness to "co-exist" at any price, the British left pictured the United States insistence on "liberation" as the needless perpetuation of tension with the Soviet Union.[7]

Verbose demands made on the world by American politicians and military leaders and the nagging qualities of American diplomacy seemed sufficient to fray the nerves of the allies and create doubt and resentment among the leaders of free Asia. European publications questioned the dependability of American policy. Said the London *Economist*, "The United States seems to have equated compromise with appeasement, and to be demanding all or nothing from the Communist world." There was danger that these unilateral tendencies would one day cause the allies to go it alone just as the nations of free Asia had been reluctant to accept American leadership from the beginning.

Not the least disturbing aspect of United States foreign relations in 1954 was the split between the United States and Great Britain on the goals of cold war diplomacy. Relations continued to remain normal, but official contacts were correct rather than warm. This decline of British enthusiasm for American policy could not be ignored. Even if our policy were entirely correct, it was doubtful if the British could be coerced into following it. Even more important, British policy was based on a realism born of long and trying experience. And the British after 1950 were becoming convinced that the possibilities for peace were present in the world. For that reason they became increasingly restive at United States moral preachments. British opinion gave the United States little choice but to play its full role in seeking accommodation if it would count on the solid support of Britain and its other allies in some future crisis.

Such British students of international affairs as Churchill, Sebastian Haffner, Arnold Toynbee, and Edward Crankshaw, in their modest evaluation of what Western diplomacy could achieve, had no interest in Eisenhower's demand for sweeping settlements. Churchill voiced his disapproval of liberation policy: "It would, I think, be a mistake to assume that nothing can be settled with Soviet Russia unless everything is settled. Piecemeal solutions of individual problems should not be disdained or improvidently put aside." The London *Observer*, one of Britain's leading newspapers, devoted its editorial of May 17, 1953, to the question of peace-making. It also decried American liberation policy as ignoring the present balance of power in Europe. Perhaps the West might secure some liberalizing of the satellite regimes, but no more. Said the editor:

The best we can hope for—and this is not a wholly unreasonable or unrealistic hope—is that a period of peace may reduce Russia's iron grip on her neighbors which six years of cold war have merely tightened—just as in Aesop's fable of the gale and the sun betting which of them could strip a wanderer of his coat, the sun succeeded, where all the violent tuggings of the gale had only made the wanderer grip his wrappings more firmly.[8]

Sebastian Haffner, a British authority on international affairs, accused American liberation policy of dishonesty and criticized the encouragement of rebellion, as some United States-sponsored radio stations were doing, as "criminally irresponsible." The President knew, he charged, that the United States could not liberate Eastern Europe— not even if the satellites themselves revolted. He believed that the United States could better translate its sympathy into more concrete action, for continued intransigence would merely perpetuate the subjugation of the region. If a Russian military withdrawal could not be compelled, then liberation would require concessions from the West. "The present American government," he concluded, "seems to be in the curious position of having to confess that it can do nothing for Eastern Europe by force, and yet at the same time being too proud to do something for Eastern Europe by diplomacy."

Haffner recognized the difficulty in re-establishing diplomacy after a long period of restraint. He pointed out that during a period of four years "diplomacy had degenerated into something like a special branch of propaganda or political warfare, and a number of habits had established themselves which stultified diplomatic negotiations and conferences from the start." He suggested that any rebirth of diplomacy, if it would succeed, be conducted without a rigid agenda, that the "round table" method be used so that the various positions would not come into direct conflict but shade into one another, and that the classical and unspectacular meetings at the ambassadorial level be exploited more fully in the reconnoitering for possible concessions and modifications of previous stands.

American students of diplomacy, like the British, preferred that American policy be based not on the illusions of omnipotence, as delineated by Senators Knowland and McCarthy, but on the admission that this nation has neither the military power nor the moral sanction to destroy the Communist regimes by force. They would see American diplomacy aimed less at unconditional surrender and more at the intention to share the same world as the Communists as long as the latter refrain from aggression. They agreed with the British that in the long run, diplomacy is the only alternative to war, and that there could be no diplomacy until President Eisenhower mastered the new isolationist forces within his party.

Successful diplomacy must emanate from strength, but most American experts were convinced that the requisite equality of power with the Soviet Union had been present for several years. Morgenthau believed that the most opportune time for negotiation had already passed by 1954, for a half decade earlier the United States has lost its monopoly of the atomic bomb and had suffered severe losses in Asia. In both respects, he wrote, the Western position was apt to deteriorate further rather than improve. Since the United States had passed the pinnacle of its power vis-à-vis the Soviet empire, there was nothing to be gained by resisting negotiating further.

Whatever the neo-isolationists might have charged, negotiation and appeasement are not synonymous. Appeasement has resulted when nations from weakness have made concessions for which no mutual advantage was derived. Negotiation, on the other hand, is the means of arriving at a settlement with adversaries which recognizes the realities of power and possession. It determines the conditions of settlement. Its purpose is to organize a balance of power which might deprive the rivals of the assurance of successful aggression, to find the formulas which allow the adversary to agree without losing face. For that reason a Secretary of State must never boast to the citizenry back home, since such action informs the opponents that they have conceded too much. Successful diplomacy does not mean that all rivalry will cease, or that both nations will be mutually converted to some common objective. It means merely that whatever differences may exist, the balance is such that they cannot afford to engage in aggression.

Successful diplomacy requires flexibility because situations of power shift. "We must not," Henry Steele Commager has written, "be frightened by words into denying ourselves essential advantages—the advantages of choosing our own ground, selecting our own issues, determining our own time and our own weapons, in so far as we can."[9] Diplomats who are constantly harassed by political pressures at home become increasingly demanding of their opponents and talk "out of the window" to those at home rather than to those across the table. It is essential that public opinion not become extreme or absolute, for absolute opinions can become a fatal obstacle to successful diplomacy.

Major powers cannot exist indefinitely in peace under conditions of tension. Eventually they must settle their differences by recognizing formally that what exists actually does exist, or they will have war. Nathan Perilman, Rabbi of Temple Emanu-El in New York has said:

Whether he prefers it or not, man . . . has to live with his neighbor however he may be fashioned, and he must accommodate himself to the differences of others, else he cannot survive, and our civilization cannot stand. . . . All of this denies us the luxury of permitting the congealing of ideas. It destroys forever any hope that some may cherish of the placid, unchanging, unchallenged way of life in which individuals and whole nations can walk alone in unalterable paths.[10]

Any persistent and deliberate reliance on military power to avoid all diplomatic concession General Matthew B. Ridgway termed "immoral and dangerous," for history, he wrote in November, 1954, "provides examples in which 'saber-rattling' precipitated rather than prevented war."

§ 4

Despite repeated Eisenhower assurances that foreign policy would not become a political issue again, it pervaded the 1954 Congressional campaign and turned it into another political brawl that threatened any restoration of a true bipartisan spirit. Knowland, in seeking Democratic support for administration measures, had assured members of that party in Congress that he did not regard all Democrats as traitors, but as the campaign evolved the Republican leadership again employed the issue of subversion in the Truman administration. McCarthy himself was immobilized, but Vice President Nixon led the attack on the Democratic party, although he carefully refrained from accusing any member of the Truman administration specifically of treason. "Communism should not be a political issue. There is no difference between the loyalty of Democrats and Republicans," he admitted, making his customary opening concession to the other side. Then he lowered the boom:

But some misguided officials of the previous Administration were blind and indifferent to the danger. They ignored the repeated warnings that J. Edgar Hoover and others including myself brought to them. . . . But this Administration is *co-operating* with J. Edgar Hoover and the F. B. I. We have not only fired the Communists and fellow-travelers and security risks off the Federal payroll by the thousands; we don't hire them in the first place. I can assure you that no one in this Administration regards communism as a red herring.[11]

During October Nixon repeated these charges from coast to coast. At Averill Park, New York, he said, "Ike found fair and effective means to smash the Communist conspiracy at home, to rout out the corruption that was gnawing like a cancer at the structure of our Federal

Government and to halt the dangerous leftward swing towards Socialism." At Las Vegas he warned that if a Democratic Congress were elected, "the security risks which have been fired by the Eisenhower Administration will all be hired back."[12]

These repeated contrasts between the alleged conspiracy under Truman and the loyalty under Eisenhower struck Nixon's audiences with clarity. This formula became the Republican line on the Communist issue. President Eisenhower, who earlier had declared his unwillingness to intervene directly in the Congressional campaign, eventually entered the fray at the request of Leonard Hall and the Republican National Committee. He warned the country that a Democratic victory would mean a cold war between President and Congress, and would paralyze the established political structure. He endorsed the campaigning of Nixon and such statements as ". . . isn't it wonderful that finally we have a Secretary of State who isn't taken in by the Communists, who stands up to them?"

Again in the 1954 campaign the President apparently preferred to maintain Republican unity than to seek a Congressional Republican-Democratic coalition on foreign policy which might free him finally from the powerful neo-isolationist pressure being exerted on his administration. Whatever the need for such a coalition, Eisenhower could not achieve it without breaking the Republican party wide open, for the new isolationists still demanded the perpetuation of the symbols of Democratic iniquity.

Actually the Republican party, to achieve success in 1954, had little choice but to campaign on the issue of past subversion. Its narrow Congressional triumph in 1952 had resulted largely from its ability to capture the isolationist vote of America. That Nixon was again encouraged to identify himself with the anti-Communist cause, as he had in 1952, was evidence of an internal conviction that without the vote of disillusionment the party would not repeat its victory. Losses in 1953 indicated that the party, canvassing on economic issues alone, would soon return to its minority status.

This Republican reliance on the isolationist vote created a genuine tragedy for American foreign policy, for the enormous revenge element in the Republican electorate militated against a positive foreign policy. In keeping alive the powerful stereotypes of Tehran, Yalta, and Potsdam, the party also perpetuated a distrust of Britain and the allies, an Asia-first concept of American interests, unilateralism in diplomacy, and the illusion of grandeur—all essential elements in the new isolationist tradition. Arousing and exploiting the isolationist emotions might bring immediate political success, but it was doubtful if the Republican party could regain its former status as the nation's majority party unless it could break the hold of negativism over its foreign policy councils.

Isolationism, whatever its political appeal, kept the Republican party divided intellectually and made it difficult for the organization to make inroads into the independent and traditional Democratic vote except to maintain those minorities which had bolted to the new isolationism in 1952. In Congress there was danger that the tactics of the campaign might alienate the Democratic support which the administration had received in its foreign policy program. Perhaps the President was assured that the basic Democratic adherence to his underlying purpose of avoiding war would guarantee further opposition support even if it were not actively curried.

Democratic victory in 1954, against which the President had warned, actually resulted in the strengthening of Executive control over American policy and rapidly broadened the confidence of Europeans in this nation's leadership. The new leaders of Congress such as Sam Rayburn in the House, Lyndon Johnson and Walter George in the Senate, plus others with long experience in foreign affairs, quickly extended the administration greater freedom in policy formulation than it had yet enjoyed. These men believed that the extensive cooperation between parties and branches of the government was a requisite for national unity and effective policy.[13]

Eisenhower soon discovered that he could count on the support of these hierarchical Southern Democrats far more than Harry Truman could have done, for they were more in agreement with him on matters of domestic policy. Their conservatism on economic issues prevented them from exerting pressure on the President to curb Republican neo-isolationists in exchange for their support of his foreign policies. For that reason the warning that the partisanship of the campaign would destroy what remained of Democratic support proved erroneous. Whereas these key Democratic spokesmen had never defended the Truman administration from Republican attacks or helped to free its diplomacy from the paralyzing effect of domestic politics, they appeared willing to use their influence to free Eisenhower completely from the limiting pressures of his own party.

This uncritical devotion of leading Congressional Democrats to the Eisenhower administration became obvious in January, 1955, when they managed the approval of the President's Formosa resolution. Senator George tolerated so little debate that the result could hardly be termed bipartisan. Vandenberg had never regarded bipartisanship as a carbon-copy process, but the new Democratic leadership actually surrendered the right of free debate on the Formosan issue. George accepted Eisenhower's assurance that he alone would make the decision to employ American forces in defending the Formosan commitment. Cried the Senator: "God keep us out of war, but if war must come let us not draw a line and say that beyond that line is a sanctuary which the enemy may occupy and behind which he may retreat. . . . I believe that President Eisenhower is a prudent man. I believe he is dedicated to a peaceful world. I believe what he says, and I am willing to act upon it."

Eisenhower's Formosan resolution confronted the United States Congress with some of the most profound questions that had plagued this nation's foreign policy in a decade. Yet the entire affair was over in less than a week. There had been five hours of testimony and discussion in the House Foreign Affairs Committee and two days of testimony from Dulles and the Joint Chiefs in the Senate Foreign Relations and Armed Forces committees, meeting jointly. The debate on the House floor lasted less than three hours and on the Senate floor two and a half days.[14]

Several members of Congress feared that the President was infringing on his own constitutional powers by bringing the resolution before Congress. Rayburn made the point that Congressional action on the resolution should not be taken as precedent. Senator Thomas Hennings, Jr., Democrat from Missouri, in a carefully prepared statement, expressed his misgivings lest "the great historical powers of the Presidency . . . be in any way limited for future generations." But he refused to push the point further. Nor did the Congress demand to know for what they were to be held jointly responsible under the resolution. It was never made clear whether the new policy would result in an ultimatum to the Chinese Reds or a withdrawal from the offshore islands of Quemoy and Matsu. One Senator summed up the Congressional action: "We gave the President authority that we don't have to give for the purpose of doing something that we are by no means agreed we want to do. And we did it in the name of national unity."

Senator George was equally committed to the Mutual Defense Treaty with Nationalist China which passed the Senate several days later with less than six hours of debate. Democrats complained that he refused to consider any amendments and gave little quarter on the floor to those who opposed him. The treaty listed Formosa among the territories of the Republic of China although Dulles assured the Senate that by "understanding" the treaty did not recognize this sovereignty. Those who questioned the juridical distinction between Formosa and the offshore islands George accused of "legalistic quibbling."

What was equally astonishing was the silence of the younger Democrats on the Senate Foreign Relations Committee—Hubert Humphrey, J. William Fulbright, John Sparkman, and Mike Mansfield. In debate these men hardly held their own against the China bloc. There was no genuine retort when H. Alexander Smith, Republican of New Jersey, asserted that the mere accumulation of a Red army could be accounted an act of war, and when Knowland added that if the Red Chinese attacked an American ship during the evacuation of the Tachens it would call for preventive action on the part of the United States. Throughout the entire discussion Congressmen asked no questions about the conditions under which the administration would seek to avoid involvement in the Formosan Straits.

Eisenhower's foreign policy, still attuned to the assumptions of the new isolationism, was questioned by Henry Reuss of Wisconsin and some of his colleagues in the House during March, 1955, but in general the Democratic-controlled Congress refused to challenge the course of American diplomacy. Democratic victory promised a re-

duction of Congressional interference with Executive judgment, but it assured no rebirth of genuine bipartisanship.
The refusal of Democratic leaders to question the administration's foreign policy illusions left the area of debate
too restricted to tolerate the introduction of either new
concepts or more limited objectives. Perhaps they believed
that the President would discard the new isolationism if
left free to pursue his own policies. If this was their conviction, their opportunity to break completely the political
hold of Congress over the nation's diplomacy occurred
during the summer of 1955. Herein lay the broad significance of the Congressional debates on the summit meeting at Geneva.

§ 5

From Bandung, Indonesia, in April, 1955, came the first
major challenge to Republican cohesion on matters of Far
Eastern policy. Here at the invitation of the Colombo
powers—India, Pakistan, Burma, Ceylon, and Indonesia—
the African and Asian nations held their historic conference to define the interests and concerns of the nonwhite,
underdeveloped world in its relation to the West. At heart
Bandung represented a dynamic racial alignment of political forces which gave new meaning and significance to
the anticolonial feeling reaching from the Atlantic across
north Africa and the Middle East to the China Sea. This
conference, predicted Carlos P. Romulo of the Philippines,
would not secure the press coverage of the Tachen evacuation, but, he added, "The free world would do well to
watch it with as much attention—and guide itself by what
it means."[15] Bandung represented the most ambitious effort
yet made to apply the principle of "Asia for the Asians."

This fateful meeting created a new aura of insistence
that the United States re-evaluate its policies in Africa and

the Far East. Yet this nation all but ignored the conference. Either the administration underestimated the significance of Asian and African nationalism or from fear of
criticism that it would appear too friendly to such Asian
leaders as Nehru, U Nu, and Chou En-lai it assumed that
political discretion was the better part of valor. Despite
its disinterest, the United States had its staunch defenders
in Romulo and Mohammed Ali of Pakistan. These men
defended their military alliances with the United States
and praised the American economic assistance program in
Asia. Only on the issue of American policy toward China
was there open antagonism, for the danger that the United
States would go to war over Quemoy and Matsu terrified
even the friends of the West.

Nor could Chou resist the pressure for peace in the
Formosan Straits. Before the conference adjourned he was
forced to assure the Afro-Asian leaders that the Chinese
government did not want war with the United States and
that it was willing to enter into negotiations to discuss the
question of the relaxation of tension in the Far East, especially in the Formosan Straits.

Red China's offer at Bandung produced such an immediate and favorable response around the world that a
reluctant Eisenhower administration could not ignore it.
Chou's announcement led one Indian official to remark,
"As a result of the Bandung conference, there is a lessening
of fear among Communist China's neighbors if not actually
a lessening of tension in that area." Premier Ali of Pakistan
believed Chou's offer was "a great move for relaxing tension, particularly in the critical Far East." Burmese Premier
U Nu and Indonesia's Ali Sastroamidjojo agreed. A British
Foreign Office spokesman said that Britain was "interested
in any idea which might provide a basis for a settlement."
U. K. Krishna Menon, India's traveling envoy, after a hur-

ried trip to Peiping, warned officials in Washington that the offshore islands would be attacked unless the United States either induced the Kuomintang to release them or started negotiations with the implication that they would be given up.

Eisenhower was caught between the pressure for negotiation emanating from Red China and the danger of a Republican split if he engaged in such negotiation. The State Department's immediate answer, approved by the President, reminded Chou that the United States had an ally in the Republic of China and would insist on that government's participation as an equal in any negotiation. It demanded also that the Chinese show their good intentions by agreeing to a cease-fire and freeing American airmen in advance. The Peiping government termed these conditions unacceptable.

At that moment Senator George, speaking before the American Society of Newspaper Editors in Washington, urged the administration to seek a Far Eastern conference with Red China without insisting that Nationalist China be represented. If Chou indicated at Bandung that he was willing to talk, said George, "this nation should be big enough and great enough, through its highest officials, to talk to him." The Senator declared that the United States could no longer be unmindful of the opinion of its friends. He reminded Dulles that he could not please everyone at home and still accept the leadership of the non-Communist world.

Thereupon Dulles modified the administration's position. Direct talks were feasible, he said, as long as they did not infringe on the interests of Nationalist China. Such administration Republicans as Smith of New Jersey, Leverett Saltonstall of Massachusetts, Clifford Case of New Jersey, James Duff of Pennsylvania, and Irving Ives of New York took the lead in supporting the administration. "The president of the United States," said their joint statement, "has a right and obligation to wage peace as well as to wage war. Waging peace is what he is trying to do." Hubert Humphrey voiced forcefully the Democratic sentiments that called for negotiations with Red China, even over Quemoy and Matsu. He warned the nation that the administration was too concerned with the offshore islands, but not enough with India, Burma, Indonesia, and Japan. "Our relations with Quemoy and Matsu are good," he admitted, "but for nine solid months we had no ambassador to Burma, which has 1200 miles of common frontier with Red China."[16] For almost a year the prime minister of Burma said he saw no important officials from the United States, but, observed Humphrey, every other weekend someone runs from Washington to visit Chiang.

But the Nationalist China bloc closed in on the administration to prevent any negotiation with the Peiping regime whatever the world pressure might be. Knowland demanded simply that Chiang be represented. "The policy of this government," he said, "is not to barter away the territory of any country without its presence at the negotiations." Representative Walter Judd of Minnesota joined Knowland in warning against any talks with the Chinese Communists. He could see no value "in law-abiding citizens sitting down with outlawed gangsters to discuss how order should be maintained." What these friends of Chiang suspected was that the United States would barter away the offshore islands. Senator Jenner warned that "the air is full of foreboding that a carefully laid plan is under way for the United States to give up bit by bit its commitments in the Formosan Straits." McCarthy rushed to the defense of the Nationalists with his resolution that they be included in any United States-Red China talks. In urging this resolution on the committee, he declared, "It involves a very important question as to whether or not we are going to sell out our Allies." Chairman George refused to change the order of committee business, and the resolution never came up for a vote.

When Eisenhower and Dulles agreed finally to a meeting with the Red Chinese at Geneva at the ambassadorial level in August, 1955, they admitted that negotiations with Peiping could no longer be prevented. Dulles assured the Republican neo-isolationists, however, that the administration would pursue the interests of Chiang Kai-shek by maintaining its commitments to the offshore islands. The negotiations of Ambassador U. Alexis Johnson at Geneva would be limited to the release of American airmen and civilians from Chinese prisons. In action the Eisenhower administration appeared to be compromising its inflexible posture toward Red China; in principle it still responded more firmly to domestic commitments than it did to the combined voice of Asia at Bandung.

8

Geneva: The Challenge That Failed

§ 1

Midway through 1955 two massive and converging forces promised to give American diplomacy greater flexibility and freedom than it had enjoyed in a decade. One train of influence stemmed directly from the conviction after the hydrogen bomb test of March, 1954, that the great nations of the world had an obligation to humanity to avoid another general war. The second impelling factor loomed from the American political scene—the belief within the Republican Party that the time had arrived to free President Eisenhower, on whose popularity the party would depend in 1956, from all domestic pressures so that his diplomacy with the world might bring distinction to himself and his party. Together these powerful trends created the first major challenge since 1950 to the new isolationism as a significant force in American politics and foreign policy.

Few scientists, writers, and statesmen in 1955 still regarded war as a rational alternative to peace. The atomic age, they feared, had come too soon, for the leading nations were not yet reflecting the realities of nuclear destruction in their policies. Shortly before his death, Albert Einstein, whose theories first exposed the secrets of atomic energy to the scientific world, wrote these poignant words: "Our world faces a crisis yet unperceived by those possessing the power to make great decisions for good or evil. The unleashed power of the atom has changed everything save our modes of thinking, and thus we drift toward unparalleled catastrophe."[1]

Increasingly, military writers and philosophers doubted that an atomic war, unlike the two world wars of the twentieth century, would be humanly supportable. When Clausewitz wrote that war was the extension of diplomacy by other means, he assumed that under certain conditions war was preferable to peace. But it was difficult to see how atomic war could ever be in the interest of any nation, for even in victory it would tend to be suicidal.[2] General MacArthur commented on the occasion of his seventy-fifth birthday in January, 1955, that the "very success of invention . . . has destroyed the possibility of war being a medium of *practical* settlement of international differences. The enormous destruction to both sides of closely matched opponents makes its impossible for the winner to translate it into anything but his own disaster."

In the days of limited destructiveness the nation with the greatest military potential could hope to win in time. When both sides had large numbers of H-bombs, the capacity to manufacture more than the adversary ceased to be a great advantage. From this realization Bertrand Russell warned that there was no escape from the choice that faced humanity. There would be peace or the annihilation of the species.

Winston Churchill was the first of the West's leading statesmen to recognize that war was not an intellectual choice when in May, 1953, he issued the call for a meeting of the Big Four at the highest level. President Eisenhower voiced the same conviction in October, 1954, when he said, "Since the advent of nuclear weapons, it seems clear that there is no longer any alternative to peace." In western Europe and in Asia, where the nations felt helpless in contemplating such a struggle without atomic weapons, this mounting fear of nuclear destruction was especially acute. Increasingly, such countries as England, France, Germany, and India were making the avoidance of war the ultimate goals of their policies. Nor could the great powers ignore this trend under penalty of alienating those countries whose goodwill their security interests required. So deepseated was the dread of war that no nation could hold out against any plan, however tenuous, that held out hope for peace.

Not in this century had the world demanded genuine accommodation among the leading nations with such insistence or anticipation of success. Eisenhower himself in a press conference reported in *The New York Times* of December 3, 1954, took cognizance of the new standards of acceptable policy. "Let us recognize," he said, "that we owe it to ourselves and to the world to explore every possible peaceful means of settling differences before we even think of such a thing as war. The hard way is to have the courage to be patient, tirelessly to seek out every single avenue open to us in the hope even finally of leading the other side to a little better understanding of the honesty of our intentions. . . ." During the succeeding months this new accent on negotiation had permeated the thinking of all important nations of the world. Thomas P. Whitney analyzed this world-wide phenomenon succinctly in *The New York Times Magazine* of May 22, 1955:

People everywhere are desperate for assurances of a long term peace so far denied them. They want to see everything tried, every possibility for agreement explored, including face-to-face meetings, not just of Foreign Ministers but of the men who give Foreign Ministers their instructions. The faith is strong even among people sophisticated in politics that the bosses together can solve some of the problems that have baffled their subordinates. It is even possible that this faith and the hopes founded upon it may lead the big men to override some of the considerations that have hitherto kept the sides apart.[3]

This confidence that negotiations in 1955 could succeed took strength from the conviction that the opportune moment had arrived. Both the Korean and Indochinese wars had terminated in a cessation of hostilities, if not permanent peace. With the calm had come a decline in bitterness and the removal of emotional obstacles to negotiations. There was, moreover, a universal belief that a genuine stalemate had been reached in the cold war; no longer could either side have its way. Western Europeans were confident that NATO, with the addition of West Germany, had created a position so favorable vis-à-vis the Soviet Union that the West could anticipate satisfactory results from any imaginative diplomacy. Third, the gradual shift in the power balance had brought the full threat of atomic war into focus. As long as the United States had held a monopoly of atomic weapons and the Soviets appeared superior on the ground, it was difficult to envisage any mortal deadlock in the event of war. By 1955, however, Russia had developed her atomic resources to the point where any general war promised such extensive mutual destruction that it appeared illogical for either Russia or the United States to procrastinate further. With irresistible logic this realization gradually pushed both nations into the Big Four conference at Geneva in July, 1955.

§ 2

Soviet leaders accepted this challenge with an air of confidence, for they enjoyed ample room for diplomatic maneuvering. Even before the death of Stalin in March, 1953, the Kremlin had embarked on its new policy of "peaceful coexistence." Having slowly created the image of a stern Russia, guided only by considerations of sheer power, the Communists suddenly struck a new pose designed to relieve a world living in dread of war. Under Malenkov—and even more under Bulganin and Khrushchev —they perfected their easy-going diplomatic techniques as men completely confident of their position both inside and outside the Soviet Union.[4]

Without altering their basic objectives, the Kremlin leaders set out to use diplomacy, economic aid, and propaganda to attract the Asian and African countries, divide the free world, and isolate the United States. By 1955 the Soviet "new look" was well under way. In April and May, after ten years of obstruction, the Russians granted a peace settlement to Austria. They next apologized to Tito for driving him out of the Cominform; they relaxed their guard along the Iron Curtain. In Asia they began to negotiate for surplus commodities.

These new offers of friendship, whatever their sincerity, reflected the pressures of the atomic age on Soviet leadership. The old classical concept that communism would expand through a series of "frightful collisions" had been rendered obsolete by the atom bomb, for any one collision could erase the Kremlin and much of the Soviet world. Russia could expect the support of her allies only as long as her leadership maintained the interests of the entire Soviet bloc. Western success in containing Russian expansion, moreover, forced the Russians to think increas-

ingly of the welfare of the Soviet masses. "In other words,"
ran Edward Crankshaw's conclusion, "even if Messrs.
Khrushchev and Bulganin have no intention of changing
their ways personally, they will find that the sheer force
of events will continue to force change upon them—provided always that the West remains strong, true, watchful
—and, above all, flexible."

What gave the Russians their supreme diplomatic advantage was an almost universal willingness in Europe and
Asia to begin negotiations with the immediate realities of
possession and power. The Soviet empire had been built
by naked force in the forties; to increase it would invite
war. But in dealing from what they had already acquired
the Soviets controlled such key European issues as German
unification, the satellites, and East-West contacts. In Asia
their position was equally strong diplomatically because
again it was based on the realities of power. Their appreciation of nationalism, neutralism, and the Afro-Asian tradition of anticolonialism, as contrasted with the intellectual
blocks under which United States Far Eastern policy
operated, seemed to assure the Kremlin leaders that they
could outmaneuver the West in Asia and in the Middle
East.

United States leadership in 1955 could no more ignore
the pressures for accommodation than could the Soviet
Union, but the Eisenhower administration revealed an
understandable reluctance in going to the summit. With
its heavy political and intellectual commitments to the new
isolationism, it could negotiate in Europe only on the basis
of the boundaries and regimes of 1939. Dulles' unequivocal
stand on liberation was predicated on the assumption that
the Communist gains of the forties need not be recognized.
His condition to any negotiation was no less than the restoration of prewar Europe. Dulles promised no similiar retreat

of the United States from its advanced positions in the Far East, Europe, the Mediterranean, and the Middle East. Much of the postwar expansion of American power and influence had resulted from Russian belligerence and therefore had greater justification. But one could hardly deny that both countering positions were based on actual power and therefore could not be wished away. It was doubtful if the Russians would forego their gains of fifteen years as a prelude to negotiation, and no leading nation aside from the United States really expected them to. The Eisenhower administration, unless it modified its policy of liberation, could anticipate little from diplomacy at Geneva.

President Eisenhower in March appeared willing to accept the inevitability of a high level conference. "I have said time and again," he reminded newsmen, "there is no place on this earth to which I would not travel, there is no chore I would not undertake, if I had the faintest hope that, by so doing, I would promote the general cause of world peace." The President visualized a formal meeting preceded by a conference of the foreign ministers. When Churchill favored informal talks without an agenda, both Eisenhower and Dulles began to lose their enthusiasm. They were no longer convinced that the Big Four conference would serve any useful purpose. But outside pressures continued to drive them toward the summit. For many months British and French public opinion had been pushing those two governments toward a meeting with the Soviets for the purpose of relieving cold war tensions. The administration, favoring Eden to Attlee, had to bolster the conservative position by agreeing to the conference.

American writers expressed concern over the national leadership's lack of enthusiasm. John Emmet Hughes discussed this in *Life* magazine in May.

For the United States to shy away from negotiations with the Soviet Union today would gain nothing for the United States, for Europe, or for abiding principles. The United States cannot win respect by assuming an air of pained reluctance about the event. It is admirable, of course, not to raise the hopes of peoples carelessly or to exploit them callously. But a scepticism and scorn for the very process of diplomacy would invite the suspicion of Europe that the United States has always feared either its own case or its own capacity to argue it.[5]

Max Ascoli insisted that this nation had nothing to fear from negotiations with Russia, and wondered why administration spokesmen did not have greater confidence in their ability to counter the Russian challenge. It was rather strange, though somewhat appealing, he thought, "to see how they are gingerly moving toward their meeting with the Russians—with the perturbed air of virtuous divinity students about to enter a house of ill repute, for no other purpose, of course, than to conduct a sociological survey"[6]

Those Americans who favored the meeting hoped that the President could go freed of Congressional pressure. Said Adlai Stevenson at Oberlin College: "If we think war is inevitable, if we regard every Soviet proposal as a trick and a trap . . . then we the people will have ruled out bargaining. Not even the President can negotiate if we tie his hands. . . . Trading used to be considered a Yankee talent and I think it still is—even by Republicans—if we don't put our traders in a straightjacket or scare them stiff in advance." Added one United States diplomat in Europe: "Flexibility and mobility are not signs of weakness. They are signs of strength. You cannot fence very well with your shoes nailed to the floor."

What disturbed many experts was the administration's continued adherence to liberation policy. During May, to the dismay of London and Paris, both Eisenhower and

Dulles spoke of the satellite problem as one of the subjects for possible discussion at the conference. Under prodding from Senator Knowland, Dulles informed the Senate Foreign Relations Committee that he was studying whether to demand that Russia withdraw her troops from Rumania and Hungary since her treaty with Austria no longer made them necessary to protect supply lines.

Sir Roger Makins, British Ambassador to the United States, struck hard at those who persisted in limiting the administration's freedom to engage in diplomacy. "I have long detected in this country," he said, "a distrust of the processes of international negotiation as being something which implies weakness and is bound to lead to appeasement and defeat. Distrust of diplomacy and diplomats is common to most Anglo-Saxon countries, and it has been particularly strong here where the mythical figure of the simple-minded American entrapped by the insidious guile of foreign statesmen dies hard." He urged the American people to accept negotiation "in the confident expectation, not so much that solutions will immediately be found, but that your strength will not be diminished, your position will not be compromised, your allies will not be parted from you in the course of the negotiating process."

§ 3

In June Senator McCarthy, assuming the role of the dauntless champion of the captive peoples of Europe, moved to limit the President's freedom at Geneva by introducing a series of resolutions into the Senate for the purpose of perpetuating the satellite question. These peoples of Eastern Europe had been victimized by the Democrats at Yalta and Potsdam; now he would prevent their abandonment by the Eisenhower administration. His first resolution—that the United States break diplomatic relations with the satellites—the Senate Foreign Relations Committee rejected unanimously.

Although the committee, with administration approval, stood firm against making the satellites an issue, it did agree to a substitute resolution that proclaimed some hope for the eventual liberation of those "people who have been subjected to the captivity of alien despotism." But it mentioned by name neither the people nor the despotism. McCarthy retorted: "The administration is, to be sure, indignant over the fate of the captive peoples—but not so indignant as to risk identifying the tyrants by name." Soon the Senator was accusing the administration of embracing the notion that peaceful coexistence was possible with the Soviet Union. He warned the Senate that any American concession would be at the expense of Germany, the satellites, or Nationalist China.[7] It was time, he said, to inform the Russians that the United States would be willing to talk "about the liberation of the countries now held captive by the Communists—and nothing else."

McCarthy backed this extremism with a resolution that would prevent the President from taking up any subject at Geneva until the Soviet Union agreed to resolve the satellite question. The Senator warned his colleagues that this was the last frail chance to free the nations of Eastern Europe. "If we fail now to make a bid to free these countries," he said, "we will have conceded them, for all practical purposes, to be Communists. We will have changed what is now a de facto recognition of the Soviet puppet regimes into what will amount to de jure recognition. And in the process we will kill off any underground movements that may now exist. . . ." Since Britain, France, and Russia disagreed, the resolution would have torpedoed the summit conference in advance.

McCarthy knew that his resolution had no chance of passage. Perhaps he thought that he could go down as the champion of the Poles while the motion would die in committee. But the Democrats on the Foreign Relations Committee had other plans. Knowland moved to pigeonhole the resolution, but the majority Democrats voted in a straight party vote eight to seven to bring it onto the floor. The committee then unanimously took the Democratic position. Immediately Jenner moved to have the resolution returned to committee and Hickenlooper supported him, but the Senate disagreed. Nor would it accept any watered-down substitute to McCarthy's resolution. Capehart, Republican of Indiana, accused the Democrats of playing politics in bringing the resolution to the floor for a field day.

Democratic leaders closed in on the new isolationists. Lyndon Johnson mimicked McCarthy by saying that the Wisconsin Senator would blame "the striped-pants boys from the State Department" if the resolution did not come to a vote. To Johnson the issue was clear. "It is," he said, "whether the President of the United States shall be sent to the Big Four Conference in a straitjacket." Then he added, "I personally do not propose to be a party to issuing a legislative fiat to the President telling him what he should do and say at Geneva." It was not, he charged, for Senators to frame the foreign policy of the United States. It was essential that the President go to Geneva backed by the "confidence and the trust of the American people."

Mansfield added the plea that the President and the Secretary of State be given the power "to negotiate with strength and conviction as the spokesmen for the entire nation." Then he declared pointedly, "But at the same time let us pledge ourselves now to spare them the indignity which their predecessors were not spared—the indignity

that would question their motives or their patriotism."
These Democratic spokesmen were effectively clubbing
McCarthy with Eisenhower's popularity—something which
the Republican leadership in the interest of party harmony
had never been willing to do.

Trapped, McCarthy attacked the men who had once
been at his side but who were now deserting him, for the
Democrats had forced the Republicans to choose between
McCarthy and Eisenhower. McCarthy turned on Hickenlooper, he ranted at Capehart, and he rebuked Knowland:
"I am not at all surprised at the position of the majority
leader. It has been the position of the Democratic party to
whine and whimper when it touches the red-hot challenge
of Communism. But I am surprised to see the minority
leader take that position." The bulk of the Old Guard
dared not oppose Eisenhower in this crisis, and McCarthy
alienated his fellow Republicans even further by accusing
everyone of pro-Communist sympathies who refused to
vote for a showdown with the Soviet Union on the satellite
issue. In the final vote McCarthy lost 77-4, with only
Jenner, Malone, and Langer on his side. At heart the new
isolationism in Congress, as reflected in McCarthy's resolutions, was forced to recede because its program was geared
only to perpetuating tension in the cold war.

But the real challenge to neo-isolationism as a political
force in 1955 sprang from the internal dilemma of the Republican party. The rampant use of the Communist issue
during the previous year indicated that the isolationist vote,
despite its significance, was not sufficient to maintain Republican majorities in Congress. The steady and gradual
decline of Republican strength since 1952 indicated that
Eisenhower had been unable to transfer his personal popularity to his party. By the summer of 1955 Republican
leaders from the Vice President to key Republican gover-

nors admitted that the party would again require Eisenhower at the head of its columns if it would control either
the White House or Congress in 1956.

Suddenly even the bitter Taftites, who had never graciously accepted Eisenhower's triumph, were climbing aboard
the Eisenhower bandwagon. They realized that whether
they liked it or not they would run on his record as well
as their own. The President's success and prestige now
loomed as the party's chief asset for immediate political
success; it reduced to narrow limits the area for internal
opposition to his leadership in matters of foreign policy.
Democratic leaders agreed that Eisenhower's re-election
could hardly be prevented, but they hoped to maintain
control of Congress. They could discern no better way in
mid-1955 than to place themselves in a position to share
Eisenhower's success in foreign affairs. The obvious support which the administration received from Democratic
leaders forced the Republican party into line behind the
administration. Republican leaders who one day might
require the President's backing dared not oppose him while
Democrats supported him. This movement toward interparty cooperation in foreign affairs was reflected almost
immediately in the announcement of the new Republican
theme for 1956—peace and prosperity.

Those who acclaimed the Geneva conference of July,
1955, as the beginning of a new day in Soviet-American
relations misinterpreted its meaning. The summit meeting
was not designed to settle the cold war. Churchill in
calling for a Big Four conference had hoped that it might
test the Russian intentions and capitalize on the world-
wide fear created by the appalling spectre of atomic war.
He desired no rigid and ponderous agenda. Specific issues
would be referred to the foreign ministers while the heads

of state could continue to talk optimistically of a new resolve for peace.

At the summit Eisenhower assumed the lead in easing tensions by assuring the Russians that the United States would never engage in aggressive war. The issues dividing East and West, he said, were "not inherently insoluble." They seemed so only because of encrusted "fear, and distrust and even hostility." Nor was it required that people think alike before they could work together. "The United States will never take part in an aggressive war," the President assured Bulganin, and the premier replied, "We believe that statement."

What gave the Geneva conference lasting significance was the agreement between the two great powers that under conditions of nuclear stalemate future differences would be settled by means other than war. The two nations, in the words of Harrison E. Salisbury, acknowledged that they had "reached a parity of horror." Henceforth rational policy would seek alternatives to armed conflict. "Once you reach that conclusion," declared one United States policy-maker, "certain other facts fall into line. You realize that diplomacy assumes a more important role, since it is diplomacy and not atom bombs which is going to settle conflicts between ourselves and the Russians. You begin to think about an atmosphere which will help the diplomats do their work."

Democratic spokesmen lauded the President's achievements at Geneva, limited as they were. Mansfield thought him extraordinarily successful. Senator John Sparkman agreed, but added that Eisenhower was "one of the luckiest Presidents in the history of the United States with respect to his foreign policy. The support he received from Senator George and all segments of the Democratic Party in his search for world peace has made it possible for him

to conduct foreign affairs the way the constitution intended
—by the executive branch." Sparkman recalled that Truman had been forced to conduct his foreign relations without such cooperation from the opposing party.

Undoubtedly the President enjoyed great advantages at
Geneva. Dorothy Thompson, with an eye on the domestic
scene, observed that "No Democratic President, whatever
his personal qualities, could have done what Mr. Eisenhower did in Geneva. With memories of Yalta and Potsdam every courteous word would have been branded as
'appeasement' and attributed to the influence of the Reds
in the administration." Only a conservative President supported by a conservative cabinet could have spoken as
kindly to the Russians as he did.

Everywhere the press commended the President for his
role at the summit conference. C. L. Sulzberger of the
New York *Times* noted his "enormous talent for impress-
ing others with the sincerity of his good will." Stewart
Alsop added: "Simply by being himself he had smashed
into smithereens the deeply rooted image of America as
inflexible and bent on war."[8] Editors did not agree, however, on what the summit conference meant for future
Soviet-American relations. *Life* magazine declared that the
West, through Eisenhower's sincerity, had captured the
moral leadership of the world—that Dulles therefore could
demand deeds as well as words from the Soviet Union.
Others were far less sanguine; they saw hope only in the
new emphasis on accommodation. The *Newark News*
admitted that the Big Four conference had settled little,
but "by opening the way to continuing negotiations on
seemingly unsoluble problems, it probably has insured
against any early transition to hot war."

This was the real gain. Geneva had witnessed the down-
grading of national objectives and the up-grading of the

destructiveness of war. Both sides agreed that whatever their differences the *status quo* was bearable, and that any future changes would be wrought through bargaining.

§ 4

Despite his success at the summit meeting, President Eisenhower was as vulnerable to neo-isolationist jibes as President Truman had been, for neither had been successful in refashioning the world of 1939. In their increasing loneliness the extremists still demanded no less than the fulfillment of the Republican platform of 1952. Those who still anticipated a reduction of Communist power in the world took seriously Knowland's warning of November, 1954: "Co-existence and atomic stalemate will result in ultimate Communist victory . . . we must face up to the fact that the Communist concept of 'peaceful coexistence' means that the United States and other free nations will be allowed to exist only until Communism is able to subvert these from within or destroy them from without." According to this doctrine the United States could not live in peace with the Communist world without eventually committing suicide. Until the Soviet leaders agreed in advance to the American conditions of coexistence, there should be no negotiations with the Kremlin.

For the new isolationists the proper course of American policy toward Russia was clear. It must never recognize the *status quo*, for at issue was not only the reduction of the Russian empire but also the liberation of people for whose oppression the United States was morally responsible. The United States must exert every available pressure on the Iron Curtain through the Voice of America and Radio Free Europe. "The status quo of enslavement," Knowland wrote in the autumn of 1955, "presents a moral question of which there can be no compromise if we are to have a genuinely peaceful world."⁹ He suggested that if the Soviet Union maintained its policy of aggressiveness the United States should withdraw diplomatic recognition "in order to rally the moral force of world opinion behind the case of human freedom." Although leading neo-isolationists declared their opposition to preventive war, they urged a bold policy that would run the risk of war while the nation still had the advantage in atomic power. Those who feared another war, charged Freda Utley, were destroying America's will to resist.¹⁰

Some neo-isolationists were still puzzled in 1955 at the continued tolerance of the Red Chinese regime. Admiral Radford commented on its lack of power. "I continue to be amazed," he said, "at the credulity of so many people in accepting the theme of Chinese Communist strength. It is indeed an amazing paradox that an offensive posture can be maintained and initiative achieved with no real substance to back it up."¹¹ Dulles himself termed Mao's China "a monster with feet of clay." It was no wonder that many Americans viewed Red China as the weakest nation that had ever talked tough to the United States. Some believed China so weak that the United States could not even blunder into war in the Formosan Straits.

This alleged Chinese weakness strengthened the belief that continued nonrecognition would eventually roll back the Bamboo Curtain and restore prewar stability in the Orient. Such Senators as Jenner, McCarthy, and Knowland warned that every plan to ease tension in the Formosan Straits was designed to erode and undermine American policy toward the Nationalists. McCarthy called the ambassadorial conference at Geneva a "sellout" and "betrayal of a devoted and fighting ally." There was every reason to believe, he said, that concrete measures of appeasement, probably relating to Quemoy and Matsu, had been agreed upon. He added later that it was "clear that the campaign to sell out free China is under a full head of steam."[12] The Senator declared that the only alternative for the United States was to encourage an all-out war on Red China by the Asiatic nations of South Viet Nam, South Korea, and Nationalist China. Knowland had long called for a blockade of the China coast to force the return of American prisoners. Pushing this concept of American omnipotence vis-à-vis Red China to the extreme, Hanford McNider remarked in August, 1955, before the Iowa American Legion Convention, "Let's get over there, put a blockade on their coast, and bomb them [the Red Chinese] off the map."

Voicing such faith in the omnipotence of American will, the new isolationists chided the administration for its inability to fulfill the party program of 1952. Before the Chicago meeting sponsored by the Committee of One Thousand Republicans in February, 1955, Senator McCarthy declared that the retreat from the Tachens proved that the administration "had abandoned all hope and intention of aiding the liberation of China." He accused the President of ignoring the Republican platform of 1952 which had pledged the party to "a policy of liberation, not coexistence." Reaffirming Truman's position in the Formosan Straits, he said, was merely an administration maneuver to cover up its retreat. General William Hale Wilbur, USA retired, continued the effort to hold the President to the platform. "The great question before us," he told the convention, "is whether the 1952 Republican platform has been carried out." The party had not balanced the budget, he said, its policies were no longer American.[13]

To the extreme right wing of the Republican party Geneva was a tragic failure because the President had not even attempted to secure liberation of the satellites. Eugene Lyons summed up the President's effort in *American Mercury:* "President Eisenhower, to his credit, did allude once—just once—to the nations and peoples in captivity, and to the mischief wrought these 38 years by world Communism. But he did it in the cautious ritual double-talk of too-friendly diplomacy, as formulated in advance by a cautious Congress." Lyons characterized the summit conference as "dismal and degrading," because no one wanted to embarrass the Russians and hearten the people behind the Iron Curtain. The end of American purpose, he reminded the President, was liberation and not a *modus vivendi* with the Soviet empire. No accommodation would succeed anyway, for any paper agreement would become merely another "mirage on the desert of self-deception."[14]

Irene Corbally Kuhn asserted that the entire movement for peace leading to Geneva originated in Moscow and was peddled by Soviet propaganda. She termed 1955 "the year of rehearsal for betrayal."[15] Republicans had become as guilty as Democrats for the existence of the Iron Curtain. McCarthy reminded the G.O.P. leadership that its critics could now say "that the American government's concern for oppressed people is a cheap politician's concern about how Americans of Eastern European descent will vote in the next election." He accused the President of seeking friendship at Geneva with "the apostles of hell." "You cannot offer friendship to tyrants and murderers, as has the President of the United States, without advancing the cause of tyranny and murder," he charged. The conference, in professing to ease world tensions when the Russians had conceded nothing, perpetuated, in his estimation, "a fraud on the American people."[16] George Sokolsky predicted that Geneva would continue to expose Eisenhower to Republican attack, for it was "clear as crystal that

Geneva was a flop and the Geneva smile the frippery of the wanton."

For those who still believed that liberation in Europe and Asia was not beyond the capability of American power to achieve there was an explanation for this failure—the persistence of the "sinister influence" in high places which was still guiding American foreign policy in the interests of the Kremlin. Jenner reminded the nation in August, 1955, that during the postwar years the Soviet Union had expanded to cover one-third of the globe. "This conflict between freedom and slavery was not lost in Asia or in Europe," he wrote. "It was lost in Washington, because the little group in our policy-making which favored the Soviet Union was stronger than the people who believed in a pro-American policy." That the conspiracy continued was proved by the fact that the promises of 1952 had not been achieved. "This collectivist machine," warned Jenner, "operated, in part, in the State Department; in part, in the White House Secretariat; in the super-Cabinet agencies of national defense, in the Foreign Operations Administration, in the CIA." It pervaded also the press, the parties, the colleges, and American business, but it emanated, the Senator admitted, "from some control tower we cannot see."[17]

That after five years there was still no proof of subversion did not render the diagnosis incorrect. The danger to America still lay at home. "We can win true peace for all the world if we will gird ourselves to defeat the enemy within," ran his conclusion. For the Indiana Senator and the declining but vehement group who joined in his extremism, nothing had occurred by 1955 to shatter the belief that the United States could have its way in all its external relations.

Whereas in 1954 this illusion that the real dangers to national security were internal still appeared to capture the imagination of millions of Americans, by mid-1955 the relaxation of tension abroad and the open Democratic support of President Eisenhower had created a changing atmosphere at home. No longer did the fears, the excitement, and the emotionalism surround the issues of communism and foreign policy. No longer was there the distrust and mutual recriminations that had characterized the previous years of the Eisenhower administration.

In this welcome atmosphere something was being overlooked—that neither the mass accusations nor the security system had uncovered much subversion. Yet in the backwash of the attacks on the past the American people had paid a heavy price in the demoralization of the State Department and the Foreign Service and in the fastening of isolationist illusions of omnipotence to American purpose abroad. It was difficult in retrospect to see how the charges had strengthened the nation or improved its foreign policy. As one Washington attorney said:

The situation is not better—it is worse. The wounds in our processes of thinking and of judgment are deep and they will take a long time to heal. If all this actually contributed to our national security, to the defense against communism, it might be justified. But the ironic part about it is that it doesn't really add to the safety of the country; it actually detracts from it by fastening attention and energies on what people said or thought or did a half generation ago, or what their casual associations were, and not on the protection of the few areas where protection is genuinely needed against subversion and espionage.[18]

For years the dogma of the new isolationism had penetrated the formulation of American foreign policy because national leadership had refused to counter its assumptions in terms of national limitations. If its influence over the nation had declined, the new isolationism still determined the goals and character of American foreign affairs.

§ 5

With its new accent on diplomacy the post-Geneva world vastly complicated the external relations of the United States. As long as the Soviet challenge appeared to be chiefly military, the American accent on alliances and retaliatory power appeared both logical and satisfactory. But diplomacy, contrasted to maintaining a simple posture of strength, required far greater imagination, variations in policy, and understanding of competing national interests.

Nor did the mere resolve that issues be settled by negotiation remove the complexity or the problems or the sharp conflicts in policy relative to Eastern Europe. The July talks at Geneva at the foreign ministers level did not presage an easy, constructive relationship between the United States and the Soviet Union. Before the foreign ministers reconvened in October it was apparent that the Russians would not concede more readily on the issues of German unification, the satellites, European security, East-West contacts, or disarmament. Molotov assured the West that Geneva did not necessarily usher in "an era of good feeling."

Russia entered the post-Geneva era with a running start and continued to reveal amazing agility and vigor in her diplomacy. By September she was becoming a disturbing factor in the Middle East, exploiting Arab nationalism through the procurement of Czech arms for Egypt and, with her new emphasis on economic and technical assistance, offering to aid Egypt in building the Aswan Dam. By January, 1956, the Soviet representative to the United

Nations had adopted a pro-Arab and anti-Israel stand. During November and December, 1955, Bulganin and Khrushchev toured India, Burma, and Afghanistan, promising Soviet trade and economic assistance while attempting to make the West appear warlike and intransigent. By February, 1956, Bulganin was offering trade and economic help to Pakistan on condition that it withdraw from its military commitments to the United States. At the same time he offered trade and aid to Latin America and a mutual security pact to President Eisenhower.

Richard Lowenthal in the London *Observer* characterized the triple impact of 1955 in world affairs:

First, it has brought the completion of the shift in Soviet *methods* of fighting the West, away from military pressure to political maneuvering and economic competition. Second, there has also been a shift in the principal *arena* of the contest, away from the extremities—the European and Far Eastern borders of the Communist empires—to the uncommitted and underdeveloped countries of the 'Middle Zone' which stretches from North Africa across the Middle East and the Indian subcontinent to the Indonesian archipelago. And finally, we have seen a growing shift in the *role* of these countries. They are no longer content to be the passive objects of the struggle and increasingly tend to become its arbiters.[19]

Neither Russia's new offensive nor the challenge of the post-Geneva world produced any "agonizing reappraisal" of United States Far Eastern policy. Not until January, 1956, did Dulles recognize publicly that the United States was in a bitter contest in the area of economic assistance in the underdeveloped regions of the world. He warned that defeat in this contest would terminate in disaster, and that the United States could lose this struggle, despite its clear superiority of wealth, unless it recognized the nature of the challenge. Vice President Nixon before the New York

Herald Tribune Forum defined the purpose of United
States foreign aid as an effort to make nations such as India
strong enough to be independent of any foreign domination. "To cut off aid or to put strings on it," he admitted,
"will never win India to our side. It is more likely to have
the opposite effect."

Tardily the administration was recognizing the new
Russian threat, but its programs still appeared insufficient
to establish communication with the aspiring people of
Asia. And they would not, wrote Averell Harriman in the
Atlantic of April, 1956, until they identified themselves
"with anticolonialism rather than with colonialism; with
peace rather than the reckless use of our great power; with
genuine respect for the national dignity of all peoples
rather than with arrogance; . . . and with a steadfast program dedicated to world economic growth . . . to help each
country achieve independence from economic colonialism
and to assure its people greater opportunity."[20] It was
doubtful if Congress, without considerable prodding, would
evince any serious inclination to meet the competition of
Russian economic aid.

Nationalism in Asia, so fully denied by the new isolationist interpretation of Chiang's decline, still received
scant attention in American policy statements. This force
was behind every diplomatic failure that the United States
had experienced in Asia. American leadership had ignored
it in China and Indochina, in the nonrecognition of the
Bandung conference, and in its persistent misunderstanding
of Asian neutralism and the aims of Nehru.

Dulles' statement that Goa was a Portuguese province
in the Far East rather than a colony was a further example
of the American tendency to underestimate the nationalistic sentiments of Asia. Retorted the *Times of India:* "If
Goa and Macao are provinces so presumably are Latvia

and Estonia. If it is not colonialism for a foreign country to hold Goa and Macao then it cannot be imperialism for Russia to dominate Rumania and Czechoslovakia. . . . Such a gesture can only imply that Washington is writing off India from the democratic slate." Similarly the *Eastern Economist*, normally uncritical of the United States, asserted that "in one incompetent, unimaginative, and unnecessary pronouncement, the Secretary of State has succeeded in alienating America's friends and giving joy to America's enemies." The London *Economist* concluded that "Mr. Dulles has been worth more than ten Khrushchevs in Moscow's wooing of India."[21] These observations were suggestive of the price of policy that ignored the vehemence with which Asia demanded equality with the West.

In the months following Geneva the administration still seemed by its action far more concerned with buttressing its military alliances than promoting the economic development on which the independence and strength of the Asiatic nations depended. Policy which looked to pacts left little room for an imaginative and constructive program. One powerful neo-isolationist tradition in recent United States diplomacy demanded that Asian nations, to receive economic aid, first join the crusade against communism. Dulles had admitted that "broadly speaking, foreign budgetary aid is being limited to situations where it clearly contributes to military strength." Tending to discount the domestic concerns of Asia, United States policies still did not penetrate far enough in the search for friends and allies.

Unable to fill its diplomatic vacuum in the Far East, the Eisenhower administration contined to rely on massive retaliation. Dulles had redefined it as a policy bent not on needless destruction but on inflicting punishment to fit the crime. He warned that any aggressor will lose more than he will gain. "He doesn't have to lose *much* more," he

added. "It just has to be *something* more. If the equation
is such that the outcome is clearly going to be against him,
he won't go in."[22] Admiral Radford agreed that American
policy must be ready to defeat aggression along the ground.
For that reason, he declared early in 1955, the administration had sought "to design a pattern for our Armed Forces
which will give us just such a military readiness—a sturdy
but flexible combination of land, sea, amphibious, and air
forces. And within this pattern our military forces are
prepared if necessary to use nuclear weapons. . . ."

Military critics doubted if national policy gave meaning
to this concept of graduated deterrence. The "New Look"
still seemed to anticipate a withdrawal of American ground
forces from the Far East and to place primacy on air-atomic
power. Together these trends seemed to allow little choice
between inaction and air-nuclear attack. General Ridgway
charged that the military budgets to 1957 were not based
on military needs, but were "squeezed within the framework of present, arbitrary manpower and fiscal limits, a
complete inversion of the normal process."[23] Ridgway
agreed with Radford that the United States required a
"fast-moving, hard-hitting, joint force in which the ver-
satility of the whole is emphasized and the preponderance
of any one part is de-emphasized." But he doubted that this
type of force was possible under the administration's budgetary considerations, for a mobile, versatile striking force
could not be purchased in the bargain basement. Chester
Bowles once observed, "Let it not be said by future historians that in the second decade after World War II freedom throughout the world died of a balanced budget."

Nor did the pressure on United States policy toward
China after Bandung alter the administration's expectations
in the Far East. No longer did many writers on Red China
anticipate the overthrow of the Peiping regime by any

means short of war. Yet American officials continued to ignore that massive fact and avoided every pressure to seek a *modus vivendi* with the present Chinese government. When Burmese Premier U Nu visited Washington during the summer of 1955 and announced his belief that most people in the capital no longer opposed the recognition of the Peiping regime, the State Department responded promptly that "this government's opposition to the seating of Communist China in the United Nations has not changed." Dulles continued to warn the world that this nation would not betray Chiang Kai-shek by giving up the offshore islands. The Secretary still acknowledged his commitment to the Nationalist China bloc and to Chiang himself that if the Generalissimo would withdraw his troops from the Tachens the United States would defend Quemoy and Matsu.

There was an element of tragedy in American Far Eastern policy. In 1955 Red China was coming into her own diplomatically while the United States still opposed her at every turn. Even Ambassador Johnson, to satisfy Knowland and McCarthy, insisted that at Geneva he was engaged in "talks" rather than formal discussions. Edmund Burke once observed that one art of statesmanship is to grant graciously what ultimately cannot be denied. United States opposition to Red Chinese recognition had been so long and bitter that if the UN suddenly voted a seat to Red China this nation would face the unfortunate choice of withdrawing or suffering a stunning diplomatic defeat. Such important nations as Britain, Canada, Italy, India, Indonesia, and Pakistan were on the verge of breaking silence in the UN, but to the new isolationists, pursuing their unilateral ideal, what the world thought of American policy on China still had no bearing on its diplomatic success or failure.

During the months following Geneva the administration refused to modify its diplomatic policies toward Russia. It continued to insist that it would never compromise on principles and therefore would never acquiesce in Soviet domination over the satellites. Vice President Nixon demanded that the Soviets prove their sincerity by agreeing to unification and free elections in Germany, the dismantling of the Iron Curtain, the freeing of the European satellites, and the acceptance of the President's aerial inspection plan. President Eisenhower himself in January, 1956, restated this primary objective of American diplomacy: "The peaceful liberation of the captive peoples has been, is, and, until success is achieved, will continue to be a major goal of United States foreign policy." At Baylor University in May, 1956, he advised the hundreds of millions of persons behind the Iron Curtain to "walk fearlessly in the fullness of human freedom" behind the leadership of the West. American policy continued to regard Communist leadership or power as no more than a distasteful and temporary phenomenon on the world scene.

No less than the freedom of East Germany and its return to the Western bloc would satisfy Dulles on the issue of unification. Perhaps this inflexible stand toward the Iron Curtain was good politics in some areas of the United States, but at the foreign ministers conference in October, 1955, it tended to anger Russia and disillusion the allies who would have preferred negotiations based on the *status quo* in 1955. Dulles' terms would have been excellent if the Soviet Union had surrendered unconditionally. But their apparent finality seemed to ignore the meaning of Geneva —that since nothing can be settled by force, it is necessary to maneuver, bargain, and trade.

Germany presented a major problem for American leadership. West Germany had joined NATO because the

West had convinced her that the pressure that would be exerted by the new military-political association would assure German unification. Instead, West Germany's commitment to the West prompted Russia to reject Dulles' plan. Nor would the Soviets accept Eden's five-nation mutual security defense plan as a guarantee against German power. This placed a burden on the United States to find a more reasonable formula, for time appeared to be on the side of the Kremlin. Moscow alone had access to both German governments and could negotiate unification without the West on her own terms of neutrality. Many German leaders, moreover, showed greater concern for unification than for a military alliance with the West. The concept of a neutral Germany had a marked appeal also to the people of France, Belgium, Italy, and Denmark who had experienced German might in the past. Dulles was convinced that he won his point at Geneva and that his inflexible stand on German unification placed that nation firmly in the Western camp. Others were not so sure. Said one Western diplomat, "What we gained in the swings we more than lost on the roundabouts."

Established policies are never easily altered, especially when they are based on political commitments as well as personal conviction. But the capacity to change is the true mark of statesmanship. Governments that are unsure of themselves reveal strength only when rigid and obstinate, and the power of the new isolationism over the administration was still too patent to be denied. Diplomacy which is geared to rigidity, lest it appear to be retreating, can be disastrous, for it accepts the assumption that all negotiation is synonymous with appeasement. Political action is expedient action, and great statesmen have often been forced to alter their demands on other nations as conditions change. Being forced to admit error or even deception in promises of success is the normal gauntlet of politics that all leaders must run.

Leadership, whether it has deceived the public or not, must never deceive itself. Amid its moralizing, its slogans, clichés, and platitudes there must be some genuine under-standing of the problems with which it is attempting to deal. Personal integrity and wisdom are the only lasting criteria of value upon which a nation can rely. "Our trust is given to certain leaders," Joyce Cary, the noted British novelist has written, "because their honor, their character, are the only things we can trust. We know they may have to change their minds, to break promises, to let us down, but if we trust them, if we can say of them they are honest men, we do not reproach them."[24]

Statesmanship rests on the willingness of leaders to break political promises, if demanded by the national interest, even though such action should destroy effective party symbols. President Eisenhower himself in 1955 informed a press conference that the H-bomb threat was "so serious that we just cannot pretend to be intelligent human beings unless we pursue with all our might, with all our thought, all our souls, you might say, some way of solving this prob-lem." This was the challenge of Geneva, but United States diplomacy revealed at best only a partial response. Whether the administration could yet satisfy the new isola-tionists and deflate the Soviet empire without war, diplo-macy, or increased military expenditures was doubtful, but its repeated policy statements in the months after Geneva indicated that it had accepted no other objectives.

9

The Task of Leadership

There is no aspect of current American opinion quite as significant as the dichotomy between the views of experts and the prevailing mood of the nation on matters of foreign affairs. During the past six years this relationship has been characterized by a strange and ironic juxtaposition. In the years preceding 1950 American policy came close to satisfying both the national mood and the intellectual foundations of coalition diplomacy. Yet that program became the victim of the severest partisan onslaught ever suffered by any American foreign policy. Today when the nation's foreign relations are vulnerable to the criticism of experts at home and abroad, they enjoy such broad endorsement and acceptance at all levels of American life that they have become almost untouchable. This phenomenon is as explicable as it is disturbing. During these six eventful years the views of the professionals have remained constant, whereas American policy and much of American public opinion have shifted from the clear internationalist foundations of Truman-Acheson policy to the almost complete acceptance of many philosophical assumptions of the new American isolationalism by the Eisenhower administration.

Whatever their quality, the nation's recent foreign policies have captured the approbation of all elements of American society which have the power to determine or modify public action. In January, 1953, Secretary Dulles announced that the Eisenhower policies would be "open so that you can know what they are and . . . sufficiently simple so that you can understand them and judge them and . . . sufficiently decent and moral so that they will fit into your idea of what you think is right." During the succeeding three years there has been a broad tendency in the United States to accept these three precepts of openness, simplicity, and morality as both adequate in concept and successful in performance.

Eisenhower and Dulles have repeatedly assured the nation that their foreign policies based on these ideals have achieved remarkable success, and the continuance of peace since 1953 seems evidence enough to prove their contention. Few Americans seemed to take exception when Dulles informed the Senate Foreign Relations Committee that the new Russian policy to destroy Western influence in south Asia and in the Middle East by means other than military was a manifestation of Soviet weakness rather than strength—that it simply dramatized the success of American action.

President Eisenhower in his address before the American Society of Newspaper Editors in April, 1956, viewed the past three years as a period of astonishing progress in American foreign relations. Enduring peace seemed hopeless, he said, when he entered the White House, but the years since then have produced "the cautious hope that a new, fruitful, and peaceful era for mankind can emerge from a haunted decade. The world breathes a little more easily today." Not for many years, he added, had there been "such promise that patient, imaginative, enterprising effort could gradually be rewarded in steady decrease in the dread of war. . . ." He outlined a foreign policy program for the United States which would pursue the goals of collective security and disarmament, economic assistance to create conditions of freedom, and every effort "by peaceful means to induce the Soviet bloc to correct existing injustices and genuinely to pursue peaceful purposes in its relations with other nations."[1] With such objectives few Americans would quarrel.

In Congress the Eisenhower policies have suffered embarrassing attack only from those new isolationist Republicans who took seriously the pledges of the Republican platform of 1952 and who believe that Dulles has had sufficient time to liberate both continental China and Eastern Europe. Democrats in Congress never believed the objects of liberation attainable and have resisted criticizing the administration for not achieving what they never anticipated. They have detected no great variance in operation between the Eisenhower and the Truman foreign policies. They have questioned neither the administration's posture toward Red China and the Formosan Straits nor the concept of liberation. In their conformism they have forced such little re-examination of neo-isolationist tendencies within official American purpose that, as James Reston has suggested, they have almost destroyed their right to criticize Republican policy.

Such hierarchical Democratic leaders as Sam Rayburn and Walter George have refused almost completely to break silence on Eisenhower's decisions. Even those Democrats who have been more rebellious have criticized chiefly what they term the "hucksterism" in Dulles' approach and his overclaiming of success. Democratic National Chairman, Paul M. Butler, for example, said that if the President "does not want foreign policy to be a political issue, let him order Mr. Hall to drop the 'peace' slogan as part of the campaign strategy."

Republican leaders have appeared wholly unconcerned with matters of external affairs; they are convinced that the future success of their party will not hinge so much on what is happening in Indochina as what is happening in Indiana.[2] Such Democratic foreign policy spokesmen as Mike Mansfield, Hubert Humphrey, Adlai Stevenson, Averell Harriman, and Lyndon Johnson have been pecking away seriously at what they describe as the sterility of ideas in present policy. They have repeatedly issued a challenge to the administration to come up with some new concepts to meet the shifting tactics of the Soviets. But they admit privately that their efforts to put the administration under fire have produced almost no public response.

Peace and prosperity are appealing slogans, and in this nation they have a unique power to make people unaware of their problems. For the vast majority of Americans peace is peace, and the current business prosperity is sufficient evidence that very little can be wrong with the world. They are in no mood to respond to any challenge based on the cry that the United States is not necessarily winning the cold war. But whatever the domestic trend toward moderation, the problems of American security have not been resolved. Continued peace and prosperity might make the average citizen oblivious to the external threats to national welfare, but the ignoring of such issues has never made it possible to avoid them. Somewhere in national political life there must be leadership that will respond realistically to the continuing challenges from abroad. Policy that is imaginative and intellectually sound cannot evolve from public insistence; it can emanate only from those who lead the nation.

This persistent complacency of the American people stands in sharp contrast to the analyses of foreign policy critics in both the United States and Europe. Seldom if ever has American policy been so unacceptable to the vast majority of free world leaders as during the months since the summit conference at Geneva in July, 1955. Harold Callender of *The New York Times* staff wrote recently that it is the almost unanimous view of Europeans best qualified to judge that United States policy lacks the resourcefulness and imagination that characterized it briefly after 1947 and that it has failed to progress and evolve with the times.[3] Most European criticism has fallen on Dulles rather than Eisenhower. David Daiches, British author and lecturer, fairly well summarized the British attitude when he said: "I'm suspicious of Dulles. . . . He seems to be in a state of confusion . . . not out of ill will, he just doesn't know how to talk like a diplomat. [As for my opinion of] American foreign policy, I'm not sure what it is, but I do know I don't like Foster Dulles's implementation." European spokesmen have been astonished at Dulles' recent claims of success.

Foreign critics believe that United States policy has not been adapted to meet the new Soviet challenge. They accuse this nation of speaking and acting too independently of its allies and of responding too vigorously to internal pressure. Recently Josephine Gilbert, a British advertising woman, remarked that "American leaders don't have enough courage to ignore elections." Europeans believe that American policy, while not abandoning the instruments of security, should direct more attention to economic competition with the Soviet Union; that it should be more flexible and less moralistic so that some of the outstanding differences in the cold war might become negotiable. They believe that United States economic policies would be improved if the government lowered its tariff barriers and handled its foreign aid program through the United Nations so that the Russians would be forced to be more cooperative and that economic assistance would not appear as a competitive system to buy support abroad.[4]

Almost simultaneously in February, 1956, three of Europe's leading statesmen launched a muffled but serious attack on American foreign policy—Christian Pineau, French Foreign Minister; Sir Anthony Eden, British Prime Minister; and Giovanni Gronchi, President of Italy. All three accused the United States of needlessly prolonging tensions in the post-Geneva world by clinging to military policies rather than shifting to a new emphasis on economic policies. Pineau pointed to the danger in the further reliance on military pacts: "We have made a great mistake in thinking that security problems were the only international problems with which we had to deal. Between two forms of propaganda, the one conducted solely in military terms and aiming at security at any price and the other constantly reiterating offers of peace, public opinion will inevitably turn toward the one that proposes peaceful solutions, even if they are not sincere."[5]

Before a joint session of Congress Eden urged the same shift from military to economic policies. "We can neither hold Communism nor beat it back by force of arms alone," he warned. "Friendship and freedom, and help of all kinds on which to base a rising standard of life, that is what we offer." He charged the United States with the responsibility to make greater efforts to allay hatred all over the world.

President Gronchi criticized the unilateralism in American foreign relations and questioned specifically Dulles' adamant stand against employing Article 2 of the Atlantic Pact which speaks of "promoting conditions of stability and well being." He informed a joint session of Congress that NATO "should be brought into line with today's realities. . . . Military co-operation continues to be very important today but it should be supplemented with new and imaginative forms of co-operation." Some European observers believed that NATO, unless its goals were adjusted to meet the nonmilitary needs of a world bent on peace, would soon cease to be a significanct factor in Europe's defense.

By the late spring of 1956 there was evidence that the Eisenhower administration was responding to the changing climate of international affairs. The President admitted in April, "A policy that was good six months ago is not necessarily now of any validity. It is necessary that we find better, more effective ways of keeping ourselves in tune with the world's needs." "We cannot undo the changes that have come upon the world," Dulles added recently. "Nor do we want to reverse what holds so much of promise, merely because it also holds some risks of loss. Our task is not to seek to reverse change, but to build constructively upon all the changes that hold a possibility of good." To promote needed unity in the Western alliance, the Secretary during April openly supported the move in Europe to employ Article 2 of the NATO pact. Europeans interpreted this shift as a direct recognition by the Eisenhower administration that broader and more imaginative policies were required to meet the Soviet threat.

But the extent of these policy changes remained uncertain. At a press conference on June 6, 1956, the President seemed to move forward another step in the new direction. Neutralism, he said, was an acceptable policy for any nation. It was not immoral or necessarily unwise for a country to avoid military pacts. Nor did it signify indifference "as between right and wrong or decency and indecency." Pouring money into military defense, he admitted, would soon reach the point of diminishing returns. "And it is better, certainly it is more profitable in the long run," he added, "to put . . . some of your money in constructive things that tend to make people respectful of the great values that we are supporting. . . ." Congressional reaction to Eisenhower's statement that a portion of this augmented economic aid might well go to neutrals indicated that the establishment of any new policy would require vigorous Executive leadership.

If Eisenhower was responding to free world pressure, Dulles' commencement address at Iowa State College on June 9, heralded as a major foreign policy address to clarify the new trends in American policy, might have been delivered three years earlier. The Secretary still accentuated the importance of confronting the Soviet bloc with military alliances and massive retaliatory power. He favored military aid to allies, but urged Congress to maintain the $800 million request for economic aid. He did not even refer to the current move to transform NATO into an instrument of economic cooperation. He attacked as obsolete the entire concept of neutralism, adding that "except under very exceptional circumstances, it is an immoral and shortsighted conception."

Again it seemed as if the President had addressed his remarks to the free world and sought to assure it that United States foreign policy was responding to the requirements of the post-Geneva world, while Dulles had reassured Congress that American policy had not changed. Both men were still trapped in a dilemma of major proportions. How could they win the approval of Congress and the nation for new economic policies unless they could rationalize them in terms of a dynamic, changing Orient? Any evaluation of policy requirements based on the revolutionary upheaval of a continent would soon reveal the necessity for overhauling the entire Far Eastern policy of the United States.

Thus there was nothing precise or novel in the administration's proposals. They were largely a repetition of the goals of Western policy which European leaders had been voicing for months. American policy statements were still marked by moralisms and restatements of common aspirations. Nor was there much inclination in the administration to push Congress toward accepting its new emphasis on long-range economic commitments. Even the highest foreign policy leaders were unclear about the President's intentions. Democratic spokesmen complained that the administration made no effort to marshal the support of the Republican leadership in Congress. It was doubtful also if a broader economic program even touched the most troublesome aspects of American foreign policy—its tendency toward unilateralism in diplomacy and its illusions of omnipotence vis-à-vis both Red China and Russia.

§ 2

Students of American foreign policy in the United States have reflected the general concern of Europeans at the persistent inflexibility of American diplomacy. Perhaps few of them would question the validity of George F. Kennan's observation of a half decade ago "that there has been in the past a very significant gap between challenge and response in our conduct of foreign policy; that this gap still exists; and that, whereas fifty years ago it was not very dangerous to us, today it puts us in grave peril."[6] In the opinion of many American writers and observers the power of will and decision are still lacking in the conduct of United States foreign relations. They fear that the nation's lack of internal coordination, discipline, and responsibility will cancel out its great potential for useful and significant leadership.

There is nothing strange or unique in the disturbing character of United States diplomacy today. The problems which confront American foreign policy have existed in some form or other throughout the twentieth century. They stem essentially from a pervading deficiency in understanding. Too often the United States since 1900 has failed to meet its external challenges because it has not recognized them. One essential reason for this phenomenon is that American democracy has labored under isolationist traditions of unilateralism and omnipotence which have rendered it difficult for the nation's leadership to formulate policy based on concepts of limited national power and genuine accommodation with the world. Notions of invincibility and morality whereby the mere declaration of utopian goals passes for policy is the stuff from which American foreign relations have been molded. Since Wilson first announced his Fourteen Points, freedom for all the world has been the goal of United States diplomacy. This moral purpose has been vastly magnified in recent years by the vigorous effort to place solely on American leadership the responsibility for the submergence of Eastern European and Chinese peoples under Communist rule.

Balance between the nation's goals (and the policies which they demand) and the limitations of national power is the essence of successful diplomacy. That characteristic which most seriously challenges this balance in the United States is the tendency toward false expectations and myths concerning past failures—"myths that indulge democracies in the fallacy that the right course is always ascertainable and practicable."[7] On the American scene this perennial tendency toward overexpectation arises primarily from the propensity of national leaders to promise too much.

Too often American politicians have argued that in the realm of external affairs unpleasant choices need not be made, that gains can be achieved without commensurate expenditures. In a prosperous economy probably no one is much the worse if domestic policy falls short of anticipation. But in foreign relations there is strict accountability between expectations and expenditures. A nation can have the policy for which it is willing to pay and no more. To demand more is to create a gap between expectation and fulfillment which divides the nation internally, casts doubt on the loyalty and wisdom of public servants, and promotes a search for scapegoats rather than solutions. Its total effect is a reduction of national prestige and power. For that reason democratic leadership must accept the obligation to destroy the illusion that a nation with even the strength of the United States can have a world of its own ordaining unless it is willing to pay a heavy price either in military expenditures or in living at the edge of war.

Recent American policy has not been characterized by any rebirth of humility in this nation's purpose abroad. At heart it still insists that the United States can demand more from its antagonists than American power can force from them—that it can expect unconditional surrender at the conference table when its antagonists have never been made to concede defeat on the battlefield. Although Dulles' demands on Russia have liberated no one during the past three years, the belief persists that somehow the moral content in American purpose will roll back the Iron Curtain without war or compromise.

Certainly there is no readily available program that would automatically reduce the scope and gravity of the tensions of Europe. It is proper also that moral values be given their proper place in international relations. Liberation is a worthy goal of a free people, but the price in demanding it as a condition of peace could be exceedingly costly in allies, goodwill, and confidence among those who expect more flexibility and magnanimity in American purpose. This hard policy toward Russia even raises doubt concerning the policy's very morality. It is not clear how the repeated declaration of such expectations alone will free the satellites or secure German unification. Nor would it be easily demonstrated that United States moral preachments were even partially responsible if the satellites again achieved their independence. This nation has obligations, furthermore, to seek some form of reasonable accommodation which might strengthen American leadership and the Grand Alliance. "The closer the West is united," Max Ascoli has written, "the bolder can be its diplomacy of movement. We can then assist the satellite peoples more effectively than by advocating the liberation of Poland on Pulaski Day."[8]

Any war fought over liberation in Europe would be difficult to explain in terms of American interest. The United States has lived with the present Soviet empire for a decade without becoming bankrupt or suffering a loss of freedom. It seems reasonable to assume that the *status quo* could continue indefinitely without injuring this nation if its diplomacy would accept the realities of power and possession in the postwar world. The time has arrived for the United States to think of improved diplomatic relations with the Soviet Union. "The Soviet position in the eyes of the world is improving," Joseph C. Harsch has warned in *The Christian Science Monitor*. "It is gaining acceptance. It is more respectable than it was five years ago. The time has come when it can be dangerous to reject the hand of friendship even when we know that the gesture is intended for propaganda."

In Asia American policy appears equally unrealistic in its limitless expectations. The Eisenhower administration continues to ignore the fact that Red China with its 600 million people is the key force in all Asia. Its intransigence toward the Chinese civil war continues to exact its heavy penalty of American policy in five significant areas: It isolates the United States from its European allies in matters of Asiatic policy, creates distrust among the nations of free Asia toward American purpose, prevents any genuine appreciation in the United States of the force of nationalism in the Far East and Africa, forces the United States to rely overwhelmingly on military policy, and perpetuates close diplomatic ties between Peiping and Moscow.

There is no particular merit in clinging to a diplomatic course that has so few adherents abroad that it reduces the United States to facing the great issues in the Orient without allies among the important nations of Europe and Asia. Britain accepts the emergence of Asia as the great phenomenon of the century and desires to win the friendship of the two new powers, China and India. Her leaders believe that the granting of diplomatic equality to Red China would make it possible to weaken if not sever her alliance with Moscow.

Leaders of free Asia regard American policy on China as an affront to Asian nationalism. Red China, with its doubtful quality and intentions, has become the focus of anti-Western sentiment in the Orient. Asia's significant neutral bloc, led by India, has little sympathy for this nation's determination to ignore the Peiping regime or to defend Formosa. Visiting Asians who stream into China—perhaps close to a hundred thousand in 1955—are impressed with the new dignity and power of the country. For

Asians everywhere Communist China represents the fulfillment of the aspirations of a continent, for that nation
has put its house in order and has proved itself the equal of
the West.[9] It is significant that no matter how belligerent
the Chinese have become vis-à-vis the United States, they
have not lost the goodwill of Asia's billion inhabitants.
Asian nationalism has buoyed up the power of China in its
antagonism toward the United States. Since 1950 it has
even allowed the Peiping regime to gain the diplomatic
initiative over this nation. If the Bamboo Curtain has not
been driven back from the Formosan Straits, it is because
the world has no sympathy with such purpose.

Nationalism is the key to the upheaval sweeping the
area from Morocco in north Africa to the China Sea.
"Nationalism . . . is the mainspring of our efforts," President Sukarno of Indonesia told a joint session of Congress
in May, 1956. "Fail to understand it and no amount of
thinking, no torrent of words, and no Niagara of dollars
will produce anything but bitterness and disillusionment."
In Asia its challenge has been clear, and too often American
leadership has underestimated its power. In the Middle
East the force of upheaval has been equally great, but the
lines of successful action for the West are blurred and
uncertain. Here nationalism involves the suppression of
minority groups, the destruction of political stability, and a
disregard for the genuine interests of the European allies.
Not every national group in the world can achieve independence. Nor could many maintain it long even if they
acquired it. Power is still an essential element in the freedom of peoples.

Many areas of the Middle East now seething in revolt
are pursuing goals that are highly unrealistic and that endanger the rights of others. The United States cannot
possibly please both sides in each dispute. It can only

evaluate each challenge to the *status quo* on its specific
merits. Successful policy need not be spectacular. In both
Asia and the Middle East the area of intelligent action is
often so narrow that American interests might best be
served by policies that are restrained, cautious, and hum-
ble rather than confident in the superiority of American
principles, power, and technology.

An American policy of humility in the Orient might
well begin with settlement of the Chinese civil war, for the
nations of free Asia and Europe demand it. To remove this
threat to peace Congressman Henry Reuss of Wisconsin
in March, 1955, suggested that the United States "ask the
United Nations to take over Formosa as a trusteeship, to
assume its defense against the aggression that threatens it
and to promote the development of self-government by the
Formosan people." This, thought Reuss, would involve no
recognition of Red China, no derecognition of Chiang Kai-
shek, and no weakening of United States determination to
defend Formosa. Under this arrangement Formosa would
cease to be a province of the United States and such nations
as India could participate in the defense of the island. Unfortunately there is no guarantee that Chiang's Nationalists
would constitute the freely elected government of Formosa, and their loss of power on Formosa would end all
hope of "liberating" the mainland. Few still regard this as
a realistic possibility anyway. Said a *Des Moines Register*
editorial in December, 1955, "You might as well talk about
the fabled White Russian taxi drivers of Paris 'liberating'
the Soviet Union."

American interests in the Far East demand a new balance
of power in that portion of the world. For the Nationalist
China bloc the answer lies in the destruction of the Peiping
regime; for students of American diplomacy it rests instead
in a policy of such flexibility and tolerance that it would

isolate the Red Chinese in Asia and permit any tensions that persist to be blamed on that government. Recognition is not the immediate issue. Rather it is the enunciation of clearly conceived conditions for recognition which the world in general would understand and appreciate. Reasonable conditions might include rectification of violations of the Korean armistice terms and the renunciation of the intention to seize Formosa and the Pescadores by force. The essential task of American diplomacy in the Orient is to make Red China rather than the United States appear as the chief threat to peace.

George Washington once warned the American people never to hate another nation, for he prophesied that hatred would propel the nation into foreign policies that would have no relationship to the national interest. Perhaps the gravest immediate danger to peace in the world rests in the tensions between the United States and Red China. The issue in the Formosan Straits is still explosive, and the threat is magnified by the fact that both Chiang and Syngman Rhee openly desire to involve the United States in a major war with continental China. Free Asia's attitude is one powerful determinant in the success or failure of any Western policy in the Far East. What such leaders as India's Nehru or Burma's U Nu believe is good for Asia should at least be considered in the formulation of American policy. To the extent that American purpose runs counter to that of free Asia it is in danger of failure anyway.

It is not clear how the continued refusal to talk of compromise with Russia or China, when the world demands that we do, is going to weaken either of them or alter their policies. The doctrine that a nation can destroy its antagonists or reform them by ignoring them is strange indeed, unless such policy be accompanied by a conscientious effort to convert the remainder of the world to the justice of its moral cause. There has been little, if any, such conversion in Europe or Asia.

§ 3

This nation's inability to isolate either Moscow or Peiping diplomatically from much of the Eurasian continent has forced it to find its security in military power. At the heart of American policy are military alliances—NATO in Europe and SEATO in southeast Asia, supplemented by special military arangements with the Chinese Nationalists on Formosa, with South Korea, Australia, New Zealand, and Pakistan, and by the "Northern Tier" alliance in the Middle East established by the Baghdad Pact. Yet any national purpose that in the post-Geneva world still must rely on the threatened use of military force, especially in the Orient, while the Russians, whatever their sincerity, speak to Asia's goals of peace, neutrality, and internal development, is obviously flouting the goodwill of many nations who desire nothing quite as much as the avoidance of war. Sukarno has warned the United States that "military aid is no substitute for Asian stability," for it reduces the value of Asian nations as "partners in the universal struggle for liberty."

To Asians this nation's excessive faith in military strength is evidence of an American premise that communism rather than nationalism comprises the real challenge of that continent. The sensitive new governments of Asia regard the threat of communism remote, whereas the memory of Western colonialism remains vivid. United States military alliances appear as Western interference in the local affairs of Asia. American military aid to Pakistan, supposedly to build United States security in southeast Asia, has been deeply resented by nationalists in India and Afghanistan. For its illusory military alliances in Asia this nation has paid a heavy political price. Neither SEATO nor the Baghdad Pact add much material strength to the West, and it is doubtful if even the signatories have any interest in them except as they open an entering wedge to the United States treasury. But to most leaders of free Asia they appear as a constant threat to peace and their determination to remain neutral.[10]

Dulles has claimed much for his military policy of massive retaliation in the Far East. In January, 1956, he said: "Nobody is able to prove mathematically that it was the policy of deterrence which brought the Korean war to an end and which kept the Chinese from sending their Red armies into Indochina, or that it has finally stopped them in Formosa. I think it is a pretty fair inference that it has." He admitted that it required risks but added:

You have to take chances for peace, just as you must take chances in war. Some say that we were brought to the verge of war. Of course we were brought to the verge of war. The ability to get to the verge without getting into the war is the necessary art. If you cannot master it, you inevitably get into war. If you try to run away from it, if you are scared to go to the brink, you are lost. We've had to look it square in the face—on the question of enlarging the Korean War, on the question of getting into the Indochina war, on the question of Formosa. We walked to the brink and we looked it in the face. We took strong action.[11]

This policy of going to the brink, as analyzed by James Shepley in *Life* magazine, January 16, 1956, has enjoyed wide and vigorous endorsement from those who accept military power as a substitute for compromise with the Communist world. President Eisenhower admitted that he had not read the article but defended Dulles from much potential criticism when he called him "the best Secretary of State I have ever known." Many believe that the Secretary has handled recent crises with skill, and that his courting of atomic war is the true method of conducting United States foreign policy.

Yet Dulles' diplomatic philosophy has come under serious charge. Teetering at the brink has been likened to playing "Russian roulette" with the lives of millions of people. Said the Milwaukee *Journal:* "It is like saying that the closer you get to war the better you serve peace. It is like saying the destiny of the human race is something to gamble with."[12] The Washington *Post* agreed with the importance of preventing miscalculation on the part of potential aggressors, but added that what remained was the advantage that the article bestowed "on Soviet propaganda through its appalling insensitivity and braggadocio, its distortions of history, its assumptions of omniscience." Summarizing the possible impact of Dulles' analysis on future American policy a *Post* editorial concluded:

What purpose is served by this boastful exercise in slanted history and massive hindsight? If it was intended as a political document to encourage the Republicans and impress the Democrats, it is likely to have the opposite effect. Electioneering of this sort will not advance the cause of bipartisan foreign policy. If it was intended to deter the Russians, the dismay it will create among our allies and in neutral nations will give the Soviet Union an undreamed-of opportunity. Like the Duke of Wellington's soldiers, the article may not frighten the enemy, but it will certainly terrify our friends. Popularity at home and abroad are not necessarily the index of effective policies; but strong policies and imaginative execution are their own best advertisement and do not require shouting from the housetops. . . . Perhaps the worst effect of the article is that its total absence of modesty serves to cast discredit on the good things Mr. Dulles has done.[13]

Perhaps Mr. Dulles overstated the success of his policies. Whatever happened, he made it appear that he had planned it that way, although in none of the crises in the Orient did he achieve his publicly avowed objectives. He overlooked the fact that the Communists were worn out by years of war in Korea, were satisfied with half of Indochina, at least for the time being, and appear to be biding their time in the Formosan Straits. To the extent that these issues have been settled at all, the threatened employment of atomic destruction was relatively unimportant.

What settled these crises, at least temporarily, was really the mutual deterrent on both sides. Certainly, the Communists have been deterred from aggression beyond the present *status quo* by fear of retaliation. At the same time, Dulles, Radford, Syngman Rhee, and Chiang Kai-shek have engaged in no liberation on the Chinese mainland from fear of Communist retaliation. In each case the United States warned the Communists not to cross the line and at the same time assured the Communists that neither Chiang nor Rhee will cross the line. In Indochina the threat of massive retaliation could no longer hold the revolutionary pressure at bay and the United States was forced to concede a Communist advance. Declarations of boldness in themselves constitute no policy unless accompanied by imagination, flexibility, firmness, and consistency in facing the concrete questions of the day. It is in the realm of understanding and diplomacy that the political battles are won or lost.

Where would the American policy of inflexibility and threatened destruction terminate? Any great nation that must live constantly at the brink of war to maintain its position is obviously overlooking the will of its allies or is demanding too much of its antagonists. Perhaps it is guilty of both. Today the margin of safety is extremely narrow. To the extent that American intransigence has won few friends in the world it has not strengthened this nation in its relation to the Soviet Union. For a nation with the freedom to pursue imaginative policies, with the goodwill and capital resources it can offer to the world, and with its real and potential allies, more can be expected of its policies than what its past diplomatic rigidity has permitted. An inflexible policy supported by enormous military potential may preserve peace for a long period, as it did in United States relations with Japan before Pearl Harbor. But such policy defies an elementary principle of successful foreign relations. Hans Morgenthau has written that "diplomacy without power is feeble, and power without diplomacy is destructive and blind."[14]

§ 4

Eisenhower and Dulles have done little to create a bipartisan atmosphere in Washington. In their policy assumptions they have allowed almost no room for Democratic influence. They have continued to bind the United States to the fate of Chiang Kai-shek, have permitted attacks on the State Department although they have been unjustified in terms of results, and have created no educational policy to acquaint the American people with the dynamic qualities of the Far East at mid-century. Although the administration has resisted every effort to destroy the Red Chinese regime, it has refused to accept officially any rationale which explains its existence in terms of the Chinese scene. Nor has it countered the neo-isolationist view that the Yalta agreements rather than the Red Army established the Iron Curtain.

If Dulles' policies in action appear little different from those of Truman, the reason is not that the Secretary so desires it. It is because he cannot wish into existence a world of his own choosing, and in each crisis Eisenhower has refrained from attempting to do so with force. Repeatedly since 1953 the President, to avoid war, has compromised with the declared purpose of the administration, but in no instance has he informed the public as to the judgment on which the alternative policy was based. If there has been no general criticism, it is not because the policies have been clearly formulated or understood, or because the administration has modified its rationale to conform to the realities of power in the Orient, but because the Congress and the people have simply trusted the President.

The Truman-Acheson containment policy intellectually recognized the limitations of American power. The Eisenhower-Dulles policy, in reality, has been forced to accept containment, but in rhetoric it refuses to adopt the conclusion that American power is limited. Nowhere is American diplomatic policy designed to regard as permanent any phenomenon which presently impedes the re-establishment of prewar American security.

Dulles recently defined American purpose as that of adopting every honorable course to avoid war, but he added: "I believe . . . that there are basic moral values and vital interests, for which we stand, and that the surest way to avoid war is to let it be known in advance that we are prepared to defend these principles, if need be by life itself." Every nation in world history has assumed the obligation to fight for its vital interests. It is essential that a nation's interests never be too rigidly defined lest they cease to be negotiable, but the Secretary has been exceedingly vague in delineating what elements in his goals are vital. If the defense of Quemoy and Matsu, or the liberation of China and Poland, are vital interests of this nation, then why is the power not being created to achieve them? If they are actually secondary objectives, and therefore negotiable, then why are they made the inflexible goals of American foreign policy? Lippmann has written that

> a foreign policy consists in bringing into balance, with a comfortable surplus of power in reserve, the nation's commitments and the nation's power. The constant preoccupation of the true statesman is to achieve and maintain this balance. Having determined the foreign commitments which are vitally necessary to his people, he will never rest until he has mustered the force to cover them. In assaying ideals, interests, and ambitions which are to be asserted abroad, his measure of their validity will be the force he can muster at home combined with the support he can find abroad among other nations which have similar ideals, interests, and ambitions.[15]

Throughout most of this century the United States has broken this principle and at heavy cost. In its policy of liberation the nation is defying it again, for at best liberation is a utopian goal which creates a commitment far beyond American power to achieve. The real question confronting the American people is what would happen if the nation in some future crisis refused to back down from its avowed purpose of liberation either in China or in Europe? What, they must ask, is the value of a diplomatic policy that so completely ignores ends and means that it is successful only as long as it is not put into effect? This continued acceptance of limitless expectations necessitates the military policy which forces the United States to live at the brink of war.

This maintenance of objectives beyond the nation's power to achieve needlessly creates a gap between what the United States and its allies or potential allies regard as the basis of a recognizable *status quo*. Policy which demands so much exposes the nation to charges that it alone is responsible for the present state of world tensions. In his continued determination to base American policy on the concept of liberation, Dulles either has not been convinced in three years as Secretary of State that the mere repetition of American purpose will not free anyone, or he cannot admit that the neo-isolationist expectations of absolute security at reduced cost were always beyond American power to accomplish.

Republicans and Democrats alike must share the responsibility of creating a balance between ends and means in American policy. For too long United States foreign relations have been intellectually sterile. Representative Reuss recently declared that for "three or four wasted years, our foreign policy concerned itself largely with reacting to McCarthyism. Now the junior Senator from Wisconsin is, at least for the moment, sulking in the wings. But the vacuum in our foreign policy, which his commotion has created, remains."[16] Neither liberation nor massive retaliation have filled the need for a flexible and imaginative policy geared to a world that can find no alternative to coexistence.

Dulles' persistent failure to achieve his purposes abroad illustrates the primary task of leadership in the United States—that of admitting the limitations of American will and educating the American people to expect less than perfect security. The issue is not whether the United States can continue to exist as a great nation, for it enjoys too many advantages in the present struggle, but whether it can live up to its challenge as the leader of the free world. Thomas Huxley said of America eighty years ago: "I cannot say that I am in the slightest degree impressed by your bigness, or your material resources as such. Size is not grandeur, and territory does not make a nation. The great issue, about which hangs a true sublimity and the terror of overhanging fate, is what are you going to do with all these things?"

Will the United States be a worthy successor to those nations which have played well the role of leadership in past history? Can it create and maintain a rational foreign policy that other nations will follow willingly rather than grudgingly? Only then can the Grand Alliance have the basic strength required to meet any crisis. The task of leadership is that of bringing the nation's military, economic, and intellectual resources to play on policy formation so that the nation might better lead the way through the present crisis and play a major role in sparing the world another general war. Above all, it is necessary again that American policy be geared not to the creation of illimitable objectives, but to discovering the means at home and abroad which will allow the Republic to live in some peace and security in a world of imperfection and continuous challenge.

Notes

Materials bearing on the relationships between politics and foreign policy in the United States during recent years are immense and varied. No bibliography could do full justice to the many books, newspapers, magazine articles, reports on Congressional debates, and other sources available in such profusion to the student of contemporary events. The author hopes that the following partial list of references will give a fair impression of the widely diverse material studied to establish the week-by-week chronicle of events and to trace the gradual development of current attitudes and opinions on foreign policy issues.

CHAPTER 1

1. Walter Lippmann, *The Public Philosophy* (Boston: Little Brown & Co., 1955), p. 20.
2. George F. Kennan, *American Diplomacy 1900-1950* (Chicago: University of Chicago Press, 1951), p. 93.
3. Quoted in Elmer Davis, "Vox Populi and Foreign Policy," *Harper's*, June, 1952, p. 67.
4. Samuel Lubell, *Revolt of the Moderates* (New York: Harper & Bros., 1956), pp. 76-84.
5. George B. Galloway, "The Investigative Function of Congress," *American Political Science Review*, XXI (February, 1927), 55.
6. James P. Richards, "The House of Representatives in Foreign Affairs," *The Annals*, September, 1953, p. 87.
7. Lester B. Pearson, *Democracy in World Politics* (Princeton, N. J.: Princeton University Press, 1955), p. 105.
8. Students of Congress generally agree that its record has been good in foreign affairs. See Roland Young, *Congressional Politics in the Second World War* (New York: Columbia University Press, 1955), *passim;* Robert A. Dahl, *Congress and Foreign Policy* (New York: Harcourt, Brace & Co., 1950), pp. 244-45; Guy M. Gillette, "The Senate in Foreign Relations," *The Annals*, September, 1953, p. 57.

9. John Foster Dulles, *War or Peace* (New York: The Macmillan Co., 1950), p. 131; Arthur H. Vandenberg, Jr., ed., *The Private Papers of Senator Vandenberg* (Boston: Houghton Mifflin Co., 1952), pp. 550-51; Dean Acheson, "The Parties and Foreign Policy," *Harper's*, November, 1955, pp. 30-31.

10. Blair Bolles, "Bipartisanship in American Foreign Policy," *Foreign Policy Reports*, January 1, 1949, p. 198; John M. Vorys, "Party Responsibility for Foreign Policy," *The Annals*, September, 1953, pp. 168-69.

11. Vandenberg, *op cit.*, pp. 518, 535-36, 547, 551.

12. Dulles, *op. cit.*, p. 181; Paul G. Hoffman, *Peace Can Be Won* (Garden City, N. Y.: Doubleday & Co., 1951), p. 48; Senator Margaret Chase Smith quoted in H. Bradford Westerfield, *Foreign Policy and Party Politics, Pearl Harbor to Korea* (New Haven: Yale University Press, 1955), pp. 379-80.

13. Vandenberg, *op. cit.*, p. 560.

14. Thomas I. Cook and Malcolm Moos, *Power Through Purpose: The Realism of Idealism as a Basis for Foreign Policy* (Baltimore: The Johns Hopkins Press, 1954), pp. 35-38.

15. Foster Rhea Dulles, *America's Rise to World Power, 1898-1954* (New York: Harper & Bros., 1955), p. 160.

16. Gabriel Almond, *The American People and Foreign Policy* (New York: Harcourt, Brace & Co., 1950), pp. 200-09.

17. Arthur M. Schlesinger, Jr., "The New Isolationism," *Atlantic*, May, 1952, p. 36. I am heavily indebted to Professor Schlesinger for much of the material in the succeeding pages of this chapter.

18. *Ibid.*, pp. 36-37; Cook and Moos, *op. cit.*, pp. 54-55.

19. W. Reed West, "Senator Taft's Foreign Policy," *Atlantic*, June, 1952, p. 52; Robert A. Taft, *A Foreign Policy for Americans* (Garden City, N. Y.: Doubleday & Co., 1951), pp. 14, 68-69.

20. Edgar A. Jonas in House of Representatives, February 15, 1951, *Congressional Record*, 82 Cong., 1 Sess., Appendix, A796. For a criticism of this view see Hanson W. Baldwin, "Dissection of the 'Fortress America' Idea," *The New York Times Magazine*, August 17, 1952, pp. 7, 54-55.

21. Schlesinger, *op. cit.*, p. 37.

22. Chicago *Tribune*, June 15, 1951.

23. Hans J. Morgenthau, *In Defense of the National Interest* (New York: Alfred A. Knopf, 1951), p. 131.

24. Bertrand Russell, "Looking Backward—to the 1950's," *The New York Times Magazine*, April 26, 1953, p. 12.

25. Richard H. Rovere, "What's Happened to Taft?" *Harper's,* April 1952, pp. 41-42; William S. White, "Almost Equal to Being President," *The New York Times Magazine,* January 14, 1951, p. 42.

CHAPTER 2

1. Arthur H. Vandenberg, Jr., ed., *The Private Papers of Senator Vandenberg* (Boston: Houghton Mifflin Co., 1952), pp. 530-32.
2. Edwin O. Reischauer, *Wanted: An Asian Policy* (New York: Alfred A. Knopf, 1955), pp. 73-94.
3. James Michener, "Blunt Truths About Asia," *Life,* June 4, 1951, p. 116; Edgar Ansel Mowrer, "What Asia Wants," *Harper's,* October, 1951, pp. 67-72.
4. *Life,* June 4, 1951, p. 110.
5. Acheson, quoted in Hans J. Morgenthau, *In Defense of the National Interest* (New York: Alfred A. Knopf, 1951), p. 258; Derk Bodde, *Peking Diary* (New York: Henry Schuman, Inc., 1950), p. 261.
6. John K. Fairbank, "China," *Atlantic,* November, 1950, p. 22.
7. Hanson W. Baldwin, "Churchill Was Right," *Atlantic,* July, 1954, p. 32.
8. Charles Burton Marshall, *The Limits of Foreign Policy* (New York: Henry Holt & Co., 1954), pp. 72-78.
9. Winston Churchill, *Triumph and Tragedy* (Boston: Houghton Mifflin Co., 1953), p. 402.
10. Chester Wilmot, "Stalin's Greatest Victory," quoted in Richard F. Fenno, Jr., ed., *The Yalta Conference* (Boston: D. C. Heath & Co., 1955), p. 83; Wilmot, "Sacrifice of Principles," *The New York Times Magazine,* August 3, 1952, p. 46.
11. Herbert Feis, *The China Tangle: The American Effort in China from Pearl Harbor to the Marshall Mission* (Princeton, N. J.: Princeton University Press, 1953), pp. 252-53; Louis Morton, "The Military Background of the Yalta Agreements," *The Reporter,* April 7, 1955, p. 21.
12. Feis, *op. cit.,* p. 428; Morgenthau, *op. cit.,* p. 204.
13. Baldwin, *op. cit.,* p. 24.
14. Feis, *op. cit.,* p. 430.
15. John T. Flynn, *The Lattimore Story* (New York: Devin-Adair Co., 1953), p. 9.
16. Felix Wittmer, *The Yalta Betrayal* (Caldwell, Idaho: The Caxton Printers, 1953), p. 12.
17. Freda Utley, *The China Story* (Chicago: Henry Regnery Co., 1951), p. 113.

18. Department of State, *United States Relations with China* (Washington, D. C.: Government Printing Office, 1949), pp. 758-59.

19. Geraldine Fitch, *Formosa Beachhead* (Chicago: Henry Regnery Co., 1953), p. 153; Utley, *op. cit.*, pp. 239-40.

20. Richard W. Van Alstyne, *United States Crisis Diplomacy: The Quest for Collective Security 1918-1952* (Stanford, Cal.: Stanford University Press, 1952), p. 142.

21. Robert A. Taft, *A Foreign Policy for Americans* (Garden City, N. Y.: Doubleday & Co., 1951), pp. 60-61; Utley, *op. cit.*, preface.

22. *U. S. News & World Report*, May 11, 1951, p. 74.

23. *Ibid.*, p. 85.

24. James Reston, "Diplomatic Stalemate, Too, Is Far East Danger," *The New York Times*, May 12, 1951.

CHAPTER 3

1. George F. Kennan, "Hope in an Age of Anxiety," *New Republic*, June 1, 1953, p. 14.

2. Arthur Hays Sulzberger, "The Bases of an Honorable Peace," *The New York Times Magazine*, December 12, 1954, p. 60; Sidney Hook, "Fallacies in Our Thinking About Security," *ibid.*, January 30, 1955, p. 15.

3. Kennan, "The Illusion of Security," *Atlantic*, August, 1954, p. 32.

4. Hans J. Morgenthau, quoted in *Des Moines Register*, May 1, 1955.

5. See Elmer Davis, "The Crusade Against Acheson," *Harper's*, March, 1951, pp. 23-29; John Fischer, *Master Plan U. S. A.* (New York: Harper & Bros., 1951), p. 74.

6. Davis, *op. cit.*, p. 24; Fischer, *op. cit.*, 75-81; Lester Markel, "The Great Need—An Informed Opinion," *The New York Times Magazine*, April 9, 1950, p. 48.

7. Davis, *op. cit.*, p. 24.

8. Herbert Feis, *The China Tangle: The American Effort in China from Pearl Harbor to the Marshall Mission* (Princeton, N. J.: Princeton University Press, 1953), p. 4.

9. Vannevar Bush, "To Make Our Security System Secure," *The New York Times Magazine*, March 20, 1955, p. 9.

10. *The Christian Science Monitor*, February 7, 1955.

11. Richard H. Rovere, "What's Happened to Taft?" *Harper's*, April, 1952, p. 41.

12. F. Ernest Johnson, "Red China and U. N.," *Des Moines Register*, October 31, 1953.

13. Leon Epstein, "Britain: Uneasy Ally," *The University of Chicago Magazine*, December, 1954, p. 12.

14. *Ibid.*; James Reston, "Why We Irritate Our Allies," *Harper's*, May, 1951, p. 33.

15. Carlos P. Romulo, "What the Asians Expect of Us," *The New York Times Magazine*, June 19, 1955, p. 61.

16. Thomas E. Dewey, "Pacific Report: Free China Must Be Saved Now—or Never," *Collier's*, December 1, 1951, p. 73.

17. For this analysis of Taft's views I am indebted to Arthur M. Schlesinger, Jr., "The New Isolationism," *Atlantic*, May, 1952, p. 34.

18. See Epstein, *op cit.*, p. 12.

19. *The New York Times*, April 22, 1951.

20. Quoted in Hans J. Morgenthau, *In Defense of the National Interest* (New York: Alfred A. Knopf, 1951), p. 269.

21. Adlai E. Stevenson, *Call to Greatness* (New York: Harper & Bros., 1954), p. 46.

22. Edwin O. Reischauer, *Wanted: An Asian Policy* (New York: Alfred A. Knopf, 1955), pp. 267-68.

CHAPTER 4

1. John Foster Dulles, *War or Peace* (New York: The Macmillan Co., 1950), pp. 136, 181.

2. William Henry Chamberlin, *Beyond Containment* (Chicago: Henry Regnery Co., 1953), p. 83; Walter Lippmann, *The Cold War* (New York: Harper & Bros., 1947), pp. 20-21.

3. John Foster Dulles, "A Policy of Boldness," *Life*, May 19, 1952, p. 146.

4. *Ibid.*, p. 150.

5. *Ibid.*, pp. 154, 157.

6. *American Mercury*, April, 1952, pp. 84-86.

7. William S. White, "Almost Equal to Being President," *The New York Times Magazine*, January 14, 1951, p. 10; Richard H. Rovere, "What's Happened to Taft?" *Harper's*, April, 1952, p. 44.

8. Thomas H. Werdel in *Congressional Record*, 82 Cong., 2 Sess., Vol. 98, Pt. 1, p. 102.

9. *Ibid.*; Usher L. Burdick in *ibid.*, Pt. 4, pp. 4836-37; McCarthy in *The Progressive*, April, 1954, pp. 52-53.

10. Henry Cabot Lodge, Jr., "Why I Believe in Eisenhower," *Atlantic*, June, 1952, p. 49.

11. Republican Platform of 1952 quoted in *Current History*, October, 1952, pp. 246-54.

12. *Newsweek*, August 18, 1952, p. 30.

13. See Richard H. Rovere, "Eisenhower: A Trial Balance," *The Reporter*, April 21, 1955, p. 14.

14. *Newsweek*, September 15, 1952, p. 25.

15. Quoted in *The New York Times*, December 4, 1955.

16. Adlai Stevenson, *Major Campaign Speeches* (New York: Random House, 1953), p. 55.

17. *Ibid.*, pp. 94, 97.

18. *Ibid.*, pp. 42, 187-88.

19. *Ibid.*, pp. 128-30.

20. Louis Harris, *Is There a Republican Majority?* (New York: Harper & Bros., 1954), pp. 22-24.

21. Thomas L. Stokes, "Democratic Tide—and Eisenhower Tide," *The New York Times Magazine*, May 15, 1955, p. 42.

22. *New Republic*, November 10, 1952, p. 5.

23. Foster Rhea Dulles, *America's Rise to World Power, 1898-1954* (New York: Harper & Bros., 1955), pp. 266-67; Richard C. Snyder and Edgar S. Furniss, Jr., *American Foreign Policy* (New York: Rinehart & Co., 1954), p. 505.

CHAPTER 5

1. John M. Vorys, "Party Responsibility for Foreign Policy," *The Annals*, September, 1953, p. 171.

2. On Taft's vigorous support of Eisenhower see Richard H. Rovere, *Affairs of State: The Eisenhower Years* (New York: Farrar, Straus and Cudahy, 1956), pp. 101-12.

3. Louis Harris, *Is There a Republican Majority?* (New York: Harper & Bros., 1954), pp. 87-103; Samuel Lubell, *Revolt of the Moderates* (New York: Harper & Bros., 1956), pp. 94-95.

4. Philip L. Graham, "Our Tory Government," *The University of Chicago Magazine*, June, 1953, p. 18.

5. Robert A. Taft, "What the G.O.P. Must Do To Win in 1954," *Look*, April 21, 1953, p. 44.

6. General Van Fleet, quoted in *New Republic*, June 1, 1953, p. 5; General Almond in *U. S. News & World Report*, December 10, 1954, p. 94; General Courtney Whitney, "The War Mac-Arthur Was Not Allowed to Win," *Life*, September 5, 1955, p. 63.

7. General Eichelberger in *Newsweek*, August 3, 1953, p. 20.

8. *U. S. News & World Report*, June 3, 1953, pp. 84, 124.

9. Geraldine Fitch, *Formosa Beachhead* (Chicago: Henry Regnery Co., 1953), pp. 258-59, 262.

10. William Jenner in *Congressional Record*, 83, Cong., 1 Sess., Vol. 99, Pt. 8, pp. 11000-01.

11. William F. Knowland, "Be Prepared to Fight in China," *Collier's*, January 24, 1954, p. 120.

12. William Henry Chamberlin, *Beyond Containment* (Chicago: Henry Regnery Co., 1953), p. 372; General MacArthur, quoted in *San Francisco Chronicle*, February 1, 1953.

13. Donald W. Mitchell, "The 'New Look,'" *Current History*, October, 1954, p. 219.

14. William F. Knowland, "The 'Instant Retaliation' Policy Defended," *The New York Times Magazine*, March 21, 1954, p. 74.

15. Hanson W. Baldwin, in *The New York Times*, January 24, 1954; Dean Acheson, " 'Instant Retaliation': The Debate Continued," *The New York Times Magazine*, March 28, 1954, p. 78; Thomas R. Phillips, "Our Point of No Return," *The Reporter*, February 24, 1955, pp. 14-18.

16. William S. White, "Joe McCarthy, The Man With the Power," *Look*, June 16, 1953, pp. 30-31; John B. Oakes, "Inquiry Into McCarthy's Status," *The New York Times Magazine*, April 12, 1953, p. 9; White in *The New York Times*, March 28, 1953.

17. *The New York Times*, February 22, 1953.

18. Henry Steele Commager, "The Perilous Delusion of Security," *The Reporter*, November 3, 1955, p. 34.

19. Quoted in Charlotte Knight, "What Price Security?" *Collier's*, July 9, 1954, p. 67.

20. Dorothy Fosdick, "For the Foreign Service—Help Wanted," *The New York Times Magazine*, November 20, 1955, p. 65.

21. *Des Moines Register*, May 1, 1955.

22. *Atlantic*, April, 1954, p. 20; William Harlan Hale, "Back to Cadillac Country," *The Saturday Review*, July 3, 1954, p. 39.

CHAPTER 6

1. See Louis Cassels, " 'Mr. X' Goes to Moscow," *Collier's*, March 15, 1952, p. 20.

2. *Des Moines Register*, December 1, 1953.

3. *The New York Times*, October 3, 1954.

4. Hans J. Briner, "The Strange Neutrals of Panmunjom," *Korean Survey*, November, 1955, p. 3.

5. *The Christian Science Monitor*, September 3, 1953. For an excellent analysis of American Far Eastern policy in 1953 see

Vincent S. Kearney, "Whither U. S. Policy in the Far East?" *America*, November 7, 1953, pp. 147-49.

6. Quoted in Laurence Lafore, "The Problem of Diplomatic Recognition," *Current History*, March, 1956, p. 154.

7. Stanley F. Hornbeck, "Which Chinese?" *Foreign Affairs*, October, 1955, p. 25.

8. Eric Hoffer, "The Passionate State of Mind," *Harper's*, January, 1955, p. 62.

9. William F. Knowland, "The 'Instant Retaliation' Policy Defended," *The New York Times Magazine*, March 21, 1954, p. 11.

10. Survey of the Indochinese crisis in *Des Moines Register*, June 13, 1954.

11. *Manchester Guardian*, quoted in Woodrow Wyatt, "Geography Closes in on the British," *The New York Times Magazine*, October 17, 1954, pp. 68-69.

12. Bertrand Russell, "A Prescription for the World," *The Saturday Review*, August 28, 1954, p. 39.

13. Macmillan, quoted in *The Commonwealth* (Commonwealth Club of California), July 4, 1955, p. 163; Attlee quoted in *New Republic*, June 8, 1953, p. 17.

14. See Chester Bowles, "A Bipartisan Policy for Asia," *Harper's*, May, 1954, pp. 24-25.

15. Quoted in Edward Crankshaw, "China and Russia," *Atlantic*, June, 1956, p. 27.

16. Hans Morgenthau, "Is 'Instant Retaliation' the Answer?" *New Republic*, March 29, 1954, pp. 11-12.

17. Chester Bowles, "A Plea for Another Great Debate," *The New York Times Magazine*, February 28, 1954, p. 64.

18. Dean Acheson, " 'Instant Retaliation': The Debate Continued," *ibid.*, March 28, 1954, p. 78.

19. Quoted in *The Commonwealth*, June 27, 1955, p. 156.

20. A. M. Rosenthal in *The New York Times*, February 13, 1955.

CHAPTER 7

1. Hans J. Morgenthau, *In Defense of the National Interest* (New York: Alfred A. Knopf, 1951), p. 234.

2. Samuel Lubell, *The Future of American Politics* (New York: Harper & Bros., 1952), pp. 25-26.

3. Adlai E. Stevenson, "Let's Make the Two-Party System Work," *Look*, September 20, 1955, p. 53.

4. Alastair Buchan, "Patching Up the Partnership with Britain," *Harper's*, February, 1955, pp. 56-57.

5. James Reston, "An Inquiry Into Foreign Policy, "*The New York Times Magazine*, January 16, 1955, p. 9. On the shift of Eisenhower policy toward that of Truman see Dana Adams Schmidt in *The New York Times*, February 6, 1955; James Reston in *ibid.*, November 28, 1954.

6. Howard K. Smith, quoted in *Harper's*, September, 1954, p. 20.

7. Peter Vierick, "Sunrise in the West," *The Saturday Review*, June 12, 1954, pp. 38-39.

8. Churchill, quoted in *New Republic*, May 25, 1953, p. 6; London *Observer*, quoted in Ernest T. Weir, *Notes on the Foreign Situation Based on a Trip Abroad* (Pamphlet, Privately Printed, June 19, 1953), p. 15.

9. Henry Steele Commager, "An Inquiry into Appeasement," *The New York Times Magazine*, February 11, 1951, p. 8; Louis J. Halle, "The Art of Negotiating with the Russians," *ibid.*, June 12, 1955, p. 59. See also Ernest T. Weir, "Why Not Negotiate with Russia?" *Harper's*, December, 1953, pp. 66-71.

10. Quoted in Arthur Hays Sulzberger, "The Bases of an Honorable Peace," *The New York Times Magazine*, December 12, 1954. p. 63.

11. Cabell Phillips, "One-Man Task Force of the G.O.P.," *ibid.*, October 24, 1954, p. 55.

12. William Lee Miller, "The Debating Career of Richard M. Nixon," *The Reporter*, April 19, 1956, p. 16.

13. For the effect of the election on Eisenhower's leadership see Drew Middleton in *The New York Times*, January 8, 1955; William S. White, "Two Parties and One Foreign Policy," *The New York Times Magazine*, August 7, 1955, p. 12; Chalmer M. Roberts, "Battle on 'The Rim of Hell': President vs. War Hawks," *The Reporter*, December 16, 1954, p. 11.

14. Douglass Cater, "Foreign Policy: Default of the Democrats," *The Reporter*, March 10, 1955, pp. 21-23.

15. Carlos P. Romulo, "Watch Bandung," *This Week Magazine*, April 17, 1955, p. 29.

16. Hubert Humphrey in *The Commonwealth*, March 7, 1955, p. 58.

CHAPTER 8

1. Quoted in James P. Warburg, *Turning Point Toward Peace* (New York: Current Affairs Press, 1955), p. 11.

2. Bernard Brodie, "How War Became Absurd," *Harper's*, October, 1955, p. 37.

3. Thomas P. Whitney, "What We Can Expect of the Russians," *The New York Times Magazine*, May 22, 1955, p. 9; Walter Lippmann in the *Des Moines Register*, May 14, 1955. See also Arnold J. Toynbee, "What Makes a Great Power Great," *The New York Times Magazine*, May 29, 1955, p. 31.

4. Averell Harriman, "The Soviet Challenge to American Policy," *Atlantic*, April, 1956, p. 43; Harrison E. Salisbury in *The New York Times*, November 20, 1955.

5. John Emmet Hughes, "The Chances for Peace," *Life*, May 30, 1955, pp. 22-23; Perry Laukhuff, "How To Bargain with Russia," *Harper's*, June, 1955, pp. 27-28.

6. Max Ascoli, "Toward Geneva," *The Reporter*, June 30, 1955, p. 9.

7. *The New York Times*, June 17, 1955.

8. Quoted in Merlo J. Pusey, *Eisenhower the President* (New York: The Macmillan Co., 1956), p. 179.

9. *American Mercury*, October, 1955, p. 6.

10. Freda Utley, "No Easy Way Out," *ibid.*, September, 1955, pp. 65-66.

11. Anthony Trawick Bouscaren, "Admiral Radford and Far Eastern Policy," *ibid.*, November, 1955, p. 47.

12. *Des Moines Register*, August 26, 1955.

13. For coverage of this conference see *The New York Times*, February 13, 1955; *Des Moines Register*, February 15, 1955.

14. Eugene Lyons, "Sum of the Summit: Moral Failure," *American Mercury*, October, 1955, pp. 29-32.

15. Irene Corbally Kuhn, "Geneva's Smile of Death," *ibid.*, November, 1955, p. 61.

16. *The New York Times*, August 2, 1955.

17. William E. Jenner, "Let's Put America First," *Facts Forum News*, August, 1955, p. 5.

18. Quoted in John B. Oakes, "The Security Issue: A Changing Atmosphere," *The New York Times Magazine*, August 14, 1955, p. 56.

19. See Dean Acheson, "To Meet the Shifting Soviet Offensive," *ibid.*, April 15, 1956, p. 11.

20. Harriman, *op. cit.*, p. 46.

21. A. M. Rosenthal in *The New York Times*, December 11, 1955.

22. James Shepley, "How Dulles Averted War," *Life*, January 16, 1956, p. 78; Alastair Buchan, "Toward a New Strategy of Graduated Deterrence," *The Reporter*, December 1, 1955, pp. 23-27.

23. Matthew B. Ridgway, "My Battles in War and Peace," *The Saturday Evening Post*, January 21, 1956, p. 46; Hanson W. Baldwin in *The New York Times*, January 22, 1956.

24. *Des Moines Register*, February 1, 1956.

CHAPTER 9

1. *The New York Times*, April 22, 1956; *Des Moines Register*, April 22, 1956.

2. See William S. White in *The New York Times*, April 29, 1956, for an analysis of public apathy toward questions of foreign policy early in 1956. See also Elie Abel in *ibid.*, February 19, 1956.

3. Harold Callender in *Des Moines Register*, April 25, 1956.

4. *Ibid.*; Thomas J. Hamilton in *The New York Times*, February 5, 26, 1956; Willard R. Espy, "Plea for a New Kind of Point Four," *The New York Times Magazine*, April 22, 1956, pp. 9, 36-42.

5. Edmond Taylor, "The Strains on NATO," *The Reporter*, April 5, 1956, pp. 12-13.

6. George F. Kennan, *American Diplomacy 1900-1950* (Chicago: University of Chicago Press, 1951), p. 93.

7. Max Beloff, *Foreign Policy and the Democratic Process* (Baltimore: The Johns Hopkins Press, 1955), p. 94.

8. Max Ascoli, "Geneva Revisited," *The Reporter*, November 17, 1955, p. 11.

9. For the appeal of the Red Chinese in Asia see Hans J. Morgenthau, "Ideological Windmills," *New Republic*, March 12, 1956, p. 21; Morgenthau, "The Danger of Doing Too Much," *ibid.*, April 16, 1956, p. 15.

10. Max Ascoli, "The New Great Debate," *The Reporter*, January 27, 1955, p. 10; Hans J. Morgenthau, "Military Illusions," *New Republic*, March 19, 1956, pp. 15-16.

11. James Shepley, "How Dulles Averted War," *Life*, January 16, 1956, pp. 77-78.

12. The Milwaukee *Journal*, January 17, 1956.

13. The Washington *Post*, January 14, 18, 1956.

14. Hans J. Morgenthau, *In Defense of the National Interest* (New York: Alfred A. Knopf, 1951), p. 242.

15. Walter Lippmann, *U. S. Foreign Policy: Shield of the Republic* (Boston: Little, Brown & Co., 1943), pp. 9-10.

16. Reuss quoted in James P. Warburg, *Turning Point Toward Peace* (New York: Current Affairs Press, 1955), p. 56.

Index

Academicians
 views of, toward fall of Chiang,
  34-37, 41-45, 79-80
 views of, toward Yalta, 38-43
 alienated from American foreign
  policy, 78-85, 239, 247-48
Acheson, Dean, 30, 34, 37, 46, 64-
  65, 68, 69, 79, 100, 117, 154, 183,
  191
Adenauer, Konrad, 151
Afghanistan, 231, 255
Africa, 103, 204
Agar, Herbert, 188
Aiken, George, 94
Ali, Mohammed, 205
Almond, Edward M., 123
Almond, Gabriel, 21
Alsop, Stewart, 223
American First Committee, 24
American Coalition of Patriotic
  Societies, 21
American invincibility, concept of
 and politics, 4-5, 7, 11, 248-49
 and American isolationism, 18-23
 basis of disloyalty charges, 28-29,
  63-66
 and new isolationism, 29, 45, 52,
  66, 92-93, 96, 121-26
 effect on public opinion, 63
 effect on foreign policy, 146-47,
  184, 191-92, 229-30
 and massive retaliation, 174
American Legion, 99, 226
American security
 and Truman policy, 18
 and charges of conspiracy, 52
 and balance of power in Asia,
  58, 60, 87, 152, 167, 253-54
 and public opinion, 62-63
 and vulnerability of State Department, 63-67
 threat to, from Russian empire,
  87-88, 224-25
 promised by Eisenhower, 128-29
American Society of Newspaper
  Editors, 129, 142, 143, 147, 164,
  206, 240
American War Mothers, 21
Anticolonialism; *see* Nationalism in
  Asia; Nationalism in Middle
  East
Appeasement
 and isolationism, 23, 196
 and new isolationism, 68, 130,
  196, 237
 opposed by Eisenhower, 101
 defined, 196-97
Armour, Norman, 139
Aron, Raymond, 135
Ascoli, Max, 180, 216, 250
Asia-first policy
 accepted by new isolationism, 27-
  28, 52
 and MacArthur hearings, 56, 59
 in 1952 Republican platform, 96
 as mandate of 1952, 109
 strengthened by denial of power
  in Asia, 126
 and Eisenhower's program, 129-
  30, 143
Asian nationalism; *see* Nationalism
  in Asia
Aswan Dam, 230
Atlantic Charter, 41
Attlee, Clement, 65, 71, 77, 170,
  215
Australia, 167, 255
Austria, 213, 217

Baghdad Pact, 255-56

crusading zeal of, 146
not defended by Southern Democrats, 201
Truman-Acheson policy; see Truman policy
Tsiang, Tingfu F., 178
Twining, General Nathan F., 165

United Nations, 21, 26, 56, 68-70, 77, 101, 107, 114, 123, 153-54, 167, 170, 171, 179, 181, 235, 244
U Nu, 205, 235, 254

Van Alstyne, Richard W., 52
Vandenberg, Arthur, 12, 14-15, 17, 34, 53, 86, 93, 112, 115, 143, 201
Van Fleet, James, 122
Viereck, Peter, 193
Viet Minh, 158-59
Viet Nam, 163, 226
Vincent, John Carter, 48
Voice of America, 9, 90, 134-35, 224
Vorys, John M., 13, 113

Wallace, Henry A., 46
Washington, George, 3, 10, 32, 136, 254
 Farewell Address, 10, 254
Watkins, Arthur, 148
Wedemeyer, General Albert C., 49, 51, 155
Weeks, Sinclair, 118
Werdel, Thomas H., 94

West Germany, 150-51, 211
West, W. Reed, 25
Wherry, Kenneth, 45, 114
White-collar vote, 117
White, Harry Dexter, 46, 185
White, William S., 135
Whitney, Courtney, 122
Whitney, Thomas P., 211
Wilbur, William Hale, 226
Willkie, Wendell, 13, 117
Wilmot, Chester, 38-43
Wilson, Charles E., 130
Wilson, Woodrow, 3, 21, 71, 97
Wittmer, Felix, 46
World War II, 8, 38, 107, 158, 234
Wriston, Henry M., 30

Yalta conference
 criticism of, 4, 38-43, 50, 120, 147-48
 defended, 39-40, 151
 and satellites, 39-41, 217
 and Nationalist China, 39, 41-45
 and charges of conspiracy, 50, 52
 as political symbol, 52, 117, 144, 200
 and new isolationism, 88, 92, 95-96
 and Eisenhower resolution, 147-48
 as barrier to diplomacy, 148, 223
Yalu River, 55, 100, 123
Yeh, George, 176